The Evil That Men Do: A Novel

Edgar Fawcett

THE EVIL THAT MEN DO.

THE EVIL THAT MEN DO

A NOVEL

BY

E D G A R   F A W C E T T

AUTHOR OF

"*Olivia Delaplaine,*" "*The House at High Bridge,*" "*Miriam Balestier,*"
"*A Man's Will,*" "*An Ambitious Woman,*" "*Social Silhouettes,*"
"*The Confessions of Claud,*" "*Divided Lives,*"
"*A Gentleman of Leisure,*" etc.

ἀλλ ἐάννοειὲν χρὴ τοῦτο μὲν γυναῖχ ὅτι
ἔφυμεν 'ως πρὸς ἄνδρας οὐ μαχουμένα
ἔπειτα δ' οὕνεκ' αρχόμεσθ εκ κρεισσόνων
αι ταῦτ' ακούειν κᾶτι τῶνδ' αλγίονα.

Sophocles, Antig., 61–64.

———

BELFORD COMPANY
PUBLISHERS
18–22 EAST 18TH STREET, NEW YORK.

812F 28
Q 3

To Professor Charles G. D. Roberts,
of King's College, Nova Scotia.

My Dear Charles :—You have so often, in your shining and capable rôle of poet and scholar, proved gracious to livelier and less tragic work of mine than this, that I shall now tax your goodness a little more, and offer you a story whose only recommendation must be its truth, and whose lack of art may perchance find in you the same indulgent critic of former friendly years.

Ever faithfully,

THE AUTHOR.

Edgar Fawcett's Writings.

Fiction.

RUTHERFORD.
A GENTLEMAN OF LEISURE.
A HOPELESS CASE.
AN AMBITIOUS WOMAN.
SOCIAL SILHOUETTES.
TINKLING CYMBALS.
THE ADVENTURES OF A WIDOW.
THE CONFESSIONS OF CLAUD.
THE HOUSE AT HIGH BRIDGE.
OLIVIA DELAPLAINE.
A MAN'S WILL.
DOUGLAS DUANE.
DIVIDED LIVES.
MIRIAM BALESTIER.
A DEMORALIZING MARRIAGE.
SOLARION.

Poetry.

FANTASY AND PASSION.
SONG AND STORY.
ROMANCE AND REVERY.

Humorous Verse.

THE BUNTLING BALL.
THE NEW KING ARTHUR.

Essays.

AGNOSTICISM, AND OTHER ESSAYS.

THE EVIL THAT MEN DO.

I.

"What is your name?"

"Cora Strang."

"Unmarried, I suppose?"

"Yes, sir."

"You belong to New York?"

"I do now; but I came here from a place up near Peekskill—a small village called—"

"Oh, never mind. . . So you want employment from us? You've references?"

"I've got this, sir."

Cora Strang handed out a slip of white paper, neatly folded. He whom she had been addressing—a little man, with a pointed nose and foxy eyes—glanced at the paper somewhat carelessly. "M—yes," he at length said, "we know Davis & Co. well. So you've worked for them, eh?"

"Yes, sir; for over a year. I've got my own machine, you know—at least I hire one."

"Oh, I see."

The man spoke those three words in a wholly new tone. It was a raw January day outside the small, blank, stove-heated room where he sat before his desk, and some sudden change of light wrought by a snow-cloud fleeting across the sun had caused a kind of glow to rest on Cora Strang's face beneath her shabby black hat.

'Good Heavens,' the man thought, 'how pretty she is!'

With a voice freed from the indifferent semi-drawl used a minute ago, he now went on : "We're not giving out very much work just at present. You see, it's between seasons."

"I know, sir," said Cora Strang, drooping her own eyes a little as his foxy ones met and tried to hold them. "I haven't always done men's wear. It don't pay well, and if times were better I wouldn't think of it."

"No, it does *not* pay well," he said, stroking his sharp little chin. "You're right there. We've got some boys' percale shirt-waists, though, all cut out and ready for you, I guess, if you choose to take them."

The girl gave a faint, cold laugh, and slightly tossed her head. "Oh, better that than nothing," she returned, with a dreary courage in the answer. "You pay for them how much, sir?"

"A dollar a dozen, each of them to have ten button-holes, thirteen buttons and wide collars and cuffs, with pleats front and back."

Cora bit her lip for an instant and then gave two or three short, decisive nods. "It'll have to suit for the present," she said, "though I'm afraid it won't bring me more than sixty cents a day while I'm at it."

The man touched a bell at his side. "Isaacsen Brothers, over in Houston Street," he said, dryly and curtly, " only give ninety cents for such work." But the girl's face at once appeared to soften him again, and as he now spoke a few words to the pale, shambling boy who had obeyed his summons, the gentle note came back into his voice. After the boy had gone away to get a bundle of work from the upstairs department, he left his desk and drew near to Cora with a smile on his lips that few daily observers had the luck to see there. He was a man of about forty years old, and his reputation for courtesy among the numerous "hands" through-

out the building was by no means great. He had not
seen in years a girl cross the threshold of that huge
Worth Street establishment who even vaguely rivalled
Cora Strang in looks. Holding a well-salaried position
and being himself quite exempt from want, he had
grown to think of poverty and ugliness in women as re-
pelling synonyms. Almost every girl with whom he
had the least intercourse during hours of business was
wan or pinched or bony, when nature had not made her
already charmless. But here throve a delicate blush-
rose in the midst of all this mirk and soilure. She must
be quite as poor as the rest; her clothes were even
meaner than some of them wore. She was without
gloves, too, and he could see on her fingers those ragged
marks that the needle gives. Oh, yes; she was one of
a thousand drudging creatures like herself. She did not
"work out"; there were a good many who did not. If
she had no near kindred in New York she paid about
four dollars a week for her board in some tenement-
house. She had a little room there, hardly big enough
to hold her bed, her trunk and her sewing-machine all
together. Oh, how well he knew the whole story, just
by looking at her! And yet . . . she was so tremendously
different from the great mass of the others. Her looks
made her so. As he stood before her, trying to put a
gleam of unwonted clemency into his smile, a new
thought passed through his mind. 'As sure as my
name's George Bass,' he swiftly concluded, 'she must be
a little trump of virtue. They're not all good—even the
ugliest aren't. But she wouldn't be taking work at sixty
cents a day, with her face and figure, unless she'd kept
herself straight as a string. . . . Well, well, how long
will it last, I wonder?'

He was a cynic, this Mr. George Bass; and with respect
to the droves of forlorn females whom chance called him
incessantly to meet, perhaps his bitterness was in a way
pardonable. It seemed strange to him that he should

assume an actual politeness toward any one of Cora Strang's kind; it was like suddenly fishing out from the bottom of a chest some garment that he hadn't put on for years. He felt awkward, of course; he had been so accustomed to a totally opposite demeanor. Several of the questions he now asked her were kind and solicitous. By the time that the boy had reappeared with a big bundle of work for her he had learned not a few details of her drudging life. Soon the boy went out again, and when they were once more alone Mr. Bass said:

"I hope times *will* brighten up, Cora." He fumbled with one hand at his rather heavy watch-chain, and then began gently to jolt its links in his palm as though he were weighing them. "You're too nice a girl not to get along better in the world." He lowered his voice confidentially. "I tell you what it is," he proceeded, "you ought to marry. Some nice fellow, I mean, that would give you a good home and a new frock every three or four months." He was very close to Cora while he thus spoke. He had left off playing with his watch-chain, and begun to finger at the draggled fringes of her shawl.

She looked at him for a moment, with her serious eyes. "I don't know anybody I care for," she replied; and then, while she slowly shook her head, the movement might have made a poet think of some tall flower-stalk in a light breeze.

But Mr. Bass was no poet. His smile grew into a grin, and it seemed to be entangled coarsely among his next words, while he showed a semicircle of uneven teeth at the recession of his thin, russet-bearded lips.

"Oh," he said, "is that it? You don't know anybody you care for, eh? Well, I guess a good many might care for you, if you'd let them?"

"Do you mean, let them—marry me?" she asked, with directness that had in it a child's candor.

"Why, yes. You're so pretty. Come, now, haven't you been told that lots of times before?"

She nodded. She had got her bundle, and had tucked it under her shawl, where it made a big, onerous bulge. "Yes; men tell me so."

"And don't you believe them?"

Her lip curled, and this gave her, somehow, a virginal look that fed her native charm. "I don't bother my head about them one bit," she answered.

"Oh, you don't?" said Mr. Bass. And then, as he drew a little nearer, she saw that a bank-note was in one of his outstretched hands. An instant afterward he slipped the other hand round her waist. "Take this, Cora," he said, with a feverish grin, and his foxy eyes kindled. "'Tisn't very much; I'll only ask a kiss for it." He drew her toward him with abrupt force, and his pushed-out lips had almost met her own when she swerved and veered, quite releasing herself from his clasp.

"Oh, that's all right," she said, going swiftly to the door by which she had entered. There was the hard ring of repulse in her tones, but she did not appear either surprised or angry.

"I'll get these done as quick as I can," she said, tucking the bundle still closer beneath her curved arm, while he stood staring at her in a sheepishly irate way. Immediately, without another word, she turned the knob of the door and glided from the room. . . . .

The day had clouded again when she got outside into Worth Street, and the lowering skies had almost a tint as leaden as that of the pavements below them. Over the resonant carts, the streams of passers, the bustle of loading or unloading cumbrous trucks, the sports of filthy children in gutters, began to float tiny crystal filaments that glistened keenly in the raw air.

'I hope it *will* snow,' Cora thought, 'for then it will get warmer.' To many of the poor in New York, snow is an abhorrence.   Its masses of soggy refuse lie on their roofs and soak through into the ceilings beneath, while for weeks the yards and courts of tenement-houses will exhale stinging dampness from its unshovelled layers.   Cora, being young and in perfect health, felt the cut and search of the cold deeper than discomforts of this more insidious kind.   She had no very stout wraps, and it now crossed her mind, as she struck into the Bowery, that she had been foolish not to take that proffered money.

But, no, she soon decided.   If it had been so much plain alms, well and good.   There had been the scent of a bribe and a lure about it in this case, and therefore avoidance was discretion.   She would put herself in no man's power ; freedom was about all that she had to call her very own, and that she meant to keep.   She had seen such sights of woe where girls went wrong.   Besides, there was always that past of hers, at home in the country, to influence her, to remind her, to smile at her from afar, as the wild, sweet light of a dead sunset smiles over distances of deserted land

The Bowery, down in this crowded part of it, clamored to-day with hobgoblin noises.   Ragged boys were yelling "extra," in voices of unusual keenness, for that morning, at the Tombs near by, a quaking little Italian wife-murderer had been legally choked to death after four years' imprisonment and three elaborate trials.   The broad street itself was crammed with vehicles, whose various wheels jarred upon its cobble-stones with every species of dissonance, and across these, in a kind of vocal sword-thrust, darted the cry of the orange-and-banana vendors, with their laden carts trundled along the curb.

In the lower Bowery life seethes as though it were some sort of bubbling broth in a cauldron—hell-broth, perhaps.   Here is no hint of the ease born from wealth as bud from bough.   It is mostly struggle and fret, with spurts of false, hectic joy sometimes, but oftener of joy that is amazingly genuine.   There are many grim faces, but still there are many in which contentment has found an abiding haunt. You see want everywhere; in the cheap goods that swing for sale from the awnings of shops; in the uncouth shoes that are festooned before the windows of their purveyors like strings of sausages, each telling you at a glance of its pegged sole and insecure stitchings; in the blistered and veiny cigars that tobacconists expose behind their gaudy-painted wooden statues, or in the vulgar, pinchbeck jewelry, flaring crudely from at least five windows on every block. If you are not of this world—if you need not hoard your nickels and dimes too diligently—you feel, amid the hubbub and meanness of it all, that Delmonico's ought to be at least a hundred miles away, and the Moorish lamps in the Hoffman House corridors even farther still.

Overhead, the Elevated roared its cacophonies, with great volumes of steam gushing down into the life-packed street, and looking now and then like the coils of a monstrous white boa. Somebody pushed Cora rudely aside as she set her foot on the verge of a crossing; the collision made her reel toward a blind man and knocked out of his frail grasp a wheezy accordion, from which he was extracting pathetic whimpers. The instrument struck the slate underfoot with a flat thud, and a bristly-haired mongrel sentinelled between the blind man's legs broke into a peevish bark. Cora stooped and picked up the accordion, while the dog snarled at her and the mendicant sounded one of those oaths which would have seemed to ears polite as a black pearl of blasphemy. But Cora did not mind the oath; she may hardly have given it a thought, it had to her so natural a ring. She felt in her pocket for a coin, found one there of small value, and threw it into the tin box pendent against the man's breast. Then she hurried along, saying to herself that this little act of indemnity had been rash, after all, and that she might rue it later. The speeding trains hurtled and clashed above her as she plodded onward. Her large bundle, clutched

beneath one arm, took its power of warmth from her shawl, and made the cold creep up one of her sides, chilling ribs and breast. The little spangles of snow had ceased to flutter earthward; the sky had grown a sullen strip of iron above the house-tops, and a blast with blades of ice in it beat straight from the north on her bowed face. She was cold to the marrow when she reached Prince Street and turned into its narrower length of transverse thoroughfare, flanked by duller buildings. All this while she had been thinking of a sum she must raise three days from now, and of the slim chances there were that the most doggedly hard work would let her gain it. Only three dollars, to pay for room and board, but without such money homelessness among these freezing streets!

She felt numb and dizzy from the extreme cold, and still had a good distance to walk. She hated both the taste and effect of all wines, but now a sort of fright beset her, and she paused before one of the corner dens where they are sold. There was the usual side-entrance for women, and beyond it a small room with the aperture and shelf drolly called a "confession-box" by some defunct satirist of feminine tipplers. Two women were already in this room as Cora entered it. "Hello!" said one, "it's you, eh?".. She glanced at her companion with a great giggle. She had a glass of some smoking drink lifted in one hand; her face was yet young, but it bore a bloated flabbiness, and mirth made her show her gums in prodigal scarlet. The other girl was bony and faded, with a hard, masculine mouth. She had once been handsome, but she was now very weary-looking, yet with a bitter bravado on every feature.

"What's goin' to happen?" she called out, with her own smoking glass held a little sideways and her dead-black eyes riveted on Cora's face. "I guess we'll have an earthquake."

"Come, Lizzie," laughed the other girl, "get outside
o' your drink quick, an' she may treat us."

"I was so cold,"shivered Cora, "that I—I had to come
in—and——" She could hardly speak, and the girl who
had been called Lizzie saw it. Her hard mouth did not
soften, but she at once went forward with a brisk step.

"Here, take a sip o' that," she said, and held her glass
to Cora's lips.

The hot fluid made a dangerous potion, but it was
pleasant in its way as would have been a cup of water to
someone parched from heat and thirst.

"Oh, thank you, thank you!" Cora said. She took a
gulp and it half strangled her, butshe laughed at the same
instant, so exquisitely grateful was the warmth.

"She'll treat *now*, sure," said the associate of Lizzie, in
her vacuous, gleeful way, with the red gums nuder than
before. "She's drank your drink, Liz, and she'll have to
pay it back, and I guess I'll ring in on the same round
when she does."

"Oh, shut up, Ellen Lynch," rebuked Lizzie. "Don't
you see she's mos' froze?"

Already Cora's eyes had begun to sparkle with re-
animate light. She handed Lizzie back her glass with another "thank you," and just then a head appeared at the
miniature window over the shelf. It was the barkeeper's,
and its hair was arranged in scallops over the brow, and
looked as if bandoline had gone to the making of their
stiff, tawny curves. He had not an ungenial face, though
it was so pitted with small-pox that his elaborated locks
gave the swift impression of an attempt to lure the eye
from these cutaneous flaws.

"Well, ladies," he began, and winked at Lizzie. Then
Cora wholly absorbed him, and in reply to the peculiar
stare she had long ago become familiar with in men, she
said :

"I wanted something to warm me a little, please.
Brandy or whiskey, I suppose. Not much. Just a mouth-

ful." Here she remembered Lizzie's last words, and
with a sudden qualm of fear thrust her hand into her
pocket where some loose silver lay.

"And they'll have something, too," she went on, with
a motion of her head toward the two girls.

"You bet we will," said Lizzie, tossing off her drink.
In another minute both Lizzie and Ellen had asked for
"the same," whatever that may have meant, and just as
the man was about to withdraw with "All right, ladies,"
Cora struck in, a little tremulously :

"How much will it be, please ? "

The barkeeper, on the point of vanishing, thrust his
head still further into the square hole.   "Oh, that'll be all
right," he answered, and then disappeared.

Ellen Lynch gave a strident laugh.   "He's mashed on
you ! " she cried to Cora.

There chanced to be one chair in the little compartment,
and Cora sank into it.   "I don't want that," she called
disapprovingly.   "I'd rather pay."   But the man had
already gone.

"Ain't she funny ? " murmured Lizzie to Ellen, in a low
voice but one that held untold worldliness and irony.

"Yes, she *is*," almost shouted Ellen, with a stare down
at Cora, who was rubbing her hands together, having set
her big, soft bundle in a near corner.   "Good Lord ! If
I had her looks I'd be ridin' round in my carriage.
Wouldn't *you*, Liz ? "

Lizzie seldom laughed or smiled at anything.   "I'd a
had some fun 'fore I was her age.   'Tain't too late *yet* for
her, neither."   And she fixed on Cora a look that teemed
with critical scrutiny.

"Too late ! " echoed Ellen.   "It's just her *time !* "   Then
came a reckless oath, which merged into the exclamation :
" *What* a fool she is to slave at sewin' when she could
cram her close with greenbacks ! "

Lizzie's voice, always lazy and frigid, had now a ruminative tone.   " *I* did, once.   I was most as good-lookin
as she is, in *my* day, 'fore I——"

"*You!*" shot in Ellen, jeeringly. "I *guess* so! When you was good-lookin' as that gal is I'd like to a seen ye, Liz!"

"Well, you didn't see me," scowled her friend. "You was too busy over to that panel-house in Macdougal Street."

"Ye don't say so!" mocked Ellen. "And where was *you*, then? On the streets—there's where you was, and strainin' yourself day and night to keep that little brat of a Phil Bradley, that's up to Sing Sing now, servin' out his twelve years' sentence for house-breakin'."

"You lie!" said Lizzie; and followed it by a chain of such lewd and uncanny names that even Cora's ears, used to all forms of blackguardly rhetoric, tingled under this abusive burst. The two women glared at each other like two cats, and from clapperclawing might soon have reached the scratches and blows drink had often before led them to, when a sudden entrance of the barkeeper and a volley of oaths more ribald than any they themselves had used put an end to their menaced fray.

"Now you two old spitfires, you get right out of here," was soon hurled at them as well; and the women, though both aflame with wrath, went muttering and glowering into the street.

"They're afraid o' me," said the barkeeper, a little later to Cora. "They know I'd have 'em run in as quick as wink.. I'm awful sorry they was annoyin' *you*, ma'am," he proceeded, putting a hand about Cora's arm and letting his big fingers, on which the nails were dead-white as those of a corpse from being incessantly steeped in liquids, press against her flesh with bold ardor. "Now jus' you wait here a minnit, an' I'll get you a nice warm drink, so I will." And then his lips came so close to her ear that his breath swept her nostrils, nauseous with those fumes which haunt the mouth of a confirmed toper. "I see from the first what *you* was. The cold weather bring *you* in here. You need a little brace agin it." He snatched a kiss from her half-averted cheek, and then recoiled, chuckling. "Jus' wait, now. I'll fix ye so's you can go out an' think the weather 's give a jump inter July."

He departed, with nods of profuse geniality. Cora did wait, but only for a moment. She was so unused to all sorts of stimulants that the sip or two from Lizzie's glass had given her a new sense of cheer and support. It was only a step into the street, and, gathering her bundle speedily once more beneath her shawl, she slipped out upon the sidewalk again with steps as fleet as though she were a thief eluding pursuit.

Home lay about seven blocks ahead. She felt able enough to walk that distance now, for the spark put into her blood had nerved her so that the edge of the blast seemed blunt and ineffectual. No doubt for this reason her thoughts began to work, and she told herself that to be dowered with a fair face meant little short of an actual curse.

"How I hate men!" she began to muse. "They're all alike—at least those I see nowadays. It makes me almost wish I'd been born ugly; they're such brutes. Those two poor creatures, Lizzie and Ellen, wouldn't be what they are but for just such treatment as I've had twice in the last hour. God somehow helps me to keep straight, though. . . . Well, I wonder if it *is* God, after all, or if it's only because I couldn't any more let myself drift that way than I could jump off the Brooklyn Bridge."

Her home was a high, brick tenement-house, and as she paused for a second at its entrance a sombre dread assailed her. But she shook off this feeling as best she could, and mounted four pairs of stairs, through ill-smelling halls, past coarsely-grained doors and "sinks" that gave out odors wherefrom not a few occupants in former years had drank malarial death. Turning a certain knob she at length passed into a small apartment which might be termed a typical lair of the poorer New York classes.

II.

Not that it was half so mean and miserable as many another in our poverty-ridden metropolis, but it had, nevertheless, its acute accent of squalor. A Mrs. Slattery was its proprietress, but this Irish name was unsuited to her as though marigold should be called peony. Years ago she had been a German emigrant, with blond braids and a little precarious vocabulary of about ten English words. Now, at fifty-five or thereabouts, she was the widow of an Irishman, with one strapping son and three rooms here on Prince Street. She slept in the room Cora had just entered, and she also did all her cooking there. Her small feather-bed bulged from one corner; a stove that diffused sickening heat crouched like some black, repellent reptile but a yard or two away. She had been a Bavarian Catholic, and her walls were hung with colored prints of the Crucifixion and the Martyred Virgin that might, in their red-and-yellow crudity, have made the bones of Rubens or Raphael rattle oversea. From the top of a pine-wood chest of drawers rose a kerosene lamp with a glass shade of muddy pink, girt by one or two tin saucepans, a bottle of melted butter for the hair, a brush with its bristles wry and flattened, a comb with half its teeth gone and little hirsute knots clogging the others. From the high, angular mantel you heard a clock ticking petulantly; and so worn and common was its triple-pointed wooden case that you might have fancied even time itself had changed in these dismal lodgings and reigned here with more than churlish rigor.

Mrs. Slattery was seated with a wooden bowl on her knees, peeling potatoes, as Cora appeared. She was a tall, broad woman, with almost the chest and shoulders of a man, yet with not a superfluous ounce of flesh on one of her big bones. Black eyebrows bushed austerely above eyes of iron-gray, whose dry glitter suited the aquiline face from which they shone. Her speech held no sign of her foreign birth, now ; it rang as nasally as any New England housewife's, and with an idiom as homespun and graceless.

"Well, you *must* a been trampin' round," she said to Cora. "But you've got a big bundle, there, to show for it. I only hope it ain't trash though, like some o' the other stuff you've brought in."

"It is," returned Cora, as she dropped wearily into a chair. "That's just *what* it is."

Mrs. Slattery nodded, with tightening lips. She was known among all her neighbors as one of the hardest women they had ever met. There was one soft spot in her heart, however, but Cora, her young lodger, had wholly failed to touch that. Indeed, she had avoided doing so, and for reasons both obvious and repugnant. These concerned the persecuting passion of Owen Slattery, her landlady's treasured son. Mrs. Slattery gave to this Owen a nimbus of perfection, whereas he did not always deserve one of even ordinary decency. Months ago Cora had quarrelled with him and bid him keep at his distance. She was getting on well with her work, then, and Mrs. Slattery no doubt valued the promptitude with which her weekly three dollars were delivered. Now it was altogether different. Cora owed board-money, and her tenure of a little room just to the rear of this looked fatally doubtful.

"I'm sorry," asserted Mrs. Slattery, in a voice that would have seemed fitter for the gruesome announcement that she was glad. "If they've been shovin' off boys' pants, or shirt-tabs and cuffs, or any such cheap rubbish on you, so's you can't catch up and pay me square no

matter *how* hard you drive, why then it'll be too bad.
But still, the room's got to go, all the same.

"Yes, I understand," said Cora. "But you agreed
that if I could let you have three dollars by next Tuesday
I could stay on for another week. And Davis & Co. told
me this morning that they expected times would brighten
soon, and that—"

"Oh, to the devil with *them !*" broke in her listener.
"I'm sick o' *their* talk. . . . Well, what did you do ?
You said you was a goin' to some new place."

"And I went," said Cora. She told her little tale,
while Mrs. Slattery smiled and sniffed, not as though she
disbelieved it, but as though she had her own opinions
about the proper stress of energy exerted by her lodger.

"And now I must set right to work," presently said
Cora, rising. She looked at the clock as she passed
toward her own little room, which she might also have
reached, if she had chosen, by the narrow outer hall.
"Four o'clock," she went on, as though speaking to herself. Then, quite earnestly to Mrs. Slattery, who had
drooped her head over the potatoes and begun peeling
them with a slashing stroke, she added:

"I *guess* I can manage it. I'm goin' to try good and
hard. If I keep the machine up till two or three you
won't mind it, I hope. It does make a good deal of
noise, I know, but—"

Oh, *I* shan't mind it," exclaimed Mrs. Slattery, throwing a blanched potato into her truncheon with vim that
implied some occult spite." "*I* sleep good enough not
to. But Oweny may."

"Perhaps he won't hear *it,*" said Cora ; and she was
about to cross into her own room when another door (the
one by which she herself had entered) was pushed open
and "Oweny," as his fond mother loved to call him,
strode into her presence.

"What's that about me ? " said the young man, in a testy
tone. He had scarcely spoken a pleasant word to his

mother for a good many years, though she would almost rather have bitten off her tongue than speak an unpleasant one to him.   He glanced toward Cora as he seated himself, a dark, keen-faced fellow, with spare but sinewy frame.   As he did so the girl slipped into her· room, closing the door behind her.

Owen leaned forward with an elbow on each knee and his big, paint-soiled hands dangling.   "Six months," he muttered, as if wholly to himself, though his mother seemed alertly listening.

"Who's got six months?" queried Mrs. Slattery, while her thoughts at once flew toward imprisonments on Blackwell's Island.

Owen snickered.   "Nobody, as I know of.   I was thinkin' o' *her*."   And he pointed to Cora's closed door.

His mother's face hardened, and she gave several quick nods.   "Oh, yes, I see.   You mean, Oweny, that she ain't spoke to you for six months."

"I guess we'll get that job down there in Rivington Street," said the young man musingly, as he looked at his paint-caked nails.   It'll be two coats for the woodwork all over the house, if we *do* manage."

"That's good news, Oweny," said his mother; and then she went back to the subject he had so coolly changed, though easing toward it, as a woman will often do.   "If you can only go on as well in your paintin' as you've been going, we can get into a better street than this and a house where the folks ain't such a low lot, neither.   And by that time, please God, we won't have *her*, any more, owin' money and puttin' on airs to one and the same time—not speakin' to you for six whole months !" Soon Mrs. Slattery continued, seeing no opposition in the blank look that her son had cast at the rag-carpet just beneath him : "Why, if 'tain't the cheekiest thing I ever—"

"Oh, God damn it, you know what I did !" Owen shot in, lifting his head, and with voice one arrogant growl.

"After that night I went drunk into her room she might have sent me to State's prison for as many years as you've got fingers on *one* hand, anyway. And what d'ye mean by sayin' we won't have her no more? She ain't goin'? You ain't been *tellin'* her to go?" And he stared at his mother with knit brows.

Mrs. Slattery laughed nervously. She feared her son as much as she loved him. But she had to tell the truth, now; she had gone too far with Cora not to tell it. Owen's iron-gray eyes—the counterparts of her own—had begun to smoulder with a surly scintillance. She let them devour her face, and then, showing a burst of mild defiance, broke out:

"Well, I *have* made up my mind to bounce her. She ain't no good here. She owes for three weeks' board, and she treats you's if you was the dirt under her feet, and—"

"So I am," growled Owen, rising. He went toward his mother, who turned pale as she saw him coming. "So are you, too," he proceeded. "She's as good a gal as there is in this ward. She's got into hard luck now, but she'll pay every cent o' that money, and you know it devilish well. What did she do for you a year ago when you was layin' on your back with pleurisy and I was drunk half my time? *She kept us both,* that's what she did! And now you want to turn her into the streets because you can't rake in them three dollars that you'd be in debt to her for if she'd chose to take count of 'em. . . Now, see here;" and Owen Slattery laid his large, soiled hand on his mother's shoulder; "I don't want to get mad with you; but so sure as I'm lookin' at them potaters in your lap, if you ever say another word to that gal about leavin' these premises, I'll make you so sorry, mother or no mother, that you won't forget it to your dyin' day!"

Owen's were perhaps the sole human threats that could wring tears from her who now heard them. She began to whimper and tremble as he drew back his hand.

"Why, then," she bleated, "does the gal treat *you* so?

Ain't that enough, alone by itself? You *was* drunk, then, and I s'pose what you did was pretty bad. But you ain't drank a drop for six months, and how's *she* troubled herself, one way or another? *She* don't care. She might see you brought home with a bullet in your skull, like Mrs. Rafferty's boy last week, and she wouldn't so much as look at you while the doctor and the priest was both to your bedside. Not *her!* Lord a mercy, Oweny Slattery, I never thought you cared for her like that! You ain't showed it if you have. You ain't never showed it till now."

He had turned away, with both hands thrust into the pockets of his paint-stained overalls. He sullenly veered round again at this point, however, and muttered between his hard, strong teeth :

"What fools you women are! Why've I kep' sober so long? Why'm I tryin' to be decent? Ain't I been waitin'? Ain't you been able to *see* I was waitin'?"

"Waitin'? For what, Oweny?"

"To marry her—the devil take her," said Owen, which he meant in a way for tenderness, and in saying which his tones betrayed a distinct tremor.

Mrs. Slattery looked thunderstricken. Then she glanced toward the shut door of Cora's room, as though suddenly roused to realization that the girl might have overheard all they two had just been saying.

But Cora had heard nothing. Shortly after closing her door, and just as she was about to seat herself doggedly at her sewing-machine, a visitor had appeared by the entrance leading from the outer hall. It was a girl of about he own age, with a sallow, frail-looking face, and eyes like two tawny diamonds. They were bathed in tears this moment, those beautiful eyes, which were all the girl had of beauty. Her thin, flat-chested figure was robed in a gown of some coarse white stuff, having four tucks at the edge of its rather scant skirt. On her bosom she wore a spray of the commonest artificial flowers—a semblance, presumably, of orange-blossoms—and round her throat was a string of white glass beads.

"Oh, Effie," murmured Cora, as she rose. "It's your weddin'-day, ain't it? And I've been so bothered I'd forgotten!"

Effie could hardly speak for her tears. "Yes," she managed, "it—it is, Cora, and it ain't brought me much fun, you can *bet!*"

"Why, how's that, Effie?"

"Oh, I'm tremblin' all over," said the bride. "Jus' *feel* how I'm tremblin'." And she put Cora's hand upon one of her bare, cold arms.

"Why, you've got a kind of a chill, Effie. Here, take my shawl."

"No—never mind. 'Tain't that. Oh, Cora, pa and ma's *both* got off—this day of all days! To think of it!" Here Effie stopped short, with quivering lips, and made an impulsive movement toward Cora, catching each of her hands. "Oh, *do* come downstairs! I know you're awful busy; you told me what hard times these was with you. But, oh, Ann's got sicker than I most ever see her, and *they're* layin'— Oh, my God, Cora, it's too much! But I won't give way! I *can't!* Jimmy's comin' at happast four, and Ann *is* so bad. Jus' come down and see what you think 'bout her. Do!"

It was only on the next floor below, and Cora went at once down through the ugly, chilly halls. As they entered a room that was but slightly different from Mrs. Slattery's in size and general detail, the sound of a hollow cough struck on Cora's ears. It came from the chamber of Effie's invalid sister, Ann, only a few yards away. Here two shapes were tumbled on a bed, not side by side, but so that the woman's prone body overlapped the man's feet, his head being buried in a pillow, while hers, fallen backward with strained throat, met the plaster of the opposite wall. Both were breathing heavily; now and then the man gave a snore like the turning of a key in a rusty lock.

The bride paused for a moment, with one arm round Cora's waist, as they were moving toward the room where Ann lay. "Jus' look!" she whined. "Ain't it too much? They've been that way ever since noon. Las' night they had a fight, and pa swore he'd kill ma, and ma dared him and double-dared him, and some o' the Rourkes and the Schmitts, here on this floor, they both come in, drawed by the screechin'. I thought you'd hear it."

"I guess I was workin'," said Cora, with a sort of plaintive apology, "and the machine drownded it."

"Well, they made up this mornin', and kissed right 'fore us two gals, and we was real happy, 'cause it was my weddin'-day. Jim dropped in for a little spell, and shook hands with 'em (he was here last night and seen the row), and if it hadn't been for Ann lookin' and actin' worse I could just a *sung*, I was so glad. But I didn't like pa havin' an off day. He does roofin' work, you know, and he came back 'bout 'leven o'clock, and said he'd fixed it so's he needn't do anything more till the weddin'. It always has a squally sound to me when pa says he' ain't goin' to work, for even an idle hour or so in the day-time 'll set him hankerin' after liquor. Well, Cora, 'fore he'd been in the house twenty minutes he got restless, and out he went with a can. He come in a little while after, and the first glance I give him I see he had a heavier load into him than the beer he was carry-in'. And ma was feelin' kind o' frisky, 'cause o' my weddin' and the make-up 'tween pa and her, so she took a sup o' the beer, though I winked at her, and tried to catch her eye, for the least taste always did set ma off. But 'twas no use o' me interferin'. Ann got one of her coughin' fits, and kep' me at her for a good while; and when I come out of our room, there was ma and pa clinkin' glasses, and the Lord knows how much more

beer they'd been havin', and ma was talkin 'bout marryin'
me to as fine a young ge'man as you could see along the
whole Bowery on a Saturday night, and *pa!*—oh, Cora, I
had one o' them tight feelin's round the heart, as if I was
goin' to bu'st, and—"

"Hark," said Cora at this point; and then they both
hurried into Ann's room, where she lay, white, cadaver-
ous, with eyes a little browner than her sister's and still
more hectically brilliant.

"Oh, is it you, Cora?" gasped Ann, between her
coughs. "I'm bad to-day—worse'n I've been for ever so
long." She grew somewhat quieter after Cora had taken
her hand, coughing more gutturally and with an evident
power to exert partial control over the paroxysm. "I'm
glad you come," she soon went on; "Effie said she'd try
and get you. Ain't it *too* bad 'bout ma and pa? They
could go to the weddin', and now they're layin' in there.
And I'm layin' here that can't go and would give so
much if I only could! Don't Effie look nice? Show
Cora your veil and wreath, Ef."

Thus requested, Effie produced from a corner the kind
of paper-flower wreath we sometimes see embellishing
plum-cakes in baker-shop windows along Avenues A or
B. Depending from it was a veil whose texture almost
resembled that of the usual mosquito-netting. She giggled
as she put the affair on, letting the veil fall over her
face.

"'Tain't much, o' course," she said, staring at herself
in a cracked mirror that overhung a ramshackle bureau;
"but I always *did* so want to be dressed like a real bride
when I got married! It kind o' comforts me, somehow," she proceeded, with a wistful look toward Cora,
"poor as it all is!"

"Why 'tain't poor a bit," exclaimed Ann, with sudden
appeal to Cora. "*Is* it?"

"I guess it *isn't!*" said Cora. And then she turned to
Ann, pulling the bed-clothes further up over the sunken

chest of the sick girl. "You ought to keep quieter," she went on. "The quieter you keep the less you'll cough."

"Oh, I feel a good deal better now," said Ann, whose voice had got to be huskier since her cough had stopped. "It's so nice to have you here, Cora. I ain't seen you in three days." Here she pressed Cora's hand with her own hot, clinging, wasted one. "You don't know what three days *is* to me as I lay here. And you're so pretty. Oh, there's nobody I ever seen that's as pretty as you are. Don't they *tell* you so?"

"She won't let 'em," said Effie, beginning to hair-pin her wreath into permanent poise. "She's got too much sense; ain't you, Cora?"

"I do so wish you'd stay with me while Effie's to the church," pleadingly continued Ann; and despite the work that waited her upstairs, with so hateful a throat brooding over its neglect, Cora could not find refusal in her heart.

Soon the bridegroom appeared, and with his entrance a little crowd gathered in the hall outside, debarred from coming further by Effie's embarrassed and pathetic veto. It wrought a visible shock in Mr. James Halloran to see his future parents-in-law supine on the bed. He was a square-built young man of about three-and-thirty, with eyes too small for his heavy, jowly face, and a bulging underlip that had come from the inordinate chewing of tobacco. He had sacredly promised Effie that he would not touch his beloved weed all that day, and the result of such abstinence had made him acquainted with nerves for perhaps the first time in his life. He had brought two carriages—a strain upon his unplethoric purse—and one of them had been designed for Effie's recumbent parents. He had brains and feeling enough to recognize that his marriage-day was being turned into a mockery and a shame. There were friends of his whom he had asked to meet him at the church, and that empty carriage might mean ambiguous volumes for the romantic inventiveness of gossip. It has often been said that the bride is always cooler-headed than the bridegroom, and on this occasion the popular verdict was verified. Effie took forth her "Jim" into the street below with a step much firmer than his own. She had promised the poor wan Ann to come back and tell her "all about how it went off"; and as Cora, sitting at the sick girl's bedside, saw the pair disappear past that tragic disclosure of the besotted father and mother, an admiration for Effie's courage and self-rule wrought its thrilling effect upon her.

Just as they neared the hall, where a curious little throng had gathered, Jim whispered to Effie, who had taken his arm with a sense of the dignity and nicety of things, even in the teeth of couchant scandal—

"Say, Ef, I'm as nervous as the devil. Lemme have a small quid into my cheek 'fore we go outside, won't ye?"

Effie scanned through her veil the dull, big face that she dearly loved. "Well, yes, Jim," she relented; "but make it small. And promise me—*promise* now, mind—that you won't spit any while we're gettin' married."

"Not if I choke, Ef," came the answer, as Jim dove with one hand into the "pistol-pocket" of his trousers.

III.

Soon after the bridal pair had taken their departure a
drowsy fit overcame Ann ; but though the lids only flut-
tered sleepily above her eyes, the brilliancy of those
feverish pupils which they threatened to obscure acquired
a dulness filled for Cora with ominous change.

'What if she should die while Effie is away getting
married?' thought the watcher at Ann's bedside.   But
soon she banished this dread by a little effort, and rose
to have a look at the medicine on the bureau, which
Effie had told her should be administered if certain symptoms of violent short-breathing set in.

That cracked looking-glass into which the vanished
bride had not long ago gazed at herself and her flimsy
braveries, now confronted Cora.   She stood before it a
moment, attracted by her own image.   Possibly some
sense of contrast between what nature had made her and
what it had made the girl who had last peered into it
may have flashed across her mind.

She could not be unconscious of her own beauty ; few
women, however deeply we plunge into the records of
either history or myth, ever are.   She stared at her
reflection for a brief time, and almost wondered at it.
She saw a body trim as a fawn's and graceful as a lily-
stalk.   Her small head rose above it, dowered with wavy
lines of cinnamon-hued hair that made two flexile upward curves at either temple.   Her eyes were of
precisely the same hue as her crinkled locks ; there
was never a more subtly perfect match between
two colors, if you waived those dark, slim rings that
gave emphasis to the liquid sweetness of her look.   She

had a small mouth, with a tiny upward bend at either corner, and teeth of the milkiest evenness. But the shape of her face was, after all, its chief charm, for the very delicacy and purity of her tinting could not have affected the same winsome spell as that which had been wrought by special outlines. The truth was, her gold-brown eyes were unusually wide apart, and from temple to chin her cheeks made, on this account, a slope that would have seemed to a sculptor no less audacious than lovely. But though her beauty was apparently of the fragile type, its hardihood almost passed credence. You might have likened it to certain orchids that we can toss here and there in idle unconcern of their lissome-curled petals and yet find them again, after hours of neglect, retaining an almost dewy freshness. Fatigue would turn Cora paler and put gloomy tinges beneath her eyes ; but the pallor and the dusk were both only a new form of attraction, and like the placing of a picture in some altered light. Anxiety, overwork, late hours, loss of sleep and even the subtle gnawings of hunger itself could thus far wreak no ravage upon her. Such as nature had fashioned her, she somehow indestructibly remained. Her funds of health were deep ; an enthusiast might almost have dreamed them fathomless.

"Cora," called Ann, softly, from the bed ; and at once the sick girl found a face that brimmed with sympathy bending above her pillow.

"Yes, I'm here," Cora said. She dropped into a chair at Ann's bedside. "You seemed to be sleepy a little while ago. Ain't you so now ?"

"No ; I feel quite wide awake."

Cora stroked her forehead and hair for a moment. "I guess you're better again, Ann."

"Yes ; I think I am. Don't leave me, though, Cora."

"Oh, no. I said I wouldn't, and I won't."

"Not till Effie comes back ?"

"No, not till Effie comes back."

"Couldn't you tell me a story, Cora—something nice and—and long? I do love stories."

Cora shook her head. "I don't know any," she answered. "I only wish I did, Ann, for your sake. I know my own story—how I came to this great, cruel city and got to be the slavin' drudge I am. But you wouldn't care for that, I guess. It ain't the kind they put into books."

"I'd rather hear it than any other kind!" exclaimed Ann, in her hoarse, eager tones. "True stories is just what I do like. I ain't been to school since I took sick —that's three years ago, and I'm sixteen now. But I've outgrowed stories with fairies in 'em. And I do hate princes and prin*cesses*, Cora. I don't believe there *is* many—not o' the kind that wears gold crowns and is always sittin' on thrones in pallerces. I guess if there is any at all they berhave a good deal like other folks. And as for fairies, good or bad—why, that's all rot, ain't it?"

"I guess it is," said Cora. "There's none in *my* story, anyway. Perhaps there's a few bad fairies In it, workin' their spite out. But I can't say; I wouldn't swear the devil himself hadn't had a hand in my fortunes, from first to last."

"Oh, Cora! Don't you believe the devil only comes when God thinks he ought to, and lets him try if he can't grip us while we're sinnin'?"

"I don't know anything about God," said Cora, with unconscious agnosticism. "But if he's good, Ann, it seems funny he don't help people more than he does; and if he's bad it seems funny he don't put his foot on all the goodness and stamp it out like a smokin' match. I was brought up to pray, and I *do* say one little prayer every night, because I promised my mother I always would. That prayer may keep me straight, but if it does it's only on account of mother seemin' to come up from her grave and listen. Seemin', I say, Ann, for she don't, and the dead don't ever come like that. . . When she died, out there near Peekskill, I thought I *must* die too. I was seventeen, and we'd been such friends! Father and I never got on a bit well. He was sick most of the time, and couldn't tend much to the business in the little store we kept, and children fretted him. He'd be cross to me, and I'd run to mother. This vexed him, and he grew soured against me by the time I was a big girl. But after mother died it was different. We'd both been so fond of her that we soon came to be fond of one another. Father'd had a frightful blow, and he showed it. I had to 'tend store most of the time; he was too weak and too queer in his head. He used to sit in a corner for hours and mutter to himself: 'Ain't it strange? ain't it strange?' He meant it was strange mother should go first when he'd been ailin' for years and she'd always nursed him and looked after him, hearty and strong. . . . But, oh, Ann, this ain't a pleasant story; it's too sad altogether for a sick-room." And Cora patted her companion's fleshless arm, and met her burning eyes with a melancholy smile.

"Oh, no," said Ann; "I like it. It sounds so true. And I guess most true things *is* sad; don't you think so, Cora?"

"I'm tempted to think so."

"Well, Cora, and how did your pa get on afterward? It was nice to hear how you and him come together and loved each other."

"But it didn't last long, Ann. Father got feebler and full of odd notions. I had to be in the store half my time, and though I did my best there, things went wrong. Custom fell off, partly for the reason that I couldn't keep in stock what everybody wanted, and partly because people didn't like the idea of havin' a young slip of a girl wait on them. And then, all of a sudden, one day, father fell off his chair just like a dead man. We got him to bed, but he only lived a week. And from that time I was alone, and I've been alone, Ann, ever since; for the few

relations I had were distant, and they behaved more so
as soon as they found out I wanted help. I was hardly
nineteen when I came here to New York. I would come.
Five or six of the neighbors tried to scare me out of it,
but I would come. There was no livin' to be made in
those parts for a girl like me, and everything I might have
got from father was wrecked by the debts he left behind him. One neighbor gave me the address of a
boarding-house in Great Jones Street, and I staid there,
usin' some money I'd saved up since I was a child and
never thought I'd have to spend that way, while I looked
round for work. But I soon found those quarters were
a good deal too dear. I moved to Amity Street after
I'd got something to do. It wasn't much—book-foldin'
in a big bindery, where I was paid seven dollars a week
for workin' ten hours every day. Pressin' down the leaves
began to blister my fingers so that I had to give up at last.
And, oh, Ann, the sights I did see in that place! Girls
almost as sick as you are, with their hands all sore and
bleedin', and some so poor they daresn't send out for more
than a five-cent lunch. I had sense enough to understand
I'd soon get just like the worst of them if I didn't stop
right short off and look for something better. I'd always
been a neat, quick sewer. The Amity Street landlady
knew a tailor in Hudson Street, and spoke a good word
for me. At first the pay was starvation itself, but by-and-
by they found out I was smarter and stronger than most
of the other hands, after my fingers got well enough for
me to show what I really could do. I hired a machine
for thirty cents a week and did men's coats, overcoats,
trousers and vests. I was baster, liner and finisher, all
in one. Mr. Rosenheim used to laugh and tell me I
was the best worker he'd ever got hold of since he first
went into the trade. I could manage the body — and
—sleeve linings and the velvet collars and the hair-cloth
inside fixin's and the button-holes ; and many a time, too,
I've put on the little silk patch that bore the firm's name

and gave the garment its last touch. All this time I was
living there in Amity Street. The landlady was a Polish
Jewess, and she had a brother that bothered me a good
deal. He thought himself very handsome, with his red
lips and oily black curls, and . . . Oh, one evening
when I was tired and nervous after a hard day's work on
a stiff corduroy shooting-suit, I just told him to go about
his business and never dare speak to me again. Many
a girl would have said it to him long before, but I'd held
my tongue because of what his sister did for me at
Rosenheim's. And now he went to her with lies about
me. I guess he was afraid I'd get ahead of him and tell
her the truth. She doted on him—and then you've seen
how Jews cling together. I had reason to find it out,
the Lord knows I had! such names as that woman called
me before I could pack my trunk and get quit of Amity
Street! 'Hussy' was the mildest of them all. And after
I'd gone away that wasn't the end of it. One day when
I went for work to the Rosenheims' they put me off with
a strange answer, and then, in a week or so, it came out
that they didn't want me there any more. That meant
the Amity Street people. The Rosenheims were Jews,
and they either believed whatever false, vile tales had
been brought them, or else it was their wish to act as if
they did and keep friends with my foes. Oh, Ann, the
sidewalk just moved up and down underneath me as I
went out of that store empty-handed. A girl I knew had
told me that Mrs. Slattery, here in Prince Street, would
give me three-dollar board, and I'd already come to her.
But in spite of the mean trick played on me that change
seemed at first to bring me luck. I got in with Davis
& Co., and there was a time last winter when I did real
splendid. But I'm beginnin' to see, Ann, that no trade is
steady right straight along. Look at feathers, gimps, flowers, plush, and all work like that. They go up and down
like see-saws, and nobody can tell why. And it ain't so
very much better with men's wear, with skirt-work at

dress-makers', with the millinery-line, or . . . Oh, Ann, what *is* the matter ? "

Seeing a great alteration suddenly take place in the girl at her side, Cora spoke those last words with sharp alarm. Ann appeared struggling for breath, and now, as she tried to give a smile of reassurance, her bluish lips made clear the distress that racked her.

" Lift — me up a little on to the — pillers, Cora," she gasped. " It's one o' them spells I—I take." And then she made an attempt at laughter, very piteous, and with indeed "a dying fall." "Don't think 'twas your story done it," she added; "that staved it off, if anything. . . . There; I'm better with the pillers put so. If it wasn't for this dreadful pain in the chest ! I—I knew 'twas goin' to begin. Oh, it's like knives runnin' in and out, or else scoopin' and twistin'."

Effie had left a few parting injunctions with her friend as to the uses of lotion and plaster in case of some attack like the present one. Cora now availed herself of the knowledge thus given, and spared no effort in seeking to quell Ann's pain. A drowsiness had come over the girl which she did not like. Faint moans would sometimes leave the pinched and tremulous mouth, finding a ghastly sort of echo in the drunken snores not far away. It was hardly pleasant to be left thus, quite alone with one who showed every sign of extreme illness. "I wish Effie were back," said Cora to her own thought; and almost as though she had mentally read this desire, Ann, with her hoarse little piping voice, called out :

" Don't you believe Effie 'll get home pretty soon, now ? "

" Pretty soon, I guess," returned Cora. Trying to speak cheerfully, she went on : " Are you so anxious to hear all about the weddin', Ann ? "

" No," said Ann ; " 'tain't that. I . . ."

But no more words came from her lips. What came from them wrung a shriek out of Cora's. The blood did not flow ; it rushed, in a horrible red torrent. And before it had stopped Effie hurried quite gleesomely into the room.

It had been the bursting of a great artery, and Ann's death was instantaneous. But her night-gown and a part of the bed-clothes were saturated with blood. Effie gave a wild cry as she saw her. She darted to the bed and in a trice her own bridal-dress and back-thrown veil were stained from the red font of her sister's ended life. But she seemed unconscious of the ghastly effect thus produced. Jim, her new husband, saw it with a shudder, and sprang toward her, trying to make her leave the bed.

" Effie," he cried ; " for God's sake !—don't you see ? " But she would not listen to him or heed him. She threw herself forward and clasped Ann's neck. The sisters had been near of an age, and very close to one another in that life of worry and drag and burden which both had led, and the vice of their parents had bound them still closer. Many a time during childhood they had shivered in their beds because quilts and blankets had been pawned for drink. The privation which had killed one of them had strengthened the mutual love of either.

Effie did not believe, at first, that Ann was dead. The blood horrified her, but the knowledge of what it truly meant evaded her perception. Cora soon made the truth plain to her, but recoiled afterward from the effect produced. It was one of madness, whether seeming or actual. Effie's eyes dilated ; she uttered shriek after shriek, until neighbors from various other rooms hurried flocking about the blood-stained corpse. This demented bride, in her tawdry gear, became touched with a new sort of romance, from which all the old elements of caste and culture were grimly lacking, and where blunt fact grinned with naked savagery. Cora sought to restrain her wildness, and failed. He whom she had just married made a like effort, but shrank from using the harsh force that occasion claimed. The noise and confusion woke the two drunkards from their sleep, and they came staggering past the threshold of the death-chamber with bleared eyes and flushed faces. At sight of them Effie, with flying veil and blood-dabbled gown, sped to where they stood.

"Look!" she shouted, pointing toward the bed. "She's gone—our Ann's gone—while I was to church with Jim! You couldn't 'tend her; you was both dead-drunk. She died while you was wallowin' yonder in your liquor. But what did *you* care? What did you *ever* care, you couple o' murderers! for that's what you've both been to Ann, as sure as a God hears me now!"

"Don't call on any god, young gal," said a voice from the little crowd. "There ain't any, and he wouldn't hear you if there was. Blame them two brutes as much as you want to, but don't fire religion at 'em. Religion's helped to curse 'em already." And here a certain little atheist and socialist shoemaker whose shop was downstairs on the first floor, looked about him, with a set of yellow, broken teeth gleaming through the tangles of an immense black beard.

"Shut your mouth," said another voice.

"No, I won't," retorted the shoemaker, who averaged at least one hot fray every week for the sake of his opinions, and had set a certain East-side hall ringing to the rafters more than once, of late, with his hot harangues. "No, *sir*! I'll be damned if I will!"

Effie's father, still dazed from drink and sleep, glared at the shoemaker. But Effie's mother did more. She was a woman renowned for daring when in her cups, looking the personal image of both her pale, thin daughters, but with a hardened aspect that dissipation alone confers.

"You won't shut up, won't ye, Bill Darick?" she screamed, and shot toward the little shoemaker with both hands made stiff and claw-like. "Then we'll see if I can't learn ye to, so we will!" The creature's conscience was piercing her with reproaches, and such taunt as she had just heard gave to her inflammable temper the easy expedient of forgetting this horror, which waited as the clear-seen phantom of soberer hours.

A man caught her wrists as she was darting onward and pinioned them, pushing her back. This brought a shout of rage from her husband, who knew the man and had been sworn foes with him for a year or so because of a quarrel over one cent in a match-game at a bar when both were half drunk.

"She's right, Bill Darick!" roared Effie's father; and he leapt to free his wife. But someone else interposed, and then, all in a few seconds, there was turmoil, screeching of oaths that drained the lowest depths of profanity, plunging of fists that struck viciously, and a stampede of scared women, who became jammed together at the doorway they strove to quit. Never were the peace and dignity of death more wantonly outraged. Effie joined in the uproar with shrill, hysteric laughter. Jim had belted her father's waist with his stout arms, eager to pull him from the little shoemaker, whose frowzy head he was pounding. A hand from behind had clutched the shoemaker's collar with rescuing intention, but his filthy shirt had given way and ripped open, showing a breast shaggy with grayish hairs and hideous with an incurable cancerous ulcer that what few friends he possessed liked to call his true reason for testiness and spleen. A woman, bolder than her mates, clung to Effie's mother, whose eyes, once of the diamond-like sort she had given to both her daughters, were now flaring a wicked, inebriate red. "Lemme loose, Bid Costigan," she yelled, "or as sure as my sweet Ann's layin' there stone dead I'll mash yer ugly mug so's the man ye've lived six years with but was never married to won't know ye when he sees ye next!"

Bridget released her then, changed by this reckless insult from pacificator to mænad. Her wide Irish mouth roared a sentence of scurrilous rage, and with a panther's fleetness her nails leapt at the other's cheek, ploughing there a deep, sanguine furrow. The wound caused a mad shriek, but Mrs. Costigan dealt her revenge unscathed, being wrenched away by a swift power that dizzied while it saved her. Someone had pushed his path in among the contestants, and every wave of his brawny hands had a sundering effect that was like an electric shock.

"It's Oweny Slattery," ran from lip to lip.

Owen stood among them in his paint-soiled gear, with his iron-gray eyes full of dry glitters, and his aquiline face a shade or two paler than its wont. They all shrank before him, afraid of the great strength which they well knew lurked in those long, lean limbs of his. Dead silence reigned in the room lately so clamorous. Effie by this time had sunk beside the bed and begun to sob with covered face.

Owen looked straight at Cora, and then went over to where she stood. "Come out o' here," he said, in a low and not unkindly voice, addressing her for the first time in six months. "This ain't no place for any decent gal."

IV.

CORA's face had been almost as pale as that which gleamed just below her on the pillows; but after Owen had spoken her color mounted in a faint, bloomy cloud, and she met his look diffidently. Then, growing herself again, she rid him of a swift, bitter fancy that she would not answer him even there and then, and said in tones as civil as they were firm :

"I can't leave Effie yet. I don't think I ought to."

Owen's lips took a sterner curve, and it seemed with him, for a moment, as though he might use some means of forcing her into obedience. But another thought evidently struck him, for he wheeled about and returned toward the late combatants.

"Clear out, now," rang his command, sharp as an officer's on the field; "clear out, everyone that don't belong here, or I'll strew the floor with your carcasses in no time!"

They trooped forth from the room, some going nimbly enough, others lagging and skulking. The little shoemaker went last, muttering curses at his late assailants, whom Owen's rough speech and presence appeared oddly to have sobered. They both stood in awe of this lank, determined young painter on the floor above them. In other days they had revelled with him among thieves and harlots, and had dreaded then his muscles of steel and his bull-dog pluck. Latterly, while for half a year he had persisted in sobriety, they had kept aloof from him and marvelled at his control of self.

Very soon Effie's parents had melted into maudlin tears. When this began to happen, Effie, as if prompted by some thrill of disgust, rose from her knees in a more or less tranquillized state. Cora had meanwhile busied herself in making the bed less loathsome, and in discussing with her friend's bewildered bridegroom what undertaker had best be sent for.

"Come upstairs, now, won't ye?" Owen at length said to Cora, in a voice as near positive tenderness as any of which he was capable. "Ye see the old man and woman is goin' to berhave 'emselves, and Jim 'll take care o' Effie; he'll git her out o' here as quick as he can, if he's got any sense to him. T'ain't a fit place for you after what's gone on, nohow. I shouldn't be surprised if the p'lice was to come in any minnit; they're always late jus' like that, ye know. And if they should they'd be mad enough to nab you as quick as the next one. . . . Say, Cora . . . come right up, now, won't ye?"

Quite soon Cora complied. Owen's appeal woke no chord of sympathy. It had seemed to her a fine thing that he had forsworn drink for so long a time. She had seen him drunk so often that the animalism excess brought out in him was quite familiar to her. But his temperate habits had never restored her lost confidence. She had known for a good while that he cared about her, having managed to learn it in that subtly miraculous way which a woman will find easy despite the man's triple mask-wearing. But since a certain night to which we have already heard vague reference, any thought of giving his regard sanction had been as odious to her as the loss of an arm. Still, even before that night, she would never have consented to marry him. The scenes among which fate had thrown her left it very clear that, as an undergrowth of human society, flourish the weeds of grossest passion, packed with bane; but the knowledge had not for this reason escaped her that where stagnated the worst moral reek and scurf a flower of sinless and beautiful love would sometimes lift unsullied leaves. Heredity and early surroundings made the desire for such a love, and the haunting dream that one day it might dawn upon her, constant in their companionship. The world wherein she dwelt was no dilettante one, as we already know. It did not merely handle things without gloves; it sometimes walked among them considerably less raimented. A good many of its candors, its nudities, its impurities had lost the power to repel Cora; but she still kept within her spirit a region exempt from all miry invasions.

She went upstairs in silence, Owen following. It seemed odd enough to be on terms with him again. Alarm, too, was mixed with this feeling of strangeness. She felt like somebody who watches the removal of one or two boards from a dangerous dam. The pent floods, having found narrow egress, might broaden it with a voluminous vigor. She would greatly have preferred to go on in her dealings with Owen just as she had gone for six months past. Once they had been intimate; how easy for him to reassume the old familiar terms now that their acquaintanceship was re-established! And Cora shivered as she thought of her own helplessness. In debt to his mother, she would be dependent for future shelter upon this woman's choice of whim; for now several hours had been lost, and the gaining of the three dollars looked far more impossible than the weaving of those twelve shirts for her twelve swan-brothers by the little princess in the fairy-tale. What, however, if Owen had seized just this time for the bringing about of a reconciliation? She knew his nature was not a crafty one, and yet there were signs that he had shrewdly planned for the present event.

Here she wronged him. By one of those cruel fatalities which make of life the mockery we so often see it, Owen loved Cora with a genuine and honest love. He had been without hope that she would, sooner or later, pardon him for behaving like the beast liquor had made him. He had often told himself during these months of abstinence that if Cora would go to church with him and be bound to him in wedlock, the least wish for a single drop of drink would never find its way into his breast again. And very probably he did not judge himself with any too much leniency. The union of Celt and Teuton in his nature had wrought it with a depth and strength of which the woman whom he so cherished had never remotely dreamed. Cora had felt indifferent to him, in the first place, because he had for her no physical charm ; he was not the sort of man whose features, body, movements, voice or smile pleased her. She even disliked the shape of his teeth, which were white and strong, and there was something about the way in which his dead-black hair grew at the nape of his neck that affected her like one of the caprices of ugliness. Let the idealists prate as they choose, it is through the senses that we sexually love, and Cora, like every healthy woman, was prepared either to love through hers or not at all. This existence of attraction on one side and repulsion on the other counts among the worst ironies with which destiny confronts us. Its cruelty is no doubt sharpened when it occurs among classes like that to which these two young people belonged, for here social vantages play no merciful part. A man is married almost solely for himself, a woman for herself. "I don't like you" is rarely tempered into "I will tolerate you" by the spell of money ; and as for birth and caste, these are impotent agents. If any preventatives are to be found among the poor and toilful for such tragedies of the heart as unreturned love engenders, it is in just these grim facts of poverty and toil that they may be said to crouch. Riches and idleness have full leisure to brood over wounds made by the magic dart ; but cold and hunger are both tyrannous and unromantic ; they veto the meditations of sentiment and put large trust in the healing forces of beef and flannel.

Owen followed Cora into his mother's room. Mrs. Slat-

tery gave the girl one of her hard looks, but there was no
acerbity in her voice as she said :

" Is Ann dead, then ? "

" Yes," replied Cora. And then she told what she had
seen happen, simply, tersely, and therefore with all the
more poignant effect.

"Ugh, what a house this is ! " grumbled Mrs. Slattery,
when Cora had ended. " I never thought I'd have to stay
in such a den for another year."

Cora was now passing towards her own room. This
lament from Mrs. Slattery made her recall with a chill
pang the work which pity had forced her to neglect.

Just then Owen gave a quick, imperative sign to his
mother. He had flung his big frame into a low chair, and
sat there in a posture that made him appear as if he might
any moment slip down on the floor, with one leg crossed
over the other, both hands in his pockets and arms
akimbo.

"Oh," said Mrs. Slattery to Cora, in a peculiar voice, •
clearing her throat. "About that money you was to
pay me next Tuesday. I guess I won't want it. . . . Er. .
Oweny's been pretty lucky this last week, and so you
needn't sweat yourself for so small a sum, but jus' work
along and. . er. . pay me when you can."

She jerked those last words forth against her will, and
Cora felt it. The girl slowly inclined her head, with eyes
drooping, and said "Thank you." She was conscious
that Owen watched her keenly, and that he no doubt waited
to have her cast him one look of gratitude. But she
would not give him even a fraction of one. Somehow,
she could not. In fact there was no real gratitude in her
heart. Relief was there, and a certain cordial gladness,
but, altogether, she had a sense of irritation against
Owen from which any thankful tendency was distant
indeed.

And now she at once went into her room, shutting the
door. A little while afterward they whom she had left

heard the sound of her sewing-machine, as it clucked stridently over seam and hem.

"If I could only get those three dollars by Tuesday," she thought, "and pay her anyway! It would look so much more independent of them both! And those Worth Street folks may have better work for me the next time I call, so that I can make up the rest I owe in another week or two."

Thus buoyant hope spread its white vans even here in this lowly little chamber and won a 'sort of music, too, from the sewing-machine's raucous din. Cora fell to thinking of a future when she might reach the grandeur of a dressmaking establishment all her own, and have girls to work under her while she moved about among them clad in a silk gown, with her hands folded. "How good I'll be to my girls!" the sewing-machine sounded as if it were saying, and exactly in her own voice, also as it had often spoken before. "Yes, indeed," it went on. "And what shall I call myself? what shall I call myself? Oh, I have it! I'll be Madame Cora. No, that won't do, either. How can I be a 'Madame' when I'm not married? And I shan't be married — no, not I! All round me I see enough of the misery marriage brings. Look at Ann's father and mother! And to think of how their own daughter, Effie, told them that between them both they'd murdered Ann!"

Then the machine, imbued with the magic of her own youth and health, began to desert such sombre themes and to tell her what kind of a man in looks and disposition he must be whom she might some day consent to marry. But suddenly, above the clatter, she heard a deep voice pronounce her name, and glanced up to see Owen standing at her side.

He had come into the room without her knowledge and had closed the door behind him after doing so. Cora flushed and bit her lip, while she let the machine slacken until it sounded like the "slowing up" of a miniature railway-train.

There was one other chair in the room, and it stood not far from where Cora herself was seated. Owen dropped his tall frame into it. "I guess you're kinder s'prised," he began, with a grin that held the pain of excessive awkwardness.

Cora made no answer. She felt anger at the rough, cool intrusion, but no hint of fear. While she pulled away her work from the machine, causing that snarl which it sends out at such times, and pretended, with half-hidden face, to re-thread her needle, Owen went on speaking.

"I want we should be friends agin, an' I've come to ask if you wouldn't be. What I done that night wasn't me but the rum that 'd got *inter* me. I don't blame *you*, though, an' I never have. I ain't got much talk, Cora. But I've been tryin' to keep straight. I've been tryin' very hard."

This touched Cora. She turned, letting both hands glide down into her lap, and gave him the full, soft light of her look. "I'm glad," she said.

"*Are* ye?" he exclaimed, while he leaned forward, with lips parting and breath quickening. "Are ye, *honest?*"

"Yes," she answered, drawing back into her chair; "but—"

"But what? Oh, I see—you don't want me to come any closeter. Well, then, I won't."

"Don't," said Cora, with vetoing dryness.

"I've been waitin' for this, an' now it's here. I've been waitin' an' hopin' for it. I said I'd let ye go right on, keepin' mum, till six months was up. They was up yesterday. Did you know that?"

"No—I didn't."

"Well, they was. An' I says to myself I'd—I'd have it out with ye to-day, *sure.*"

"Have it out? You mean—you'd ask me to be friends with you again? If so, I—"

"No," shot in Owen, with a scowl that ill became a wooer and yet meant only an ardor which he could but express in this uncouth way. "No, I—I mean more'n that. Oh, yes, consid'rable. Damn *friends*, Cora! I want ye to—to marry me." He rose, with pale face, glistening eyes and working lips.

Cora saw that he was greatly excited. But still she was not afraid of him. He was fierce at nearly all times ; in his cups he was lawless, barbaric. But now, knowing him as she did, she found in him no formidable image.

She shook her head, growing almost as pale as he was. "No," she returned, "I can't mar—" and then she abruptly paused and looked up at him where he stood close beside her, with a frown gathered plainly above her sparkling eyes. "Do you think it's a square thing," she asked, with a tart tang in her voice, "for you to come to me like this, after we haven't noticed each other so many weeks, and—and speak as you're speakin'? Ain't you got more—more sense—more bringin'-up—more ——?" Her tones faltered, then, and the tears visibly moistened her eyes. But with the access of emotion her anger seemed to deepen. She struggled to her feet, pushing away her chair from the sewing-machine. "I'll go into the streets and beg," she cried, "if *this* is the reason for that change in your mother! I won't stay here another hour! I don't care what becomes of me. I'd rather starve like the worst tramp than be forced to tell you I'll marry you because I'm in debt for my board!"

"No," exclaimed Owen ; "it ain't that!" He did not make any attempt to touch her as they stood and faced one another. "I only *said* it, Cora. I wasn't tryin' to force ye. What made ye think I was? You can stop here ten years if ye want. I ain't *that* kind, an' if mother is, she's got to 'count to me for it when she plays any of her dodges. You can bet on it, Cora. I'm givin' it to

ye straight. P'raps I *was* too sudden. I hadn't ought
to a spoke so soon. I give in—I hadn't."

"So soon!" said Cora, with plaintive sarcasm.
"Don't ever speak of it again, Owen Slattery! Don't
ever speak of it again as long as we're both alive!"

She was so lovely to him, in her indignant maiden-
hood, while she thus replied, that he forgot the real significance of her words. "I won't—I won't," he answered, with a soothing intonation that some of the men
and women among whom he had mixed would hardly
have recognized as his own. "The fact is, Cora, I
didn't come in here to talk spoony a bit. I come to—to
ask you if you'd show we was friends again by—by doin'
me a favor."

"A favor?" she repeated. The tears were still wet
on her cheeks. Her anger had already begun to lessen.
She thought of what this man might have power venge-
fully to inflict upon her. Begging and starving had
seemed heroic alternatives but a few seconds ago, now
they made for her calming brain, the old chill, despairful
perspective. "A favor?" she repeated, and thought that
perhaps she might in some manner propitiate him, so retaining his own and his mothers' tolerance until she could
gain enough by labor to find food and a roof elsewhere.

"Yes," Owen said, slowly. He drew something from
a side-pocket under his paint-stained blouse while he
spoke. "I've got two tickets for the ball to-night. It's
the Matthew J. Quinn Society ball, over to the Bowery.
I want ye to go along with me. There'll be dancin',
an' a lot o' ladies. That'll show me you're willin' to
make up. I'll treat ye right! There'll be liquor round,
o' course, but you know I don't touch nothin'. We can go
at eight an' leave at 'leven. Come, now! what d'ye say?"

Cora shook her head most obstinately, recoiling while
he held out the two tickets for her to examine.

"No," she replied; "I don't like goin' to balls. I—I
can't. You needn't ask me any more, for I can't and I
won't."

4

V.

But in the end she let herself be persuaded. A sense
of expediency, of politic tact, strongly wrought with her.
If she accompanied Owen it might help her future position as a pensioner upon his mother's mercy. These
were his days of abstinence ; he would prove a most
efficient guardian so long as he kept free from drink. Besides, the ball itself would be a diversion. And then she
had that dark-red merino frock with the white satin belt
and bow for the throat. She had bought it in an extrava-
gant hour, months ago, for two dollars and sixty cents at
a second-hand clothing-store in Canal Street. It was
rather shabby, and the satin of the belt had got yellowish, but it became her. There were those red-glass ear-
ings, too, that went so well with it. Their hooks were
brass and inflamed the lobes of her ears if she wore them
much, but three hours or so wouldn't matter.

Her final consent gave to Owen's aquiline face as joy-
ful a look as it could ever wear this side of positive insanity. He had achieved a great triumph, and felt as proud
of taking Cora to this ball as though he had been some
ardent struggler for social honors and she were the reign-
ing queen of an exclusive set. He let his mother see how
happy and victorious he was, and Mrs. Slattery at once
shone with a reflected glow. They took an early supper of sausages, bread, tea and the cabbage without
which Owen hardly thought any meal complete, and
which he shovelled into his mouth wholly by the aid of
his knife. At this meal Mrs. Slattery was the soul of
blandness. She heaped a second helping of sausage on

Cora's plate, though the girl protested she could not eat
another morsel. A few hours ago Cora would have been
glad of this extra supply, for Mrs. Slattery's gaze, forbid-
dingly frigid, had made her nearly always rise hungry from
the table. But now the horror and pain caused by Ann's
death, and the excitement of a certain still more recent
interview, had tellingly blunted the edge of appetite.
Besides, it was a source of more excitement to think of
the coming ball. No amount of crushing and cooping
can twist youth into something vitally different from itself. Cora had seen but very few festal nights. Dancing came as natural to her flexile young limbs and small
American feet as its note comes to a thrush. Even the
ghastliness of what had happened downstairs that afternoon could not chill the pleasant little fever of anticipa-
tion which had begun to warm her veins.

While she stood before her looking-glass, arranging the
white satin bow at her throat, Mrs. Slattery entered and
laid with grimness upon the bureau a big brooch of blood-
red coral.

"I guess that'll show good on top o' your white neck-
bow," she said. "Besides, it kind o' gees with the culler
o' your dress."

"Oh, thank you—thank you very much!" exclaimed
Cora, to whom the vulgar bauble seemed priceless.
Once or twice she had seen Mrs. Slattery wear it, but
only on occasions that fitted its fine importance. "Still,
truly, Mrs. Slattery, I—I daresn't borrow it. No, I
really darst *not!*" And in spite of some actual persuasion
on the part of this woman who had treated her with so much
hard acrimony but a brief while since, Cora went on re-
fusing the proffered ornament.

And yet the alteration in her landlady wrought its
enlivening effect. It was almost with her as though the
coming sound of the dance music cast its echoes before.
When Owen came into his mother's room and found her
there ready to accompany him, he told himself that she

was 'goin' to take the shine out of every other gal in the place.'

"Wrap up as warm's ye can," was all he said, however. "It ain't snowin' no more, 'cause it's got too cold. I put my head out o' my winder a minnit ago, an' thought I'd have it froze off 'fore I could get the winder down."

"I've only got this shawl," said Cora, as her face fell.

Owen looked at his mother. "I guess I can get ye somethin' warmer'n that," said Mrs. Slattery, and soon the girl felt the folds of a large woolen shawl, thrice the size and thickness of her own, drop about her shoulders and breast.

"Oh, how good that's goin' to feel !" she cried, with a trill of glee in her voice. And Owen laughed aloud, and his mother joined him, though a little feebly, and said to herself as she did so that Oweny hadn't once before laughed out loud and hearty like that since his "swear-off" began, six months ago.

As Owen and she were passing downstairs together, Cora recollected the dead Ann and the living Effie with a guilty pang.

"I'll just run in a minute and see how they're gettin' on," she said, pausing at the door, which had of late been beset by a curious rabble."

Owen slightly frowned. "Well, I'll wait here," he said, with a touch of sullenness.

Cora softly turned the knob and slipped inside. The first room was quite empty and very dim. A light shone from Ann's room, however, and there were signs that the undertaker had been and gone. At the head of the big, dark ice-box were five candles, and in their mellow glimmer Cora saw a crouched form. But the light was queer and almost elfin to her, coming as she did from duskier regions. It seemed as if the shape of Effie's bridegroom, Jim Halloran, had suddenly resolved itself out of naught. There he stood at her side, and in another second she heard his clumsy whisper.

"That's Ef, squattin' over there by the ice-box," he said. "No use a speakin' to her ; she's kind o' funny in her head *yet.*" Here Jim Halloran heaved a great sigh. "This is a fine weddin'-night for me, hey ?" And then he grinned with excessive melancholy at Cora, who stared back at him with her lovely brown eyes as though she longed from her inmost soul to help him, and could not, and sorrowed that she could not.

"The wake'll begin putty soon," re-commenced Jim. "Ye see, ther's a few parties here now."

Cora looked closer at the walls and perceived that some vague murmurs of converse which had lately reached her must have been uttered by these "parties," just referred to. She had not been bred in the Catholic faith, but more than once she had assured herself that even if this were true and she were an Irish girl as well, she would heartily have detested "wakes." They had often struck her as simply the lugubrious pretexts for orgies held past midnight on till the white challenge of dawn itself failed to repress them.

"You'll stay, now, won't ye?" Jim here asked, and just then Effie lifted her colorless face, on which the candle-light streamed weirdly. Without seeing that she had done so, Cora answered :

"I—I don't think I *can* come to-night. I—"

And then Effie's mother strode up, reeking with the fumes of liquor, and yet having grown sober enough, since her strange arousal of the afternoon, to vacillate leeringly between grief and jollity. Cora felt that to strike her would have been pleasanter than to speak with her, and yet, civility, like death, has its insistences. This repulsive woman (who was far from being anything of the sort when she kept free from drink) almost caressed Cora while she spoke, in a cracked whine, of the daughter that lay dead.

"I haird you was so good to her, me darlin'," said the tottering, dishevelled creature, "jusht afore she died!"

"Oh, no, Mrs. Flynn," objected Cora; "I merely staid with her while Effie was gettin' married."

"Shure ye done more nur that!" said a gruff male voice, and Effie's father joined his wife, collarless, in his shirt-sleeves. "Ye woiped the blood from her poor lips as she was a dyin', so ye did," said Mr. Flynn; "an' the Lord be praised that so good a gurl as yerself was there to shtand in the place o' the priesht."

Mr. Flynn was more drunk than his wife. He had seized Cora's hand and was ardently pressing it. Cora was about to tear the hand away, when her tormentor dropped it of his own accord, because Effie had just come forward and joined her friend, and such a sight proved keenly unexpected.

"Cora," said Effie, speaking in a lifeless, neutral voice, "I'm so glad it's you. Now you'll stay, won't ye?" She put her lips close to Cora's ear. "Do, please stay with me," she pleaded. "They'll all begin to drink as soon as the wake's once started. Oh, Cora, pa's got two demijohns o' stuff hid somewhere. I heard him say so. I dunno how he managed to pick up the money for 'em; I s'pose somebody's lent it to him, or perhaps he's got trusted. In a little while folks 'll come in and the bottles 'll be passed round, and you know what *that*'ll mean. I wouldn't mind so much if pa was sober; but bein' as he is now he'll jus' want to drownd everybody in liquor. So do stay, Cora; do, *please?*"

Thus flowed the swift entreaty of Effie, in a vernacular so different from the brogue of her parents; for she and Ann had been "this country born," as it is called, and had no more of the Irish touch about them than Owen Slattery had of either Irish or German.

It was Owen who now prevented Cora from answering, for he had grown impatient out in the hall and had just marched into the room where she stood. As he joined her he said, with some austerity of manner—"Come away!"

But Effie's imploring eyes were upon her, and Cora let the thick, dark shawl drop from about her person, right before Owen's clouding eyes. "*I must* stay a little while," she said, looking at him, while she took one of Effie's hands and pressed it.

The next moment Owen had stooped and growled in her ear: "Don't ye do it! God knows *what'll* happen here 'fore the night's over."

But Cora shook her head. "I'll have to stay for a half-hour or so," she murmured, "with Effie."

"You needn't do nothin' o' the kind," Owen contradicted. "There'll be plenty here without *you*. Come on!"

But Cora turned away, almost forcibly drawn by Effie, who had heard all that Owen had said. "I thought you an' him wasn't great no more," she began. "Where does he want ye to go?"

"Oh, somewheres or another," replied Cora, with a plain reluctance to tell the real truth amid these sombre surroundings. . . .

But they soon changed from sombre to ghastly. More people came in to the wake, for a report had got about that Mr. Flynn was well supplied with whiskey. Both he and his wife had coolly circulated bottles and tumblers. Talk waxed louder and louder. Some of the women would not drink, but all the men did, and freely. Jokes were cracked, and bursts of laughter followed them, timid at first, as though asking a sort of permission from death to let the sounds of revelry intrude upon its mute little domain. Then there would be apologetic sighs and whimpers, in which Mr. and Mrs. Flynn would join with what appeared repentant if transitory zeal. Faces that had screwed themselves into at least the semblances of pain and mourning would bend over that small square of glass, below which the white features of the dead girl glimmered vague in the candle-rays as a lily under water. Bursts of elegy would be heard upon Ann's untimely taking-off, upon her Christian gifts of character, upon her matchless patience through many months of suffering. These expressions were all cast in language of blent slang and illiteracy, and sometimes their droned intonations would clearly bespeak the hypocrite. Cora and Effie had gone into a corner, not far from where loomed so cumbrously the box by which Ann had been hidden. In the assemblage and yet not of it, they could note the gradual increase of sociality, hilarity, profanity. Effie did so with pure terror. It was not solely that she believed her sister's offended spirit might deal some punishing blow to her blasphemous parents, but that she feared a worse desecration than any which all this ill-timed mirth had yet dared to manifest. A few more guests now crowded in, and the smaller bedroom became thronged, while the larger one, which was also kitchen and dining-room, soon grew rather densely filled besides. The chairs had long ago given out, and in some cases men sat on women's laps or women on men's, amid giggles and chucklings from both observers and participants. A hot, rank, almost fetid smell began to exhale from each apartment. Some people, of a more decorous type, rose and disgustedly withdrew. Meanwhile the drunkenness augmented. Suddenly a corpulent man, with a face that looked like an abnormal preserved cherry, and a piece of white flannel bound about his uncollared throat, commenced the telling of a somewhat obscene anecdote, in tones at once tipsy and shrill. Cries of "Put him out!" sounded here and there, these being drowned in a storm of reproachful hisses. The corpulent man was extinguished, though not ejected. But presently there was a good deal of commotion at the hall doorway, and it flew from tongue to tongue that the Fat Woman belonging to a Dime Museum over in the Bowery, and living down on the first floor of this same house, had mounted four pairs of stairs for the purpose of appearing at the wake. Her time was just up at the Museum, where she had been on · duty all day, and the news of Ann's death had reached her only a few minutes before. Ann and she had been on good terms with one another in earlier times, and now Mrs. O'Grady bitterly rebuked herself that she had allowed even so solid an obstacle as her avoirdupois to separate her from the little sick friend four flights up. As she waddled through the parting crowd there were titters on every side of her. The ascent had been a difficult and even perilous one for her to undertake, and she was now sadly out of breath. She had long ago got used to being laughed at ; it was a portion of her professional career. Still, after all, society was different from trade, and a certain heed of " manners " might reasonably be expected from those who had not paid ten cents for the privilege of despising them. The poor flesh-burdened creature winced a little at the amusement she created, as she dragged her monstrous body along, with arms hanging exhaustedly and yet so enormous of girth that they might almost have been the thighs of a giant. She panted hard as she reached the threshold of Ann's room, and her purplish face appeared to indicate that the horrible malady of fat which victimized her might have a sudden and apoplectic end. Her triple chin shook like a jelly, and the sweat began to course down her bulging cheeks from pretty rings of blond hair, which in other girlish years might have lent loveliness to a visage once endowed with it. We often hear and read of what dire ruin emaciation will wreak upon the human frame; but its ravages are, after all, not half so ruthless as those which may be effected by smothering, overwhelming masses of animal tissue. Physical attenuation has at least a certain woful dignity ; but the being cursed with swinish obesity lives in a perpetual lonely interspace between the tragic and comic, and lips that are one moment drawn in pity before so piteous a monster as was poor Mrs. O'Grady, may broaden, a moment afterward, with uncontrollable derision.

It is notorious that fat people are easily moved to emotion, and this new-comer had no sooner reached a place which enabled her to look down upon the dim, peaked countenance of Ann before she burst into a tremor of tears and moans. Doubtless she had been genuinely fond of the pale little girl who would visit her of old and talk with her sociably, frankly, as if she had been an ordinary mortal, and not the Living Curiosity described in her chromatic portraitures. As it was, Mrs. O'Grady's lamentations must have made the very spiders in their cobwebs up on the ceiling tingle with a sense of some threatening besom. "It ain't been me, Ann, that's neglected ye," she wailed; "it's been the azmy that gript me an' the weight that pulled into me whin I wanted to mount them stairs! Ah, the Holy Vairgin's got ye nQw, mee darlin' an' she'll keep ye better nur ever ye was kep' down here!" Here the mourner gave a laugh hysteric of key, and leaned closer to the square of glass into which she peered. "Ah, little wan, do ye remimber how I ushed to tell ye I'd loike to shpare ye twinty pounds or so off mee own damned carcass, so I wud, an' not feel I'd losht it, nayther!" This quaint apostrophe caused a ripple of laughter, at which Mrs. O'Grady threw back her head with that droll result nearly all her motions produced, and tried to look thunder-clouds out of her small eyes, whose very lids were wads of fat. More laughter ensued, and then Mr. Flynn, who chose to regard her threnodic mood as highly serious, cried out hot reprimands to the irreverent scoffers. Personality bristled from his remarks, and one or two of the assembled mourners, as drunk as he was, chose to pour resentment upon their savagery. Perhaps with sudden lively recollections of what had happened, Mr. Flynn promptly grew peaceful. He was sorry he'd hurt anyone's feelings; he hadn't meant to ; but Mrs. O'Grady had been "wan o' the besht frinds " his beloved daughter had ever had, and because the lady's bones were a little further under the skin than most people's, that wasn't any reason why she shouldn't be treated with respect. Here Mr. Flynn lurched insecurely toward the massive object of his defence and tried to put an arm about her waist. But the waist had once been and no longer was. His effort sent reckless guffaws from several masculine throats, and one of the men who had laughed gave Mr. Flynn a violent push. He fell heavily against the fat woman, who shrieked, jumped forward, tripped, and then toppled over upon the ice-box, dislocating it from its trestles and causing it to crack and split beneath her enormous weight.

An uproar swiftly prevailed, disgusted cries mingling with amused ones, and alarm making itself loudly heard, as well, for the safety of Mrs. O'Grady. "She's kilt." "She's bursted herself!" "Look at her chokin'!" "It's an ice-box that *she'll* soon be wantin'!" leapt from mouth to mouth.

To the dead girl a revolting thing now happened. As the ponderous box fell, the glass over Ann's face had broken into a hundred bits. Its receptacle being suddenly flung upon one side, the corpse became discomposed, and to the amazement of some, the horror of others, Ann, a few seconds later, seemed to be putting her head out of the aperture as though she were literally roused from death.

While several shrieks of fright rent the air, Cora felt an arm slipped about her. She was drawn into the hall with stern though uninjuring force ; to have resisted would have been to beat the air. At last, breathing quickly and with eyes enkindled, she was brought to a stand-still in the stout grasp of a man she had good cause to know.

"How dared you do that, Owen Slattery?" she broke out indignantly.

They were alone together in the cramped little hall.

He looked down at her, without real anger, but instead of it a sort of exasperated calm.

"Didn't I tell ye this afternoon that devilish den in there wasn't no place for a gal like you?"

"But poor Effie—" began Cora.

"You ain't Effie's keeper," he struck in roughly. "Now come 'long to the ball. Come, as you promised ye would!" And he put his arm within her own, rather, perhaps, with the aim of accompanying than of leading her.

"Let go of me!" insisted Cora crossly, not stirring an inch.

She felt his eyes burning down upon her—those eyes that some women would have thought so virile and soldierly a grey, with their unshirking crystal pupils and their short, coarse black lashes. But Cora never thought anything at all about them, except vaguely to tell herself they were too small for the lean face from which they shone.

"D'ye mean to say," Owen asked, "that ye're goin' back on me after givin' me your consent? Is *that* the way the land lays? Eh? *Is* it?"

"What I've been seein'," said Cora, "ain't put me in much of a humor for dancin' at balls. . . . Besides, I don't like what you just did. It's made me lose faith in you—a good deal as I lost it once before."

He smiled bitterly, with a brief, curt nod. "You're wrong now, if you was right then—an' I give in you *was* right then. I got ye out o' that room in a jiffy 'cause it made me sick to see ye there. . . Well, it's settled, is it? You won't go to the ball?"

Cora looked at him. He was dressed in a suit of black broadcloth, whose low-cut vest showed between the lapels of his open overcoat. It had come from a second-hand clothing-store, and its gloss was that of age, not of newness. But such as it was, it meant, like the dingy white-satin tie at his throat, an absolute and rarely-donned "best."

Cora had a twinge of pity for him, and showed it. "Well," she said, with softening voice, "I suppose I ought to go since I *said* I would."

He stepped up to her and clutched one of her hands. The narrow hall was quite empty. In another minute she felt his lips on her cheek, so hot that they seemed to burn. They almost made her cry out, because terror was born with a sense of their severe heat. It was not that she feared the potency of his passion for her—at least she did not fear it then and there. But what woke her dread was a thought that some day the action of his will might prove stronger than her own, and she might give herself loveless to his hungry arms. This now flashed upon her as she drew back from him.

But she had no need of drawing back. Into that one kiss Owen had flung the fervor of ten. A second afterward he stood quiescent at her side. And yet his words, while they left him in a bass whisper, disclosed some volcanic tumult as their source.

"I love ye so—I love ye so! My God! there's times when I wish I'd never seen ye, an' then there's times when I curse myself for not bein' thankful I even got that much luck!"

"Come, if you *will* go," said Cora, not at all graciously. She was thinking of Effie and listening to the loud hub-bub that floated through the near doorway.

After that they went downstairs together, and were soon in the open street, where bitter winds were surging under heavens cleared of all cloud and gemmed by a moon that looked like a globe of blue ice.

VI.

THE ball was in full progress when Owen and Cora arrived. It was held in a great hall, whose appointments and decorations were garishly cheap. It was by no means the lowest kind of entertainment given in New York. Such dance-houses as the Cremorne Garden, the Haymarket, Allen's, or the Buckingham contained revellers of a more abandoned breed. Here were possibly some few women as virtuous as Cora and a fair number of men honest enough not to steal if chance favored. A lancers was going on as Owen and his companion made their appearance. They waited till it was over, and then joined the promenade that followed. Cora's face caught many an eye and held it. The ugliness of her dress hid her beauty only in the way that a rubbish-heap hides the tints of a rose. Contrast brought out her face, too, in delicate and lovely relief. There was no other feminine face without some touch of coarseness in lines or coloring ; hers appeared naturally separate and apart from the rabble that engirt her. And yet her heart had already begun to pulsate in accord with the falsetto fiddles and the wheezy trombone. Soon, as a waltz struck up, she turned to Owen with delighted eyes. "I guess I can manage it with ye," he said desperately, and they set forth together amid the sea of bobbing, skipping or prancing couples.

But they had smaller success than any of the others. Owen was simply bovine as a dancer, and plunged hither and thither with so coltish an infelicity that Cora at length begged him to pause. He did so, and she took his arm again, biting her lips. After he had placed her on one of the wooden settees that lined the wall, he said, with evident depression :

"I guess I don't 'mount to much at heel-coolin'."

"No, you don't," said Cora.

Owen was proud of his fair young associate, besides adoring her. "There's some first-class dancers here," he said, and he recalled while thus speaking some friends of his own sex whom he had seen walking about the floor.

One of them came up almost immediately. He looked like the ordinary "rough," a young fellow with shorn face and a dull smile that suggested infinite knowledge of evil. Owen introduced him to Cora, and it would have been in the order of things for her deserted escort to seek another partner. But Owen did not. He stood and watched Cora as she glided along the floor with her new devotee. All women were flat and insipid to him beside Cora. He had had paramours, in his old days of drink and disorder, who had bowed with a kind of idolatry before the vigorous animal that he represented. One or two of them were here this evening, and they cast looks of blandishment at him as they came within the scope of his glance. But he replied merely by a careless lifting of his dark, composed brows. He was absorbed in Cora, and loved the despotism of his reverie.

As for Cora, her enjoyment had now commenced. She had no sooner ceased dancing with her new acquaintance than certain friends of the latter gathered about them both. Again an arm encircled her waist and she was whirled off on the spacious floor. Her step was elastic; the motions of her exquisite shape stimulated him with whom she danced. Once more she paused, and four or five new partners promptly sought her. But she was tired, and looked round for Owen. She discovered him just at her elbow, but he seemed buried in the proceedings of a shooting-gallery, which dipped away from one side of the wall against which he was stationed. This pleased her; she was glad to be temporarily forgotten by him; his proximity always irked her. She had as yet seen no one whom she cared for, and it was in her temperament either to be interested in men immediately or not at all. Still, she had enjoyed her dances very much, and as soon as her breath should again come equably she had already decided that another dance would be no less delicious than those which had gone before. She ran her eye with a critical boldness over the faces of her assembled admirers. Most of them were of a type already wearisome from long recurrence. But just as she had made up her mind that no one stood near her for whom she could feel the least thrill of attraction, a new form quietly dawned upon her sight.

In a second she perceived that this was some one of a higher social grade. His dress told her that. He was tall and large, and in the button-hole of his neat black, double-breasted coat he wore a big white flower, presumably made of two or three carnations bunched into one. As her gaze flashed over his face she saw a ruddy blond complexion, a pair of humorous blue eyes, a curled yellow mustache and an expression of mixed sensuality and unconcern. She did not dream of asking herself why this face fascinated her, but she had no sooner become clearly conscious of it than a desire took sharp hold of her to know and talk with its possessor.

Nobody seemed to be acquainted with him among those who surrounded her. Indeed, several gloomy and unfriendly glances were levelled at him. He did not appear to mind these, however; he had the air of not minding anything in particular—of simply following the trend of his caprices and enjoying himself as the hour, even the minute, allowed.

"Won't you let me have a little turn about the floor with you?" he said; and Cora was at once willing to grant his request because he had put it in so easy and genial a tone, with so gay and spontaneous a courtesy.

"I'm a good deal out of breath," she replied. "I've been dancin' ever so much."

"Yes," he replied, "I saw you."

Somehow he seemed also to tell her, in this dry little phrase, that he had both seen and greatly admired her. Soon afterward they danced together, and the secure spring of his step gave her pleasant thrills. When they stopped it was in a part of the ball-room many yards from where she had stood before. If Owen's distant eyes had kept track of her, that only showed how keen and vigilant they were.

"You trip along like a little fairy," said Cora's companion. "Who taught you how to dance so well?"

"Nobody," she answered, laughing.

He laughed, too, and she saw that his teeth were as white and perfect as her own. He drew out his handkerchief, and passed it once or twice lightly across his forehead. An odor of cologne floated from it, delicious to Cora, whose hard, mechanic days were haunted by no such welcome fumes.

"Well," he said, " 'nobody's' the best teacher, after all. That is, the persons who dance best are those it comes natural to."

"How nice that smelt," said Cora, as he was putting away his handkerchief. "What kind of scent is it?"

"Plain cologne. I hate those fancy perfumes. Do you like them?"

She looked at him with a winsome vacancy. "I don't know anything about them," she said.

His eye was quick and his ear sharp. He had already noted certain points in her dress, caught certain tones in her voice that made him, so to speak, suspect her of innocence. One did not often meet pure women at places like this. Her beauty had won him to her at first, and he had been prepared to find her a loose enough bacchante behind its apparent refinements. But the swift disappointment had most agreeably shocked him. He was not easily deceived by women ; he had spent a good deal of time in making it difficult for the sex to deceive him.

5

" I suppose," he now said, " you go to few big affairs like this."

" Balls? I've never been to but one before."

" Only one? . Isn't that strange? You must have had lots of fellows ask you to go to others, of course."

" No—I haven't."

" Why, how's that?"

" Oh, I don't see many fellers, as you call 'em. I live quiet—ever so quiet. I'm workin' all day, and I'm mostly pretty tired when night comes."

They were seated side-by-side, now. He had discovered the needle-marks on her fingers ; nothing in her appearance or attire escaped him ; he was telling himself that in spite of her having evidently come from low surroundings it was wonderful to see how brilliantly fresh and virginal she looked. He had been lied to a great deal by women in his rather vulgar and voluptuous life of seven-and-twenty years, but already he had concluded that there was faint risk of his having met some phenomenal arch-hypocrite now. Ah, no ; as well fling charges of duplicity against a pansy or a primrose ! Guilelessness like this must be genuine, for it was so naturally mingled with the simple awkwardness of ignorance.

" It's too bad such a girl as you should be hard at work all day," he said.

Cora liked " such a girl" ten times better than if some adjective had gone with the sentence, like " pretty," " handsome," or even " nice." The suggestion of a compliment appealed to her more strongly than the mere paying of one, though she would have found it a task to formulate this preference.

" Oh, I might be much worse employed than hard at work making an honest living," she replied, jauntily and piquantly. " You needn't pity me, sir, if you please. I shouldn't be a bit discontented, myself, if times were not so bad. . ."

And then, a little while later, he had got her to tell him

just how bad times were, and had asked her soft, kindly questions which proved easy to answer and indeed made her glad to receive them because ostensibly so brimming with interest and sympathy. They sat out one entire dance. and Cora forgot that they were doing so until just as the strains of the band died away.

" You're sorry you missed that polka, Cora," he said. He had managed to learn her name by this time. " I can see in your eyes how bad you feel."

She laughed. She had begun to think that she knew him very well indeed, all in this little space of time. She was not afraid of his bright blue eyes any longer ; she could look right into them fearlessly enough. But to do so made her heart flutter queerly, and she knew her cheeks were burning, more because he kept so ceaseless a watch on her face than from any unwonted heat in the ball-room.

" I guess I needed some rest," she said, " after the way I'd been gallopin' round."

" Perhaps you did, Cora—especially as you tell me you're such a continuous little worker at your sewing-machine and with your hands as well."

" Yes, I do work pretty hard. But I don't feel tired to-night. I guess it's excitement."

" What's excited you ?—being here among all these gay folks ? "

" Yes. That, and—well, something else."

" Tell me what the something else is. Won't you ? "

" Oh, no. Never mind it ; I'd rather not talk about it.'

" Very well. I shall hate it as much as you do—and because you do. I don't want to like anything you don't like. You can understand that kind of a feeling, of course."

" N—no," she loitered coquettishly ; " I'm afraid I can't."

" Well," he· said gravely, " it all comes to this—that I

like you more than I've the courage to tell you on so
short an acquaintance."

She laughed, loudly and heartily. " You're not such a
coward as that," she exclaimed. " I'm dead sure you
ain't."

" Oh, yes, I am—when girls like you are 'round."

Cora lifted to him a pair of lips that seemed to pout and
smile both at once. " Oh, come, now ! Girls *like* me !
That won't do a bit !"

" Won't it ? Well, I'll take it back. There's no girl I
ever saw that was like you. The girl that tried to be
would have to get up pretty early in the morning—you
can just bet your bottom dollar she would ! . . . But why
don't you care much about this Owen Cafferty, Slattery—
what's his name ?—who brought you here ? Don't you—?"

" Oh, hush," said Cora, with fleet admonition. " There
he is now."

Owen had come quite close to where they sat, and it
looked as if he were about to confront them, when suddenly a dapper young man, with a waxed black mustache and a diamond scarf-pin of rich radiance, clapped
Cora's new friend familiarly on the shoulder.

" Well, Casper," cried the new-comer, " you appear to
be having it all your own way." He glanced at Cora,
and made her a pranksome, dipping bow, to which she
did not respond. She somehow felt that he would ask
her to dance, which he presently did. She hoped that
Casper would object, but he showed no signs of even the
least unwillingness. The two young men seemed to be
excellent friends, and Cora found herself surrendered with
entire complaisance.

He did not dance so well as her previous partner, and
he babbled with a garrulity that almost made her giddy.
She had not yet learned either his own or his friend's
full name, and he at first appeared loth to talk on these
subjects. Presently Casper rejoined them, just as they
were dropping into the circular stream of promenaders.

But at the moment he appeared, Cora had withdrawn her
arm from that of her escort and was betraying a nervous
displeasure in her clouded eyes and tightened lips.

"Why, what's the matter?" said Casper, as he paused
at her side. "Are you afraid Owen will come after you
with a big stick?"

"No," she said, bluntly. "But I should go back to
him, and not waste my time with them that's ashamed to
tell their real names."

"Oho!" laughed the young man who had been so
loquacious. He thought her good-looking, but by no
means pre-eminently. "You better learn to take a few
reefs in your curiosity," he pursued, mirthful yet satiric;
"it's dangerous to go sailing round with so much."

Cora shook her head in brisk negation. "It ain't
that," she affirmed stoutly. "But if people want to hide
their names, they're not apt to do it out of any good
meanin'."

She saw Owen leaning against a pillar, with both hands
in his pockets and just below a flaring gas-fixture that
showed how irate had grown his face. She was about
hurrying over to him, inspired by a strong nervous distrust, when he who had been called Casper on a sudden
caught her hand and held it firmly.

"Look here," he said, "you're dead right, every time.
Don't mind that chap's devilish nonsense. He don't mean
what he says; he's too fond of his own chin-music." By
this time Casper had drawn Cora's arm within his own,
and they had begun to move onward with the train of
couples whose passage they had hitherto rather seriously
interrupted. "We'll leave Rudie in the lurch; he often
does get left; he deserves to be; he's always shooting his
mouth off a good deal too much. We're the best of friends,
but I don't mind telling you his name, since it's come to a
point of—of eti*quette*, as they say. He's Ru, or Rudie, or
Rudolph Champny—a nice, kind-hearted, cheeky sort of

Cora broke in here.   "Why do you say that you don't *mind* tellin' me his name?" she asked.   "Had you minded before?   Had *he* minded?   Or did you and him both come here wantin' people not to know who you are?"

Casper threw back his head, laughing.   "Of course we did!" he exclaimed.

"Of course?   *Why* of course?"

"Oh, how good that is!   Don't you know that this isn't the kind of a place where two fellows like us—? Well, no, I won't say what I was going to, because—"

"Because you might hurt my feelins?" queried Cora. "What do I care about the place?" she went on.   "I suppose you're 'way up in the world—better off than most of them that's here.   But if the men and women *are* nearly all of 'em bad, it don't make any difference to *me*. I'm always mixin' with people like that.   I have to.   I can't get rid of 'em; I sometimes wish I could; I'd always wish it if I let myself think about who's who.   But I don't; I try to forget.   And then there's my work, and that helps me to forget.   Besides, it's none of my business. I've got enough to do lookin'. after whether I go right or not."

He pressed her arm with his own as they walked along. "And you *do* go right, Cora," he said, with a burst of feeling that was quite native and sincere.   "My poor little girl, you don't know what a glimpse of your own goodness those few plain words of yours give me!"

Cora slightly tossed her head.   "Oh, I ain't so awful *good*," she said, "I'm honest, if you mean that, and I live a clean life.   I don't go as some girls go; not that I'm soundin' my own horn.   I've heard 'em do that when I knew they hadn't the real right, if it came to proof. . . . But you and your friend—" she suddenly broke off.   "Are you and him *'shamed* of givin' your names?"

"Yes—a little."

"Oh, well—"   And she paused.   Then, in another

minute she added : "If that's so, what's the reason you
came here ? I woudn't come to a place where I was
'shamed to be seen."

"You're right—you're right again," he said. "Now,
look here, Cora, my friend and I had been dining together. We drank a good deal of wine. We both got
pretty full. I'm pretty full now. Perhaps I don't look
it, but——"

"You don't, and you *ain't!'* said Cora, with vehemence.
"Lord a mercy ! I guess I know what *that* is ! I've
seen enough drunkenness in *my* time ! "

"Oh, no ; I don't mean that," he replied, laughing, and
with an inward amusement whose subtlety of exposition
did not reach Cora at all. "I only mean—well, never
mind if I don't explain ; you're so shrewd that you can see
it. Anyhow, we wouldn't have come here, Rudie and I,
if we hadn't been having a lot of champagne."

"Champagne," murmured Cora ; "yes, I've heard of
that. It costs piles of money, don't it ?"

"It does if you take too much of it. It's a very nice
tipple, though. I wish you'd try a glass——"

"Oh, no," she shot in, sharply.

"Only one glass, downstairs. I dare say they've got
some, and I'd like to see how you liked it. It's a lady's
drink, you know ; it wouldn't hurt a child, it's so smooth
and pleasant."

"But I don't want any. I——"

"Oh, all right. That settles it. You might care for a
sandwich, though, and some . . . well, some lemon-soda."

"I guess I might," she answered, with a slow sort of
candor that he found exquisitely diverting. "But" . . .
and she tried to pull her arm out of his. . . . "I—I
mustn't keep too much company with you," she went on.
And then, while he retained her arm with gentle force :
"Owen brought me here, as I told you, and he won't like
me to go off with somebody else so long ; and then you

don't want to tell me your name because you're 'shamed
to be seen here ; and—"

"I *do* want to tell *you* my name," he struck in, with
low, eager tones. "It's Drummond—Casper Drummond.
And it's my true name, too. I give it to you because I've
never met any girl in all my life that fetched me as you
do. That's gospel truth, Cora ! Here's my card. Now. . .
just read that. Do you see ? I'm not lying to you, my
little darling ! God knows I'm not !"

She read the card that he had thrust into her hand. His
latter words had a familiar and yet a keenly novel ring.
She had grown so accustomed to the amatory attitude and
epithet from men, and yet all that this man said teemed
and tingled with so original a meaning ! Hardly knowing, in her charmful confusion, just what reply to make,
she hit upon one of challenge and provocative reproach
while she thrust the card, after a glance at it, into her
pocket.

"It's funny you should think this ball ain't . . ." (she
hesitated for a word and soon found it) ". . . respectable.
It looks ever so, to *me*."

Casper Drummond made a kind of groaning sound in
his throat. "Respectable ! Good Lord ! Just look round
us ! "

VII.

His implied condemnation was not unjust. No doubt the assemblage had its brighter gleams of membership, but moral dusk prevailed there. Some of the men's faces were hard as bronze and with a flash in their eyes like an assassin's knife-blade. Some of the women were reddened both by paint and liquor, carrying themselves with a laxity that told its own lewd story. The floor was well-sprinkled with thieves, and with courtesans on whose wages of sin they kept sleek; for perhaps the saddest part of all social degradation in our vast town is just this feeding of lawless men upon the sustenance vilely got for them by guilt-bathed women. In many of the costumes poverty and vanity were drolly allied. Among the men, false rubies and emeralds glittered from frayed neckties, impure shirt-cuffs went with a coat of thrifty nap, boots of patent-leather gleamed below trousers with fringy hems. Among the women, pinchbeck jewelry would help to adorn a gown worn and soiled; slippers that had lost all semblance of satin peeped from skirts crackling and smart, or per-. chance a spray of fresh-looking artificial roses would rest on a bodice of threadbare velvet. The ball itself was the gathering of a clan, the tribute paid to a congressman of his district by a band of supposably devout voters. Mr. Matthew J. Quinn was a State candidate gifted with that nicety of political conscience which has for many years helped to heap credit upon our civic records. He was wise enough in his generation to realize that ambition without dollars must mean, for New York statesmanship, the ladder without the wall. He had " put up " a sum not less than three thousand dollars and perhaps as large as six thousand, and somebody who "bossed the boys"

in the district had gone to work for him as the faithful
custodian of this rich deposit. Mr. Quinn had bought his
way to the polls with a serenity that could scarcely be
called unblushing, since he had doubtless thought no more
on the subject of his action as a venal one than he had
felt a sense of turpitude about eating his dinner when the
time came. So much distinction and triumph, so much
jugglery and fraud : thus ran his formula of procedure,
and thus has it run with his predecessors for almost half a
century, in the greatest city of the greatest living republic.
Votes must be purchased with a free purse, or defeat
would quickly show its teeth at economy in a snarl there
was no propitiating. Once having secured his nomina-
tion, Mr. Quinn must settle in hard cash with the
"leaders." It was one of the penalties of fame. The
henchmen would see that his ballots had been properly
"run out" from the boxes, and that no such paltry impedi-
ment as the American citizen's right of franchise should
stand in the way of his happy and honored election.
Votes must be bought up, here, there and everywhere.
Of course they must. It had been that way with many a
previous Mr. Quinn, and why should this particular publi-
can set himself in the beaten path of governmental prece-
dent ? Tramps, housebreakers, professional "heelers,"
the grimy little gang of sots who would sell their sisters',
wives' of mothers' good names for a hot spiced rum
when they beheld all other avenues toward drunkenness
obstructed, and that larger throng of half-starved toilers
who find probity a void pretension beside the dulling of
hunger—these formed the bevy of loyal "constituents"
who would send Mr. Matthew J. Quinn to Albany. Able
and upright men, interested in the maintenance of soil-
less rule, kept silent for "party reasons," with the knowledge of such black briberies in their brains and hearts.
Quinn would go to the Legislature and was ready to sell
his votes there as he had trafficked for those of others in
getting there. And this ball, flocked to by his myrmidons,

meant the infancy of his victory. The turnkeys down at
the Tombs would have recognized not a few of to-night's
revellers. Do not let us even dream that the would-be
"reformers" countenanced so dingy a rout with their
presence. They were up-town in their mansions on
Murray Hill, or lounging at their select clubs, or crying
"bravo" at some Delmoniconian dinner where the
Honorable Mr. Smoothtongue told them, with bursts of
pungent epigram, how delighted the Pilgrim Fathers
would feel to cast an eye on this glorious common-
wealth . . . Well, there lies a gulf between winking at
corruption and openly dealing in it. Of course, depravity
and criminality are the horrors of all politics. But the
vile ways of these minor city elections are endured by
the millionaire eaters of terrapin and sippers of cham-
bertin with a prescient resignation. When the Presidential
election comes, and the thirty-six electoral votes of New
York are coveted in a close division of parties, Johnny
O'Rafferty, for all his rascality, may be useful, and the
scampishness of Mike Mulligan cannot with prudence be
counted as a cipher. Besides, this Mr. Matthew J. Quinn
himself has a voice up there at the State capital, and though
he value it as highly as if it belonged to Madame Patti,
still, the boldest railroad scheme can't be pushed without
a charter.

One or two thoughts like these may have passed
through Casper Drummond's mind as he gave his brief
ironic reply to Cora. A little later he said, "Just let's
step downstairs and see what's going on there;" and she
was allowing herself to pass with him into lower regions
when some disturbance on the floor caught their attention.
A number of the dancers had massed together and were
staring across one another's shoulders. The music had
struck up again, but their clatter of voices rose above it.
All at once a shriek rang out, and presently the crowd
parted and a woman who appeared to be in sharp agony
was borne speedily toward one of the doors. Drummond

inquired of several people what was the matter, but secured no satisfactory answer. At last he put the question to a man who came along giggling with some deep secret amusement, and was met by a response which made him bite his lip and say "Oh,". rather grimly. As Drummond rejoined Cora, she at once inquired, "What did the man tell you?"

He hesitated, and then, with slight jerk of his head, replied: "I hoped you wouldn't be curious to know. But since you are, well—it's that stout woman with the yellow dress and the red wreath round her head, who—"

"Oh, yes," said Cora, "I remember." And a wave of rosy color swept to the roots of her hair. Drummond observed this, and drew his own conclusions.

The woman referred to had been galloping over the floor with various partners, and it needed hardly more than a glance both to tell that she was half drunk and that the exercise might imperil her own life, not to speak of another's besides her own. And now, in the midst of her orgy, she had been flung prostrate and writhing under the pangs of childbirth.

The man with the giggle glided up to Drummond soon after their little talk. He had evidently received still fresher tidings. "I'm blowed," he said, "if the baby ain't been born a'ready, 'fore they could git her into a kerridge. They say 'twas born dead, but I guess they meant dead-drunk." And his giggle sounded again, with a less rasping inflection, as though he had somehow succeeded in getting it oiled.

Drummond and Cora went downstairs. Here were two spacious apartments, in one of which you heard the click of billiard-balls and in the other occasional bursts of bacchanalian song from couples that were seated about the slim wooden tables. There was an immense bar in this room, with mirrors on which certain shibboleths or maxims of the Matthew J. Quinn Society had been recorded through majestic flourishes wrought by the agency of soap.

Drummond chose chairs at one of the tables, and soon a waiter shuffled up to them along the sandy floor. Cora felt both hungry and thirsty, but she would accept nothing in the way of beverage except the mild one which her companion had already mentioned. Drummond ordered a pint of champagne and drank it while she dealt with her sandwich and lemon-soda. Some of the women leered at her with inebriate grimaces; others gave her coldly critical looks and whispered about her to their masculine mates. The billiard-balls went on clicking in the next room, and blent their thin, keen echoes with the long adagios of a waltz upstairs. Now and then you heard an oath from one of the neighboring players, and sometimes it would be reduplicated with tipsy yells from a convivialist near at hand. Cora soon saw that the women were not alone her interested observers, for several of the men grinned at her and sought to catch her eye. But more than once there was the filmy, libidinous glance that she had learned to know and hate, and that changed itself to hostile insolence when resting upon Drummond. He had drunk more than his light words had expressed, and his new refreshment did not tend toward sobriety. He was not, however, quarrelsome in his cups. Realizing the difference between himself and his present encompassments, he preserved an air of happy good-humor even while privately teased and irritated.

"It does me good to see you get away with that sandwich," he said to Cora, as her white teeth bit into the layers of ham and bread; "most girls I meet don't want to show when they're hungry. They nibble and mince, and make believe they've only got the appetite of a bird. Now I love to see a girl that doesn't mind who looks at her while she goes to work on a bit of supper. But they've got turkey here, and oysters, and—"

"I couldn't take a bit more," broke in Cora. "I took this only to kind of stay my stomach. I'd get sleepy if I should have a big meal. I ain't 'customed to eatin' *any-*

thing so late. And it *is* gettin' late, ain't it?" she went on, somewhat anxiously. "Look here, Mr. Drummond, I'd like to go upstairs. Yes, I would—right away."

"Oh, pshaw," he said, draining his second glass of champagne; "I could sit here forever with *you*. I could, really! But I suppose I've begun to tire you."

"Tire me?" she murmured. "Oh, no; it isn't that. I—I like to have you with me. I like it ever so much, sir."

"Please don't call me 'sir.' Call me 'Casper,' won't you? A good many people do that I don't care a fig for. Why shouldn't you?"

"Me?" laughed Cora, though the laugh was a factitious one. "Why, you're only a passin' acquaintance. I ain't ever goin' to *see* you, after to-night."

"Yes, you are," he insisted, and clasped her hand under the table. She knew no reason why he should not so clasp it, and yet he had roused in her that feminine feeling which made her get the hand away from him as soon as possible. It was rather hardened with work, and not like the soft hand that she instinctively deemed he would desire her to have. And after she had released it from his hold she stole a covert look into his face, to see whether he showed the least sign of repulsion or disappointment.

Fond and genial devotion, however, was alone evident there. "Do you mean to say," he went on, "that you won't even let me come and see you after to-night."

"Come and see *me*! A gentleman like you are!"

"Oh, hang the 'gentleman' part! If I want to drop in, that's all there is to it."

"Drop in!" she sighed, with a slight laugh full of sadness. "You'd better say drop *up*. Why, it's no place for such as you." And then she made plain to him just what sort of a place it was. He seemed indeed nonplussed when he heard of the tiny bedroom that held the sewing-machine, and the door of communication between this and the combined sleeping and cooking apartment of Mrs. Slattery herself.

"But you can meet me somewhere, some evening," he said, "after your working-hours. We can have a bite of dinner and then go to some theatre like Tony Pastor's or the Windsor. Don't you think that would be ever so jolly?"

"No," said Cora, with actual severity of mien and tone. "I've seen other girls begin that way."

"Begin what?"

"Oh, well, never mind. I don't want to follow in their tracks; that's all."

He either was or assumed to be offended. "But you'll go to a ball like this with—somebody else."

"Owen? Well, I had reasons that I don't care to tell you of."

"Ah! no doubt of it!"

"Besides, I only went to-night as a very unusual thing—oh, very!"

"And Owen had it in his power to persuade you? He must be a pretty fetching kind of a chap."

"Oh, no; it ain't that."

"Come, now, what is it? If you're not fond of him— if you don't expect some day to marry him—why do you go out with him at night to a place that's packed with loafers and queer women?"

She hesitated for a moment before she answered. The demand in his question was flavored with a native jealousy and no mere counterfeit of it. This pierced her with a furtive pleasure; and yet pain quickly followed, for had not he himself just reminded her that future meetings between them could not take place? If the hereafter bore such fruit, it would be poison to her lips. Between what he was and what she was yawned a social abyss. She had no fastidious insight regarding the grades that separated one gentleman from another. He might not be as high as this one or that one, but he was far above herself, nevertheless. For him to marry her would bring ridicule if not disgrace on his name, but for him to be with her abroad, either by night or day, would cast an instant slur upon her own. Perhaps the accusation would have little mattered, for there were many in her round of acquaintanceship who gave her the discredit of sly and wary immoralities. But still she clung to the outward form of stainless behavior, loving it as do nearly all women to whom the spirit of it is likewise dear.

" I went out with Owen to-night," she presently replied, "because I—I'm in debt to his mother. There!" she added, with flushing face; "I hope your satisfied *now*, "

He looked at her with a stare of pity in each of his blue eyes. "Oh, my poor, poor girl!" he murmured, and in his voice was passion. She knew then that he loved her as well as she knew that she loved him and must go on loving him from now until she died. "And I'm rich, Cora," he pursued. " If 'twasn't for my infernal extravagances I'd almost have more money than I knew what to do with. Let me help you a little bit." He had bowed his head and was fumbling with some bank-notes held between both his rather unsteady hands, and shadowed by the wooden abutment of the table. "I say, now, Cora, let me just give you—or lend you——"

" Put up your damned money, if ye please. This lady ain't for sale while I'm round."

VIII.

It was Owen who spoke these words, and he seemed
to both of them, in their preoccupation with each other,
a presence of almost phantasmal abruptness. Cora saw
swiftly how angry he must be, for his face had a chalky
pallor, and his iron-gray eyes were two discs of fire. It
flashed across her that he had been drinking ; and she was
right, for after he had got down here and seen herself
and Drummond seated together, a madness had made
him toss off three large glassfuls of liquor. He looked
upon Cora's treatment of him as a most contemptuous
affront. Even if it had sprung from ignorance of received
codes its effect was all the more wounding ; for the willing-
ness to do without his own company showed with what
ease she could slip his image entirely from her thoughts.
If you had asked Owen Slattery why he had stood for so
long a time apart from Cora and made no attempt to
pit his powers of fascination against those of Drummond,
he would have told you, with all the illogical abandonment of the jealous, that her preference had been written
on every line of her face and that from the first she had
flaunted it at him with wanton mockery. He would quite
have forgotten the devotions of that ball-room babbler,
Mr. Rudie Champny, since these had been met with no
visible marks of favor. And he knew each lineament of
his beloved Cora so well ! He had studied them with
stealthy glances through all those six long months when
she and he would meet at meals and a barrier of detested
silence rose between them !

After all, the autocracy and tyranny of his present conduct had their excuse. He was on amical terms with
some of his fellow-guests to-night. Bringing Cora hither,

6

and having her lean on his arm as "his gal" was to be the palpable seal and witness of his new, triumphant joy. I am far from asserting that his love belonged among those loftier emotions with which a certain species of biographer likes to accredit men of his earthy stamp. The brute cannot love except brutally, and if Owen transcended mere animality by several clear degrees he was that sure product of his time, his town, his rearing and his inheritances which no erotic thrills could dematerialize.

As Owen spoke those few fierce words to Drummond, Cora felt her blood freeze. Her companion did not once quail or waver. He rose from his seat and faced the man who had just addressed him, with a good-natured bluffness.

"I suppose you're Owen," he said. "You appear to be riled at something. Sit down and let's make it up. I dare say we can. Don't scowl so, Owen ; it isn't becoming to your style of beauty. . . Look here, old boy. Sit down and have a drink. What shall it be?" And Casper Drummond laid one hand on the shoulder of his new enemy.

"Be careful," muttered Cora, wishing that only Drummond should hear her.

But Owen heard, too. He shook off the pacificatory hand. "I'll take no drinks with you nor none of your breed. I ain't one o' them that such a chap as you be can play it over, *no*how ! "

"I'm the best fellow in the world, Owen," said Drummond, with an audacity of familiarity that terrified Cora. "Just sit down and try if I'm not. There's no use of our standing here and staring at one another, like two Kilkenny cats."

Drummond was on the point of nonchalantly reseating himself, when Owen, with a stifled oath and a nimble spring, aimed at him the sort of blow that can make a man's brain one sick blur and blacken both eyes for a fortnight. But the other was too prompt in his own defence. He parried the blow just as a crowd came surging up from the different tables. Owen made another dash at him, and this time with better success. Drummond had drenched himself for years past with the science of boxing, but he could not wholly divert the course of that mammoth and leaden fist. It more than grazed one temple and brought out a bloody welt there in no time. Then the usual thing happened, and at least ten forms darted between Drummond and his assailant. But Owen had tasted fight. His hard, gloomy nature held an almost murderous grudge. Drink had begun to feed once more the ruffian in his veins, that had lain there half-dormant for six months, like a hibernating viper.

He grappled with the men who strove to restrain him, and it looked as if he would get back to the object of his rage in spite of their efforts. Meanwhile Drummond stood with a handkerchief pressed against his bleeding temple. He burned with a sense of outrage, and yet no wild imp of wrath had got hold of him. This partly was because of his equable temper and partly owing to the contempt he felt for such an antagonist as Owen. Two or three fellows of blackguardly air and speech now attacked him verbally ; they were friends of Owen's, or perhaps only admirers of his fine muscular gifts. One took for granted that Drummond had ''picked a row'' with the young athlete of Prince Street, and jeered accordingly ; a second knew of how ''this 'ere sport'' had ''gone an' froze to Oweny's gal,'' and a third, more insolent than the others, wanted to learn ''What in thunder's name is a dude like you a doin' round here to the Quinn ball, *any*how ? ''

''Ah, Rudie,'' exclaimed Drummond, recognizing his friend across a little sea of heads, and taking no more notice of his persecutors than if they had not spoken. ''That rascal over there has been going for me in the most infernal way ! ''

"Yes," grumbled a voice, "and he'll go for ye worse yet if he gits the chance."

Rudie heard this, and shouted out, as he pushed imperiously toward his friend. "No, he won't, not if I'm round!" This raised a laugh among the bystanders, who had quickly compared Rudie's alert yet small stature with that of the struggling and infuriated Owen.

"Good for you, Rude," returned Drummond, with a glance at his blood-stained kerchief, which he promptly reapplied to his temple. "But the fellow's a regular devil. You'll help me, I know, all you're able, and that might surprise some that saw you getting in your fine work. But why don't the police turn up, I'd like to inquire? Three or four officers were in the ball-room. I'm damned if I'll run away from that bully!" Here he appealed to the gathered mob, sweeping his enkindled eyes over its numerous male faces. "Can't somebody fetch a policeman? I've a charge of assault to make against that man."

Just as he ended this rapid train of words it looked ill with Casper Drummond; for Owen had twisted himself free from a detainer of specially stubborn sinew and now plunged forward, all angry glare and hostile purport. Those who stood guardingly before the young man receded in dismay. Drummond himself thrust away his handkerchief and stood his ground. Jarred and unstrung, though he felt, it was not in him to budge for all the Owen Slatterys in rowdydom.

But Rudolph Champny, whom a sight of his friend's blood had wrought upon tellingly, confronted Owen by a fleet sidelong swerve. He appeared dapper, plump and composed as when Cora had been bored by his loquacity about an hour ago. He squared himself, and there was a flurry of laughter as he did so. Owen, livid and breathing hard, paused before him, overbrowing him. Then, in the twinkling of an eye, something happened that had in it the surprise of pure miracle. Champny had man-

aged to land his fist on Owen's cheek, and to flash backward with amazing speed. Owen struck out, but his
burly hand raked air, and the man he had thought to
level dealt him a fresh bruise, harsher than the last, that
set him dizzily reeling with a spirt of blood from the
nostrils. It was the quiet splendor, on "Rudie's" part,
of pugilistic science. Owen had thrice his strength, and
a few more seconds of contest between the two might
have brought forth prowess that would have made Champny's fate a sorry one. But at this juncture two stalwart
policemen, with raised clubs, hurled themselves upon
Owen, presumably the assailing party because of his
better height and build.

Owen was beaten back. Another policeman dashed
after his mates, and seeing that one combatant had been
taken charge of, turned upon Champny. "Officer,"
came his cry, "what I've done has been self-defence."
As he spoke he threw back his coat, and on his breast
gleamed the badge that policemen of New York bow
to. Already Drummond had joined Champny, and
shown a like sign.

"We're ready," shot Drummond, "to make a charge
of assault against that loafer. He attacked us both
without the least cause. We're here as peaceable citizens.
I'll give you my name if you want." He leaned toward
the policeman and whispered a few words, among which
"son of the alderman" may or may not have been heard
by eager surrounding ears.

Cora had seen all this. And now she perceived that
Owen, with his face stained luridly by blood, was being
clubbed about body and shoulders. Soon after came the
click of handcuffs. It leapt through her mind that she
was without protection, that Owen had been arrested,
that she must not and would not accept assistance from
Drummond or his friend, and that if any one course were
more discreet than another, flight would alone be advis-
able.

No one seemed to notice her, and she sped at a cautious, gliding pace toward the stairs which led to the ball-room. Mounting, she made haste toward the dressing-room where her shawl and hat had been deposited. Her head swam while she gave her check and received them. Then, across a draughty hall, she made her way to the front entrance and passed by another stairway into the street.

It was still arctically cold. She had gone three or four blocks before she realized that to return home would be to encounter a storm of questions, ending in . . . what? Expulsion, perhaps, from Mrs. Slattery's doors. For had not she, Cora Strang, been the chief cause of Owen's calamity? Afterward, too (even if she were still allowed to live there), what persecutions might not assail her? Then there was the danger of Owen's vengeful fury. He might come back to-night, or in the morning before she was up, or just afterward. . . The ways of police-courts were happily dim to her. . . And so, in the mordant cold, in the rushing blast, under that austere moon which floated through so mercilessly distant a heaven, she stood and told herself that to re-seek those Prince Street lodgings would be madness.

But suddenly she recollected the shawl that she wore. It was Mrs. Slattery's loan to her. 'Well,' soon came the decision, 'and if she *did* lend it! Better I borrowed it a little while longer and sent it back afterward than risked my life to-night! All the luckier I never took her coral breast-pin, for that *might* have weighed on my conscience. . . . Yes, I'll go to Em Cratchett. She'll take me in for a few days at least. She's up now—God help her, this is her *time* for bein' up!"

Em Cratchett was a sewing-girl who supported a bed-ridden mother, an idiot brother seven years old, and two sisters, aged about nine and eleven. This family had once occupied two rooms in the Prince Street tenement-house, and there Cora had got to know Em even better than she knew Effie and Ann Flynn. Em had been forced to find cheaper quarters, and a tenement-house close to Grand Street had supplied them. It was a den of filth, but its two yet smaller rooms were a dollar and a half lower per month, and to Em that meant a great sum. She had more than once told Cora that she believed if it wasn't for the strong tea, starvation would have killed her long ago. She took it as black as ink, and no doubt it buoyed her up among the fearful sights and smells on every side. Not a cent, with Em, but counted ; and when they raised the electric light within a few yards of her windows it brought her one more chance to save. For a monstrous iron structure had been built, of late, just over the way, and its bulk had darkened the sunshine, so that morning seemed like afternoon and three o'clock in the day was like dusk. But when night came the electric light flooded Em's front room with its keen, pale splendor, as though it had been the marvellous moonlight of another planet. One evening a sudden thought seized the girl, and she tried those acute white rays to sew by. Always afterward she did her work at night, and took what rest she could get between morning and the hours that followed. Soon others in the house imitated her—such as were not too slothful and drunken among the womenkind. Those cold and colorless beams poured in upon bent shapes and wan faces, night after night. The late feasts of luxury and dissipation in other parts of the town were copied here with tints of frightful parody and irony. These were revellers with cups of gall for their wine, and spectres of want to serve as footmen. Sin rioted in the reeking house, whose very stairs had rotten creaks when you trod them, as though fatigued by the steps of sots and trulls. To enter some of the rooms was to smell infection and to face beastliness. Fever lived in the sinks and closets along the halls, where festered refuse more rancid and stenchful than stale swill, and so vile that to name it would be to deal with words which are the dung of lexicons. Those halls had nooks of gloom whence miasma might have fled in fright before the human grossness that spawned there. Little children dipped their chastity in poison between the scurfy-grained wainscots of every corridor, and twisted their soft lips into the shaping of oaths that would scare brothels. Now and then, in the lull of midnight, while the sewing-machines clattered from rooms like Em's, and her toilful sisters' high yells would ring out as the beaten wife cowered and shivered, murder had been done here. There was a room with the ghost in it of a hanged desperado, which had so lowered its rent by its uncanny pranks that an Italian couple with six little ones had got it cheap after quitting the steamer. Malaria forever kept busy her minions of disease, and the just historian of this noxious house must have collected his annals ill if he forgot to tell how often the pine-wood coffins of the Potter's Field undertaker had been hustled over its noisome floors.

Em Cratchett gave a great start as Cora's hand touched her on the shoulder. She was working away at her machine, and had heard no one enter because of its clamors. "Well, I do declare!" she exclaimed, and looked up at her visitor as though she had been a wraith. "For the Lord's sake, Cora, where did *you* drop from?"

Cora made it all plain in a few words. "You ain't a bit to blame," decided Em, after she had mused a little. "You didn't do a thing you hadn't ought to a done—not a *thing!*"

"Oh, yes, Em, I left Owen——"

"Stuff! Couldn't he a follered you if he'd a mind, an' took you from them other parties? He always *was* a big, sassy bully, with a cheek onto him like the hull of out-doors—'cept when he was drunk, an' then he was a heap sight worse. If I was as pretty as you I'd turn up my nose at a beau like that. I don't have any of 'em look at me nowadays, but when I did they never tried to bulldoze me, *you* can bet, without they got consid'rable left doin' it ! "

This reference to a time when Em bore the dower of comeliness was fraught with a terrible pathos and satire. She had once been rosy as a sea-shell and straight as a reed, but you would not guess it to-day if you noted her pallor and her stoop. Not much past twenty, she was a mere haggard wreck of womanhood. She used to say, with a laugh bitterer than any sob could sound, that she had kept her character and now she was being rewarded. Lots of the girls whom she had grown up with had lost theirs. "But after all," she would dismally announce, "I can't see just where the difference lays. Such as us, unless we can marry some good man and quit the awful grind and fret of our lives, must die young anyhow. I guess them that go crooked has a good deal the best time. I don't see why so many *does* go if 'taint that way. They get nice clothes and food, for a few years at least. If most of 'em didn't drink along with the other badness they wouldn't end half so quick. But there's very few women that coins dollars out o' their self-respect without cravin' to deaden the self-disgust it brings."

Em, for all that she had made a sad failure of her life, was no cynic philosopher. She had striven with that sublimity which is not embalmed in epic tragedies, but which has obscurity for its theatre, and for footlights the uncouth old flickering lamps of side-streets and alleys. Yet defeat had answered her struggles, and this defeat had in a way been typical of her entire class ; for she was one of hundreds who learn that they cannot support themselves in decency by being honest and biding separate from the tens of thousands who reap the lucre of profligacy. She had not yielded, and now she began to doubt if for soldiers like herself the battle held any palm of victory. A mind conscious of its own virtue ? Ah, yes, there was perhaps guerdon in that ! But how did it serve when both spirit and flesh were enfeebled by fatigue, and the shadow of untimely death had already spread its veil across the sun ? And then if there were only those who cared whether a girl went astray or not ! But how many ever did care ? How many even knew whether if she had sunk or no into the black gulf, or still was busy keeping the wash and lap of its waves from that slim raft she clung to ?

" Of course you can stay here, Cora," said Em, a few minutes later. " But you ain't used to our kind o' livin', though you have roughed it, sure enough. I swear to God," the girl went on, lifting one bony hand in the elfin glare, " that I ain't got but forty cents to my name this night, though I ain't missed a single workin'-hour for six weeks. We've had to keep the stove red-hot just as you see it, or we'd half froze up here ; and then there's the victuals, of course, and milk for Stevie, 'cause the child spits out everything else you give him, and medicines for mother—"

" Oh, I thought I'd hear something o' that kind. My sakes, I wish I was dead an' buried in the same grave with your poor father, an' not layin' here a nuisance to my own flesh an' blood ! "

Worriment had swept over Em's hollow-cheeked face as these words were whined forth from a bed in one of the corners. At once she left her chair and went toward the bed, saying while she did so :

" Now, mother, you just know that's all fiddlestick ! If you *was* to go I'd give right up, an' be after you in no time."

Here she tucked the bed-clothes deftly and nimbly round a skinny, white throat, not very much larger than the stem of a stout grape-vine, and peered down, smiling, for a moment, at eyes that made one think of two big brilliants aglow in a skull. For years Mrs. Cratchett had been as much the derision of death as the victim of disease. Her trouble was a spinal paralysis that left her wholly helpless. But no resignation had come with the

affliction. Her tongue was waspish in its discontents and
sarcasms ; there could not have been a more embittered
invalid. She loved to moan forth melancholy remarks
about graves or shrouds or the decomposition of the dead,
and such tendency would reveal itself more strongly
while the room where she and Em slept was illumined
by that eerie radiance from the street. Its glamorous and
cheerless power seemed to provoke her morbid meditations and make her deliver them aloud with a sinister
gusto. Em had implored her, at first, when the plan of
night-sewing had first been formed, to have a bed put up
in the next room beside the children's, and thus escape
the worst disturbances of the machine. But no ; she
appeared to see a new chance for obstinate revolt, and
declared that the machine " soothed " her, and that she
didn't want to "pop off " while out of her daughter's
sight. She was always prophesying a moment when she
would "pop off ; " she had been expecting it and brooding over it for years, and if she had said nothing at all on
the subject Em would have missed the doleful utterance
as though it had been a lack of the familiar pungency in
her own too frequent cups of tea. Long ago the unhappy
woman could have gone to a hospital for incurables, but
she had rebelled against that idea with characteristic
mulish hardihood. Doctors of eminence had seen her,
and wondered what latent vigor kept her alive. It might
be said that she had been alive only mentally for a longer
time than common credence would have cared to accept.
Mortification hovered over her like a vulture above its
carrion. But somehow the thrust-in beak had never left
its plunderous mark. A subtler disintegration, however,
had bitten with invisible fang the tissues of her brain, and
she lay, the object of a malignity more severe than that
which any physical dissolution could have wreaked.

" Excuse me for not seeing you when I came in, Mrs.
Cratchett," promptly said Cora. " But perhaps you were
asleep, and didn't see *me.*"

" Oh, no, I wasn't," said the sick woman. " I heard everything you told Em. I don't blame a spry, pink-faced gal like you for likin' goin' to balls. I used to love 'em. But Lord ! what's human happiness, even for such as lives onto Fifth Avenue an' hangs their winders with lace? Why, we're all nothin' but skeletons with a little flesh put round the bones, that's all we are. An' somewheres, either in the lumber-yard or the tree itself, is waitin' our—"

" Let me boost your head up a little higher, mother," Em here broke in, with the natural wish to curtail speeches of so pessimistic a dolor. And while she proceeded to rearrange the flabby and flimsy pillow, a laugh sounded in a near doorway, quaint and chuckling, as if some gnome out of a fairy-tale had made it in a dream.

" Oh, come here, Stevie," said Cora, and she held out one hand to a tiny shape with straw-colored hair and huge blue eyes made empty by idiocy.

But the boy would not obey her, and was running back into his bedchamber, when his two sisters, Maggie and Katy, emerged thence and pushed him forward between them. The girls were both in their night-gowns, made from some coarse gray flannel, whose thick woof could not hide the wasted outlines of their bodies. They both knew Cora well and were fond of her, and rebelled when their elder sister ordered their return to bed. They had little, pinched, bluish-white faces, and the younger was disfigured by a deep scar on one cheek, which had come to her a year or two before in a fight with an Italian boy of about thirteen years old—a juvenile Don Juan of the slums—who was now in a reformatory for this and similar assaults. Maggie went to the stove, declaring it was so cold in her room that she could not sleep there, while Katy put one pipe-stem of an arm round Cora's neck, and whispered that she was " awful hungry."

" I don't think much about the cold," rang Mrs. Cratchett's nasal tones from the bed. "What's the use, when we're all bound to be a good deal colder 'fore we git through with this queer job they call life ? "

"Hee, hee ! " laughed Stevie, in his eldritch way. He had climbed upon his mother's bed and sat beside her, with his legs crossed and his arms folded, like a droll little pixie, while the searching and crystalline light gave his queer, long face an unearthly vacancy. He always laughed like this whenever his mother spoke one of her funereal sentiments ; he of course had no conception of what they meant, but something in the tone of her voice he would always appear to recognize and to make a signal for his impish mirth. His mother's illness had begun the day he was born, and it had been alleged that the "dear dead husband" whom Mrs. Cratchett was so fond of talking about had kicked her in a drunken rage. Stevie was born idiotic, and his mother became the lingering and piteous invalid we have seen her.

"We ain't got bed-clothes enough in there," said Maggie, as she crouched in front of the stove. She had her mother's querulous temperament, and gave Em twice as much trouble as Katie. "Besides, 'tain't fair to have one room all het up an' the other like an ice-house. Now Cora's come," she added, "p'raps we may have a little beer."

"Beer ! beer ! " cried Stevie, who knew the word ; and he clapped his little waxy hands together as if in applause at Maggie's courageous hint.

"Hold your tongue, Mag," reproved Em. "The less beer you git the better for yourself and them that's got charge of ye."

"She was drunk on beer, night 'fore last, Maggie was," whispered Katie to Cora, but in a tone loud enough for all the rest to hear what she said.

Maggie scowled, with the round red-hot stove glaring at her side as though it were the head of an evil spirit.

"You hold your nasty little tattlin' tongue ! " she cried to Katie ; and then, forgetting the "company manners" which Cora's presence should both have evoked and fostered, she poured out a sudden torrent of profanity, each oath of which seemed to fly up and hammer the low ceiling with peril to its cracked and swollen plaster.

Em shrieked her name in expostulation, and then rushed toward her with an evident design of taking her by either shoulder. But the project failed, and miserably; for Em stood still in a sudden dazed way, and putting one hand over her heart slipped limply as a dropped garment to the floor. Cora was kneeling beside her in an instant and scanning the worn young face that this wild, fairy sort of light made deathly.

"Em !" she called in alarm, "Em ! What *is* it ?" and almost at once the fallen lids were lifted again, and a laugh rippled through the chalky lips. "Oh, it's nothin' —just one o' my spells. I take 'em sometimes, but they pass off as quick as they come."

"Yes," said Mrs. Cratchett from the bed, "an' some day, Cora, *she'll* pass off *in* one of 'em. It *might* be that she'll go even 'fore *I* do, an' if she does, that *would* be a joke ! "

"Hee ! hee !" cachinnated little Stevie, who seemed to think it would indeed be a fine joke, though he really thought nothing at all about it except that his mother's voice had sounded in the old sardonic tones.

"Em," Cora murmured, after the collapse had given place to a half-recumbent languor, "if you've a bit of brandy it would be a good thing just to take a swallow, and——"

"Oh, no," hurried Em, whispering the words, with a glance at Maggie, who crouched sullenly by the stove; "I never dare keep *anything* like that here, because of *her*. She's only a child, but that curse is on her, and she'd drink anything she could get. . . Oh, *Cora !*" and here Em burst into tears, laying her head on the shoulder that was so close to it. "There's been changes even with such as us since you was away from us. I didn't want to tell

you, for I know your lot ain't any too easy ; but I've just
got to stay chained to my work day in an' day out an' see
that little thing go right down to—to the very dogs. . .
Well," she broke off, with a great gulp that showed she
was heroically swallowing her tears, "don't mind my
blubberin' a bit. There, now ; it's over. Lemme get up. .
Oh, yes, I can ; don't be afraid." And she rose with even
a certain nimbleness.

"Some day she won't get up. She'll lay there," said
Mrs. Cratchett. And Stevie did not laugh, this time, for
some reason that his own topsy-turvy little brain best knew
about.

"Em," now said Cora, in a low and very earnest voice,
remembering Katie's recent words to her, "I wish you'd
let me get you a bite of something. I—"

"A bite ? Why, Cora, I've had my supper. We all did.
It's my breakfast, you know. All I need, now, is a cup
o' tea ; an' the tea-pot's there on the stove. We'll both
have one."

"I hate tea," grumbled Maggie ; "it's such wishy-
washy stuff."

"I like. coffee, though," said Katie wistfully. "You
can get a big cup to a place a little ways from here, with
a hunk o' sugar into it an' lots o' milk, for three cents.
An' if ye've got five you can get a piece o' the yaller
mushy pie—punkin, I guess it is—throwed in."

"Em," Cora pursued, after this epicurean outburst was
ended, "I do believe the tea hurts you a good deal more
than it heals. Now I'll tell you what it is. I'd like a cup
of hot coffee myself, and if you've got a dish of any kind
I'll just try to bring in some little relish from that place
Katie spoke of."

The place was not hard to find. It was a narrow little
eating-house with a tawny dish of baked beans in the
window, flanked by a few sanguinary beefsteaks. At
first the proprietor would not give Cora a dish of his
corned-beef hash to take away, though this was the viand

much amused. "Are you referring to my new maid, Rob?" And then, with some hesitation and an evident doubt as to the approval with which her little story would be received, she made known just where and how she had secured Cora's services.

"And *don't* you think her a perfectly lovely creature, Rob?" at length finished the narrator. "Did you *ever* see a more truly bewitching face?"

"I didn't notice much about her," he returned, "except that she wasn't that cat-like French thing of yours, with the black moustache. I'll look at her better the next time."

This was a falsehood on the part of Mr. Robert Conover. He had seen Cora with great distinctness, and had thought her curiously charming. But he had long ago made it a point never to praise any woman in the presence of his wife. His reasons for this course may not have been very astute ones, but they were at least sufficient unto himself.

"I hate to see you so indifferent to every earthly woman except me, Rob," murmured Mrs. Conover, who really took secret delight in the belief that he was thus indifferent. "It might make people imagine I keep too tight a rein on you, or some such absurd thing . . . But I'm glad, Rob—ever so glad—that you haven't felt like scolding me for taking this poor girl from the Lodging House."

"Oh, that's your own affair," he laughed. "The spoons belong to you, not to me."

"Oh, *Rob!* They say at the Lodging House that for seven or eight weeks she's been a perfect saint."

"M—yes. What was she before that?"

"A poor sewing-girl. Oh, horribly poor! Some of the things that she's told me have made my flesh creep. But I haven't heard half yet; she's going to tell me more."

"Indeed! You want your flesh to go on creeping; you like it that way. But I don't see why. These are measurement. But she now did a thing which materially differed from her usual method. She spoke to Miss Tefft in an altered voice—one so much below her customary tones, in fact, that it made numerous inquiring eyes glance up at her again on the instant.

"Do you know, that girl over *yonder* with the reddish-brown hair, is just *too* fascinating!"

Cora happened at this moment to glance from her work and catch the speaker's eye. She did not hear Mrs. Conover's words, but it became speedily plain to her that she was their subject. And then, in a minute or two afterward, Miss Tefft's voice mildly called:

"Cora. . . Cora Strang. . . Just step this way, if you please."

Cora rose, with a glad hope at once tingling through her blood. She had not thought Mrs. Conover vulgar, for she had no standpoint from which to judge commonness or its reverse among those plutocrats whom any such woman would inevitably represent to her. The new-comer had simply appealed to her as some one who was pompous and rich. It had entered her mind that to live as a servant in the palace (of course it must be a palace on Fifth Avenue) where so prosperous a being dwelt might belong among the possibilities. But she was ill prepared for the summons that in a trice made this remote chance promise to become proximate.

She found it very embarrassing to stand before Mrs. Conover and be devoured by that person's gaze as though she were poor Ann Flynn's friend, the Prince Street Fat Woman. Besides, giggles and titters had begun to sound from some of the girls, who realized her discomfiture.

"So your name's Cora," said Mrs. Conover. "That's a pretty name. I like pretty names because my own is a great ugly mouthful. Miss Tefft has just told me that you're American and a good plain sewer. You've never lived out, though, have you, Cora?"

"No, ma'am."

8

figure in overcoats amply furnished with trimmings of fur, velvet or braid, and none but the boldest patterns of plaids or stripes would have struck him as too daring for trousers. On the smallest finger of one hand sparkled a superb diamond, sunken in a heavy hoop of gold—a ring that princes might have envied him. This precious bauble had been bestowed upon him by his wife soon after their marriage. He would sometimes jocularly mention it now, as his " wedding-ring."

We have seen how Honoria Conover adored him and on what a pedestal of virtue she placed him. But he was so completely unworthy of both her confidence and her esteem that it would not be far from truth to call the terms on which he lived with her those of revolting hypocrisy. Her friends had long ago circulated a bitter little tale that flung satire upon her devout uxoriousness ; for, as we all know, friends are by no means too reluctant at times when their silence would bear merciful fruit and their gossip merely facilitates a sort of poisonous telegraphy. "I let my husband go to the club three or four evenings in the week," Mrs. Conover was reported to have declared, "and I'm only too happy to think he *can* sometimes enjoy himself in gentlemen's society." An ordinary remark enough, and yet one made pregnant with humor to certain of Mrs. Conover's hearers ; for these, who were all women, and most of whose husbands were at this particular club every evening of their lives, had long ago learned that wherever Robert Conover *did* pass the interval between nine o'clock and midnight, his passing it at the club was a most rare occurrence.

In other words, his infidelity to his wife had been a theme for derision among their acquaintances. Time and again his name had been bandied about in connection with that of some woman whose repute was fatally tarnished, and not long since he had found himself the prey of a guilty dread lest one specially notorious intimacy should reach Mrs. Conover's ears. If she had been a

woman less given to extolling the perfections of her
spouse, enmity, not to say the sly caprices of friendship
itself, would have whispered to her concerning this or that
misdeed. But no; her fool's paradise was its own safe-
guard against disillusion. Then, too, no one knew her at
all well who did not also know the hot leaps and starts
of her loose-bridled temper. Meanwhile Conover's life
might be described as one of semi-genteel profligacy.
The facts went brazenly to show that his career was profitless except through mild spurts of speculation, that he
had married under difficulties, with sordid obstinacy, a woman whom he had never cared for, and that he was now
quite dependent upon the funds allowed him by this wife
whose faith and fondness he daily insulted.

Cora soon heard from Mrs. Conover just how she had
married her husband. The lady appeared to grow fonder
of her with a speedy augment of indulgence and gracious-
ness. Cora had gained some knowledge of her peppery
irascibility, for she had heard her upbraid the butler and
one or two of the other servants in terms that trenched
on an almost ribald syntax of reprimand. Besides, the
growls against her shrewish moods were often fierce in
regions below stairs. But to Cora she continued the soul
of tolerance and suavity. "You are getting along ever so
well," she said to her new maid one morning. "You're
bright as you can be; you take hints and act on them; I
like that; it encourages me to go on teaching you. With
a very few more lessons you'll succeed in doing my hair
quite nicely, so that I shall need nobody except you to
manage it, no matter how finely I want to get myself
up."

"I'm very glad to hear that," said Cora, who clung to
her place, now she had received it, with grateful tenacity.

"Perhaps," Mrs. Conover went on, "you'll also be
glad to hear that my husband likes you and—and ap-
proves of the way in which I found you out. I sometimes
regret that he should have such a cold way of showing

preference whenever it's a matter which concerns one of my own sex. But such is really the fact, and there's no altering it. I may as well say right out just what I want to say : he's perfectly cold to all living women except myself."

"Oh, yes, I see, ma'am," said Cora ; and she knew that her cheeks took at least a slight pink tinge, and hoped that her interlocutress would not observe it. For Mr. Conover had already shown her marked attention both in word and look while his wife chanced to be absent.

"*Per*—fectly cold," proceeded Mrs. Conover, with a drawl that had the effect of intensified repetition. "It's always been precisely like that, ever since we were married. You see, Cora, I was an orphan, living in a rather dull manner with my uncle, Mr. Abner Prime. Uncle Abner is immensely rich, and a bachelor, and nobody has ever doubted that he will leave me a large portion of his property when he dies. No doubt the Children's Aid Society and the Cancer Hospital for Women, and a number of institutions like that, will get a great deal of it, for Uncle Abner is tremendously charitable. But he's as good as told me that I shall inherit more than half, though there *was* a time when it looked as if he were going to cut me off with nothing. That was when I married Mr. Conover. He was poor, and besides, Uncle Abner didn't like his family. My husband's father had been mixed up with New York political affairs—you wouldn't understand just *how*, even if I tried to explain it to you, for I've never quite understood, myself. I was a girl just out of school when I first met my future lord and master. He wasn't *quite* as handsome then as he is now, but still he was wonderfully handsome. He'd no sooner been to call on me than Uncle Abner forbade him the house. There were several awful scenes, and then I quieted down. I'd made up my mind to run away and be married if ever my darling Robert asked me. At first he didn't show the least sign of doing so, but we used to meet and have long walks together, and we contrived it all in the queerest fashion ! At that time there were several vacant lots behind our house in Forty-Eighth Street. If Robert passed through Forty-Ninth Street of a morning my window-shades would give him full information of just how the land lay. One shade up and the other down meant that it was doubtful if I could get out that afternoon. Both shades half-way down meant 'probbable.' Both shades three-quarters down meant 'very little hope.' One shade down and the other up as far as the top window-pane meant 'sure.' And so it went on. Well, in the end I eloped with Robert, got married, came home again, and told Uncle Abner I was a bride. I expected to be killed on the spot—truly, I did, for though he's a Quaker he's got a frightful temper, as nearly all the Prime people have except myself. But he was ever so much quieter than I'd expected him to be, and in the end I carried my point. He gave us this house, and he allows us a handsome sum every year. But he never speaks to my husband. It's shameful, of him, but he doesn't. It's shameful, Cora, because Mr. Conover is so devoted a husband, and works so hard down in Wall Street, and is respected by lots of first-class business acquaintances. They say runaway matches are apt to turn out well. I'm sure mine has ! I've only one thing to be sorry for, and that is my husband's coldness to other ladies." Here Mrs. Conover laughed a little, and threw back her high, mettlesome head and showed her white, irregular teeth. "'Pon my word, Cora, I'd *like* him to be a little sweet on Mrs. This or Miss That, just to see how a *slight* fit of jealousy would make me feel."

"Oh, no, ma'am," said Cora, shaking her head in respectful reproof. "I'm sure you don't really mean what you're sayin !"

But afterward, thinking over everything she had heard, the girl caught herself wondering whether this constant allusion on Mrs. Conover's part to the flawless behavior of her husband might not conceal a lurking suspicion.

The brilliant black eyes of Robert Conover soon began to steal many glances into her own. Cora must indeed have been silly not to realize that those long, bold stares were evidently not born alone of friendliness and good-will. She had seen the same gaze so often before! Why should she not recognize the latent fever and fierceness of it now? And yet she strove against any conclusion that would subvert the testimony of Mrs. Conover's fond praises.

'Perhaps I'm wrong,' she thought, 'and he only looks at me like that because his wife has told him how smart I am and how well I'm gettin' along.'

Still, his manner worried her, and a haunting fear grew upon her lest he might take occasion in the future to seek her when she was alone. Quite often during the afternoons Mrs. Conover would be out in her carriage, shopping or paying visits, and not seldom her husband returned before she did.

One morning a somewhat startling thing happened. Mr. and Mrs. Conover were seated at breakfast, when Cora was summoned to the side of her mistress for the purpose of bringing a forgotten handkerchief. As she paused by Mrs. Conover's chair, the head of the house, who was reading a letter apparently just received, broke into a loud, blithe laugh.

" Oh, how funny ! " he exclaimed.

" What's funny, Rob ? " said his wife, who was pouring out coffee. " You haven't even told me who your letter's *from !* "

" Haven't I ? " he said absently. " Why, it's from old Casper."

" Casper Drummond ? "

" Yes. He and Rudie Champny got on one of their big sprees down at St. Augustine, the other day, and raised such a row that the hotel-people bounced 'em both, bag and baggage."

" How scandalous ! " declared Mrs. Conover, frowning over her luminous coffee-urn. The next minute she turned to Cora. " That's all ; you can go," she added.

Cora left the room. But she felt a little dizzy after she had got into the hall outside.

" Casper Drummond," kept ringing in her ears. It was he ! It must be ! And these people knew him ! . . . As she went upstairs her heart throbbed so wildly and queerly that she had to pause, with one hand clasping the banister.

XII.

MEANWHILE she had been brought face to face with another cause of discomfiture. The chambermaid, Martha, was a woman of about five-and-thirty, trim of figure, with a sedate, shrewd face, and movements nimble as a weasel's. At first she had been all smiling affability to Cora, but of late her treatment had markedly changed. This was because of the butler, Joyce, whom she deeply admired and expected one day to marry. He had not yet proposed to her, but the near future had seemed big with that event at the time of Cora's coming. Soon afterward, however, the sky of Martha's hope grew dismal. She secretly gnashed her teeth with jealousy and felt herself almost capable of putting poison in Cora's coffee. Joyce was a huge fellow, with the solemn visage that became his calling, and not a little secret reverence for self. He had learned of Cora's association with the establishment of Mrs. Montrose, and for this reason, perhaps, regarded the conquest of her affections as one which would be fraught with ease. His advances had an elephantine slowness, which he no doubt intended for dignity. They confused Cora, at first, not a little. The man was certainly fifteen good years older than herself, and she was prepared to have his devotions take a merely fatherly form. They soon revealed, however, one that was decidedly less grave. She drew back from him, then, with that physical antipathy so many men had already roused in her, though there bristled for her a special repulsiveness in the languishing looks and amorous undertones of this particular swain. She had made short work of it toward the last; the idea of his court-paying was so unpleasant to her that she told him in flat terms to discontinue it. He closed himself, after that, in a shell of taciturnity with a kind of turtle-like snap. His behavior gave Cora a grisly feeling of dread. She seemed in rebuffing him to have offended some sort of creature that might combine the feigned torpor of the opossum with a snake's coil and strike. Majestic and melancholy, Joyce no longer gave her the least heed, though there was something in the bilious yellow of his complexion and the morose redundancy of his clean-shorn upper lip that made her dimly conscious of ambuscaded craft. He had gone back moreover, to Martha, and there could not be much doubt that Martha failed to like the new maid any more on this account. It is possible that women really do exist who are willing to pardon others of their sex for having fascinated their lovers away from them ; but to extend forgiveness for having disdained a faithless lover's attentions—that is quite beyond the best resources of feminine benignity.

In the privacy of her own treasured little room Cora found time to think over this double hate that had sprung up against her—for such she drearily felt that it must be called. The sense of savage persecution from destiny deepened in her mind as she added Joyce's name to a list already large. Why could she not escape from the fatality of making men her devotees against their wills and against her own? Was this what women were so fond of possessing?—this power to enslave and captivate where they could not bestow a single real emotion in return? How strange that they should care for such a barren sort of gain! She would be glad enough to go through the rest of her life without winning more than the most casual heed from any except a single man on earth. That man was Casper Drummond, and he!—why he had no doubt long ago forgotten her existence! It was pleasure and yet fear to think that he and Mr. Conover were friends. How would he act if by some chance

they were brought face to face in this very house?. . .
How would *she* act, for that matter? Her cheeks began
to burn and her pulses to flutter as she shaped from the
yielding element of fancy a vision of their possible
encounter.

Three or four days later she happened to be seated in
her mistress's dressing-room, mending some awkward
rents in a large lace flounce which Mrs. Conover had
worn at the Charity Ball on the previous night. The
lace was very expensive, and Cora had mistrusted her own
deftness in repairing it. Still, Mrs. Conover had said
that she could do so, and this confidence in her capacity
had spurred both energy and ambition. She sat near
one of the bright-lit windows, with her head bent sedu-
lously over the gossamer fabric and a needle of extreme
delicacy, filled with the finest thread, slowly moving
between her rather dubious fingers, when all at once
she became aware of a neighboring footstep.

She looked up, startled, alarmed. "Oh, Mr. Conover!" she said, and rose, putting aside her work.

"I guess I kind of scared you, didn't I?" said Conover, as he sauntered toward her with his hands in his
pockets. "Mrs. Conover hasn't got home yet?"

"No, sir."

He turned a little away from Cora and stared at an
engraving which hung on the wall near by. Mrs. Conover had bought it for reasons of a tenderly suggestive
sort ; it represented a farewell between two lovers, the
attitude of the male figure being Romeo-like in its expression of fondness.

"*How* she does go gadding about in the afternoons!"
he said, as if he were addressing the picture and not Cora.
"M—m—did she say *where* she was going?"

"Yes, sir. It was to a reception, I think. A—a—tea-
drinkin', I believe she said, sir."

He threw back his head and laughed heartily. "A
tea-*drinking*! How funny! You haven't got over your

country phrases yet, have you ? You must have picked up that one in Peekskill. You see, I know you came from somewhere near Peekskill before you landed here in this big, wicked town. It is a wicked town, eh? don't you think it is? Eh? Don't you, now?"

"I—I suppose it is, sir," answered Cora.

He had drawn so close to her by this time that an anxious doubt beset her as to his coming closer still.

"You *suppose* it is, eh? Don't you *know* ?"

"Well, yes, sir; perhaps I do."

"Aha, I thought you'd have to own up that it was a pretty bad sort of a town. But it's never been able to lead *you* into any mischief, has it?"

"No, sir." She had been avoiding his eyes, but she now let them shine full and dark into her own. "And it never will, sir, either, if I can help it."

She stooped down and lifted the filmy garment that had fallen at her side. She wanted to re-seat herself and begin work upon it once more, but she feared to do so while he stood thus near ; it might seem as if by such an act she were hinting that he should remain where he had already paused, and above all things this was what she just then least desired. He reached out one hand and began fingering the white fleecy fabric with an assumption of carelessness. His hand once or twice almost touched hers, though she did her best to keep it from doing so without the plain disclosure of effort.

"That's the dress she wore last night to the Charity," he said, the indefiniteness of his pronoun seeming to intensify an air of harmless familiarity which he chose rather subtly to cultivate. "It was a real fine ball, too. Were you ever at a ball, Cora ? "

"Yes, sir ; once or twice."

"Once or twice? Is that all? I suppose your sweetheart took you there, didn't he ? "

"I haven't got any, Mr. Conover."

"Oh, come, now—that won't do a bit, Cora. As fine

a looking girl as you are not having any sweetheart!
Who's going to believe such a thing as *that?*"

"I can't help who believes it, sir; it's true."

"True! Why, then, what's the reason of it? I dare
say there's many a chap dead gone about you that you
don't care a button for. It can't be you're fond of anyone that doesn't care for *you*. No, indeed! I'd like to
see the fellow that wouldn't jump at the chance of stealing a kiss from those jolly little lips. . . ."

"Oh, no, no, no!" now shot from those lips.

There was not any jollity, either, in their swift appeal;
there was only terror, and the plaintiveness born of it.
The arm that had curved its way round her waist and the
assaulting kiss that was rather snatched from her mouth
than taken from it were to Cora like hateful confirmations
of ominous former fears. She had been dreading it from
this man, and it had come! She had suspected him as
the merest masquerader and trickster before his credulous
wife, and her suspicions were verified. In those few
seconds of time despair seemed breaking the ground
from beneath her feet. She had won a happy hold of
refuge outside the inexorable storm of need and struggle,
only to find this curse waiting for her here, as it had
waited in the squalid home of Owen Slattery. For how
could she remain in this house any longer? How could
she dare look Mrs. Conover in the face again? She felt
already as if her mistress were accusing, arraigning her.
She had twisted herself from the man's embrace, and now
stood staring at him with eyes that were like liquid flame.
But not a trace of anger was in the words that she soon
spoke. Each sentence fell from her, indeed, sadly as
though it had been a heavy tear.

"I'm so sorry for this! God knows it isn't my fault!
Your wife might blame me—*will* blame me, if she ever
finds it out!"

"Finds what out?" he returned, with a sidelong jerk
of his head and the flash of a vicious mirth under his

dead-black moustache. "Who the devil's going to tell her? *I* won't, certainly, and I can't think *you* would. No, Cora; you're not half such a little goose as you're trying to act like. Not you, indeed! You must have been admired before now. By Jove, a fellow can't help admiring you . . . Look here, now; let's have just a short, serious talk together."

She had got a few yards away from him, but as he attempted to shorten by several quick steps the space between them, she made a gesture that was a mixed entreaty and command.

"No; stay where you are, sir! This is your house—you've a right to go where you please in it—I'm only a servant and can't ask you to leave me here in your wife's room. But it *is* your wife's room, and I was at work on something she'd given me to do, when you . . . "

"When I made a fool of myself," he broke in, with a ring in his tones at once conciliatory and repentant. "Yes, you're right—you're all right—I give in you are. You've made me feel awfully ashamed of myself. I hadn't any business to go over there to the window and bother you, poor little thing, in that devilish rude way. But *please* forgive me this once? Won't you, Cora, like the good girl you are?"

"Forgive you?" she said, looking at him with a sudden wistful surprise. "Oh, do you mean, then—?"

"I mean that I ought to have kept myself under better control!" He slipped nearer to her while he thus spoke, and his next words were hurried out with an impetus and seeming frankness that were like those of a penitent boy. "You looked so lovely as you stood over yonder (you are the very loveliest girl I've seen in ages, with those brown eyes of yours, and that curly reddish hair, and that sweet pink-and-white complexion!) that I—well, Cora, I'm only a man, you know, although I *am* a rather weak and shabby specimen of one—that I . . I lost my head. Yes, there's just the truth of the matter—I lost my head. You'll despise me, now, after this. You'll think a lot of hard things about me. But you'll be wrong if you do. Yes, ever so wrong, Cora, for I'm your friend, right down to the ground. Just give me one more trial, now, and see if I ain't!"

He was at her side again. His gentleness and humility had disarmed her. She had never known but one other man in the same sphere of life as himself, and that one had been Casper Drummond, met transiently, though still kept so fresh an image by the photography of recollection. She compared, instinctively, the demeanors and attitudes of the two men, and perhaps, in a certain way, Conover profited and gained a point, as it were, by the comparison.

"If—if you're my friend, then," she faltered, "let me beg that you will always behave as one. The way to do that, Mr. Conover, will be to treat me as the servant that I am. There's no other way—none other at all!"

He laughed a little sadly and gave his moustache a quick, embarrassed sort of pull. "True enough," he said. "You're right again. But I *can't* help thinking it's a shame you *should* be a servant. It's no place for such a beautiful little creature as you are. Why, bless my soul, child, there are thousands of ladies that would get down on their knees to you with envy if they should see you in a real fine frock—the kind you were born to wear— the kind nature must have meant you *should* wear."

All this was said with an art peerless in its delicate diplomacy. Resistance is but a spur to men of Conover's long-indulged greeds. They are often laggards enough in their ordinary paces along life's highway, but when it comes to the pursuit of their own peculiar pleasures they can show a neat skill of action that would tax the gifts of lauded nerves and thews. Cora fell partly into the little shining snare of his flattery, and looked at him with a grave though mollified shake of the head as she answered :

"I never could be a lady; I ain't educated, and I

haven't got ladies' manners. If I'm good lookin', that don't make any difference. I've seen what comes to girls like me when they want fine clothes and soft livin'. They're fools, and pretty soon they find it out."

"*You'd* never find it out, Cora. Now, see here. Let's put it like this. We'll suppose you didn't care to stay here and said some day you thought you'd go—and went. Well, instead of going into another place you take a first floor in some respectable side-street (see?) and put in big gold letters along the balcony, *Madame Cora, Modes.* You're smart with your needle, and you've learned dress-making, and—"

"Ah, Mr. Conover," she broke in, "I—I'm not smart enough for that! *Indeed,* I ain't! And, besides, it costs a lot of money to set up the kind of 'stablishment you mean."

"Oh, it doesn't cost so very much," he said softly. He had got quite close to her once again, and with the merest movement of his own hand he could touch hers. "It costs a few twenty-dollar bills,—like this,—but not such a very big lot of 'em. Yes, yes, Cora, take—*take* it! Don't be silly, now. I hurt your feelings a little while ago. We'll call this a peace-offering. What! you won't, Cora!"

She had receded from him, while his hand, with the money in it, still remained oustretched. She had folded her arms, and he saw the firmness of her refusal before she made it audible.

"I will not take a copper from you," she said. "I can't, and I won't!"

"But look here, now, Cora," he persisted, with the same persuasive tenderness which had all at once become as obnoxious to her as his former bluff joviality. "There's no use treating me as if I didn't mean fair and kind by you. There's no use—"

"Fair and kind!" she exclaimed, with a forlorn vacillant movement of her head and a sudden outspreading of her arms that implied the pathos of desperate supplication. "Oh, Mr. Conover, go away from me—go, please do!" She darted toward the window at which he had first found her seated. She took up her dropped work again, though she groped for it with tear-blurred eyes. Her hands trembled piteously as she strove to re-apply the tiny needle to the almost ethereal meshes of the lace. But her voice was no less tremulous than her fingers, as she now hurried on : "Oh, go, *do* go! Mrs. Conover may be home any minute. She'll think it queer if I ain't through with these mendins. I—I don't want anything, sir, but to be left in peace. I'll take my wages, and that's every cent I *will* take. I'm *her* servant, and yours, too, if you'll treat me as one." Here the girl raised her bent head and momentarily let the ball-dress lie limp again in her lap. The tears were now streaming from her eyes, and her breath was coming in a series of short gasps. "Don't be afraid I will speak of—of this to —to your wife. I'll—I'll never mention a word of it! I —I promise you, I won't!"

Conover had already felt one or two anxious qualms of fear lest his wife should burst inopportunely upon the present conference. But Cora's last appeal had for him, nevertheless, the nature of humiliating rebuff. It showed him what he estimated as a cold-bloodedness of rectitude and reproval far more unpleasant than if she had offered him an ireful blow in the face. Her disarray, her entreaty, her valiant little stand against surrender, had all affected him as new details of picturesque piquancy. But the calculation in her final flurried sentences fell on him like an abrupt bath of chilly water. He flushed, frowned, gave a smothered cry of impatience, and walked to the door by which he had entered.

"You can say what you please to my wife," he retorted, curtly and defiantly, with his hand on the door-knob. "She wouldn't believe you, no matter what you said!"

The next instant a stifled oath left him. Cora
rather surmised than heard it. The sound of all vilest
oaths that human lips can swear had become so familiar
to her of old ! As he quitted the room she burst into
uncontrollable tears. A dense cloud of gloom seemed to
have closed over her, with the hate of her mistress's husband piercing it like a scintillant sword. For of course
he would hate her now ! She had done nothing to
deserve his persecution, and yet it had come in this insidious and serpentine form ! A passionate surge of exe-
cration swept through her brain while she sat there,
shaken by sobs. 'Oh, how I despise men !' she said to
herself. 'They're always wantin' to drag me down.
Every one of 'em I meet has somehow got his hand
against me. I wish I was either dead or else that there
wasn't a man in the whole world ! I do ! I do !'

But an afterthought crept across the tumult of her distress. It was a remembrance of Casper Drummond.

Still, it brought no comfort, for she recalled her recent
knowledge of the Florida letter. This wrapped her in a
still darker despondency. It only clad her future with
new peril and made her more hopeless of security and
rest within the household whither, not long ago, a very
miracle of luck seemed to have drifted her !

10

XIII.

ABSORBED in her woes, Cora had lost all recollection of her mistress's return. But it was reasserted in an almost brutal way by the sudden appearance of Mrs. Conover.

"Well, Cora, here you are," came the odd, identifying shriek of her mistress. "How did you get on with that torn flounce?. . Oh, what a bore this afternoon's been!" She was twirling her heavy silken skirts about the room, addressing herself one moment in the mirror and the next tossing off a velvet fur-trimmed mantle into the shadowy cavern of an arm-chair. "Deliver *me* from literary receptions! If ever you meet the rag-tag and bobtail crowd anywhere, it's just there! Pooh! talk about the snobbery of the ' Four Hundred!' I'd four-hundred times rather hear what *they've* got to say than the gush of Mrs. Ellen MacIntosh Briggs, with a hat on that looks as if it came from Division Street, or the simpering twaddle of Mr. Leander J. Billings, who raves over the downfall of art in the nineteenth century with filthy gloves and a false diamond for a shirt-stud! Oh, *what* a rabble! Newport next summer? Well, if I'm alive we'll have a cottage there and just try *what* we can do!. . . Oh, Cora, I forgot you. Do come here and get this confounded shoe off. It's been pinching me till I'm half mad. I'll *never* go to that man, Delongchamps, for another boot, as long as I live. He's all price and politeness, and no fit worth a cent. . Ugh! That's right. Pull it off, Cora—pull hard! There! now I breathe again. . . Mr. Conover's got home? Yes? It's almost dinner-time, I suppose. Well, you can help me off with this dress, and then get me my heavy white wool wrapper; that will do to dine in. I shan't see a soul but Mr. Conover, and I'm going to bed early because the Charity last night

and this deadly thing I've been to this afternoon have
fagged me out so. . . Why, Cora, you've been crying!
You're crying still! and you're trembling! What *is* it?
What's happened, girl? *Tell* me!"

'*He* won't tell *her*,' sped at this moment through Cora's
confused mind. 'He'll keep it all a secret, and there's a
chance for me to stay here yet if I only don't lose my
wits.'

Ah, the traditional craft of womankind! If cynics do
not err and women have ampler store of it than men,
Cora's now served her in excellent stead.

"I—I *have* been crying, Mrs. Conover," she stammered.
"I—I ain't yet through that torn flounce you left me
to do. I'm very sorry ma'am, but it was because—
well, ma'am, because I got—thinkin'."

"Thinking, Cora? Why, what do you mean? How
could thinking make you cry? Aren't you happy here?
You told me yesterday that you hoped you could stay
along with me for years and years."

"Yes—I did, Mrs. Conover. And I meant it, too,
ma'am; I meant it from the bottom of my heart. But—
but there are times when I feel very wicked."

"Wicked? Why, what do you mean?"

"It's this, ma'am: I get cryin' when I'm alone by
myself, 'cause I feel there's people not far away from me
at this very minute that would be willin' to swear I
wasn't honest." And then she told about the work which
she had taken from the Worth Street factory and never
brought back to it, about the unreturned sewing-machine,
and about the shawl that belonged to Mrs. Slattery. She
was so unstrung by what had just passed that her sobs
and tears would not cease. But the narration upon
which she had launched gave them an excuse for being.

Mrs. Conover was completely deceived; it never occurred to her that behind this perturbed mood lay any
cause or incentive which was not plainly revealed by
Cora's half-choked words.

"Why, what perfect humbug!" she at length cried, with her voice pitched a little higher than usual, as if in consolatory tribute to the unhappiness of her maid's recital. "You're not a bit to blame, and it only shows me what a thoroughly good girl you are when I hear how such comparative trifles have affected you. Why, Cora, you—you carry honesty in your face. Yes, you do. . . . Just get me my fur-lined slippers—the dark-red kid ones, not the velvet ones. . . . Only yesterday Mr. Conover spoke about your face to me. Yes, he did. Now stop crying. Stop, I say! This will brighten you up. But I won't tell it to you till you've brought the slippers. There, you conscientious little lunatic, go along!"

When Cora returned with the slippers her eyes were dry and she looked much more composed. But while she knelt at her mistress's feet and slipped on the easy encasements demanded for them, no question came from her with respect to the comments which had been passed upon herself by Mr. Conover.

His wife, however, disregarded this lack of interest. She continued where she had left off. "Oh, yes, Cora," she said, "my husband told me that he had hardly ever seen a face which expressed more real honesty than yours. Upon my word, Cora, he's *delighted* with you! And that means a great deal to me, because I put strong faith in his likes and dislikes. He's *so* keen about such matters! He never liked Josephine, my last maid, and always warned me I'd have trouble with her. . . . Well, now, you've got over your nonsensical crying, so I'll talk to you about that other matter. Don't you care a pin for those percale shirts delivered you by the Worth Street people; they're the merest trifle; it's ridiculous to *think* of them! I'd drive down some day and explain it all if there were the least use, but there isn't. Just let the whole thing pass out of your mind. And then the sewing-machine! Pooh! Stuff and nonsense! Don't give it another thought ; your deposit and your payments afterward more than cover the price of it. And that shawl ! I dare say Mrs. Flattery, Pattery—what's her name ?—ground fifty times the worth of it out of you long before you went away with it ! "

"I am glad you think so light, ma'am, of what I've told you," said Cora. Her tones were quite collected. She had made good use of her little feint. It had served her as masque and domino for the distress in which she had been caught. And she was not sorry for her confession ; she had designed to vent it sooner or later. After all, it had only come earlier than apparent fate had prophesied . . . .

The next day was Sunday, and all the afternoon was given her to do as she would with it. She went down to see Em. The fetid purlieus almost roused nausea in her now. She had ten dollars to give Em. Her wages were not so liberal but that she would have needed them for clothes, had not Mrs. Conover supplied her with both dresses and undergarments in handsome quantity. These her mistress had bestowed on her, half from a random generosity and half because tired of them, paying for all requisite curtailments on account of their different sizes. Cora felt very glad of her power to donate those ten dollars. Nearly three weeks had passed since her former visit to Em's quarters. The day outside was so fair and bright that as she looked at the blue sky above the murky buildings, an odd sense of its extreme cleanliness came to her. She mounted the dull, ill-odored stairs and reached Em's door. She knocked. There was no answer, and she knocked again. Still no answer. She tried the knob of the door, and at once perceived that it had not been locked. As she pushed it open a little cry of dismay fell from her.

The room was one blank vacancy. You saw nothing except its bare floor and its four staring walls. Cora hurried into the next room, where the children had slept. This was denuded in just the same way. Cora now remembered that she had seen during her ascent several open doorways which had shown her, beyond their thresholds, rooms of a similar emptiness. A sudden misgiving overcame her. She hastened into the hall and knocked at one of the other doors . . . A little later she had discovered that the entire house was deserted precisely as were Em's two apartments.

Out in the street, however, only a few yards away, sat a little old Italian woman with a leathern face and an arching back, before a stand that held dusty pink and white cocoanut cakes and other sweets, equally soiled, in tawny sticks or ruby blocks. Her English was less precarious than that spoken by most of her race, for she had been oversea a good while and had sat on that special corner a good while too. Cora soon found that she knew all about the empty house and why several others in its neighborhood were also abandoned by their inmates. Moreover she could give tidings about the Cratchett family, and to these her auditor listened with breathless interest.

"Ze smallpok took zem ze first. Kadie, she catch it and die before ze Healtz-Boart find out. When zey come leetle Steefie was dyin'. Zen, when zey want to take her away ze ole laty she go crazy. She screech so you could hear her all over ze street. But zey take her. Zere was no money to bury Steefie, so zey bury him in Potah Fielt. Em and Maggie zey was very sick when zey was took away. I donno if zey be deat now or not. I guess so. I hear a good many dite zat was took away. Zere's been bad times 'ere—awful times. Ain't you seen in ze noosepapes?"

"I—I haven't read the newspapers," replied Cora.

The old woman laughed, showing two yellow tusks, with a gap of shrivelled gum between them. "Ze street is so lonesome," she said, bobbing her head to right and left, "it kill my bizness. Nobody come here if zey can help come. You're too pretty a young laty to come. Zere is daingaire yet—daingaire—oh yes ! "

"Danger yet?" faltered Cora. She cast her eyes up and down the street. There was scarcely a soul in sight. The fact of its being Sunday had prevented her from re-marking the solitude just mentioned. "Oh, poor, poor Em !" she burst forth.

The dark, faded eyes of the old woman were fixed up-on her face. She looked like some sort of prophetic imp as she lifted a brown, grizzled forefinger and shook it at Cora. "You got pretty skin—verra pretty, you ! Take care. Zere's daingaire—daingaire ! "

"And you can't tell me anything more about poor Em?" Cora questioned. "Do you think she's dead— really dead? "

"I guess so. Zey took 'em all to a place—I donno ze name—it's on ze watair. . . A place vair zey die wizou anybody ever to hear about it," continued the old woman, her voice now changed as though she had suddenly fallen upon a self-communing mood. "Ah, yes ! a place vair I sink death must be vaintin to messur zem for zair graves like tailors messur peoples for zair close."

Cora could scarcely hear these low-spoken words, yet she half divined them. Fear of contagion made her soon quit the quarter, and yet this was not the sole motive that spurred her departure. She felt conscience-stricken at the thought of what Mrs. Conover might say if aware that she had entered a part of the town infested by small-pox. Speedy flight therefrom was surely a duty which she owed her mistress, outside of the least self-preserv-ing impulse.

And yet, poor Em ! Those few vague sentences of the old Italian candy-vendor were like the feeble rays of a lantern shot into a noisome den of darkness and anguish. She saw the whole bitter tragedy in hues of despair and terror as she took her way up-town. The mad shrieks of Mrs. Cratchett rang again and again in her ears. Em, dizzy and weak with the approaching illness that had probably proved her death, bent over little Stevie's dying form. And then the torture of poverty that made charity bring its pine box for the unburied dead! Ah, those ten dollars of hers! Why had they come so late? What must Em's agony have been as they dragged her away from her screaming mother? Oh, the ghastliness of it all? And such things happened under this bright, cruel, indifferent sun! And people went to church and prayed to God, and gave him thanks, and lauded his infinite goodness! Em was only one among racked and persecuted thousands. How she had struggled on, and yet all her pluck and grit and bravery had only come to this! What a lesson, what an example! Suppose she *had* gone wrong when the glow was in her eyes and the roses were on her cheeks. It might have been a shorter life; but could it possibly have been a more miserable one?

She made no reference whatever, before her mistress, to the crucial experience through which she had passed. Indeed, she felt secret alarm lest Mrs. Conover might allude in some questioning way to the "friends" whom she had previously spoken of going to visit. But no such issue had to be met. Another, far more vital and pregnant, awaited her.

For a week Robert Conover did not deign even to glance at her when circumstance brought them together. He had all the vanity of the successful libertine, and her marble negative had dealt it a severe bruise. That she might tell his wife what had occurred, by no means took the form of an anxiety with him. He felt perfectly confident that he could cripple in a trice any charge that she might bring against him. One glance from his beloved black eyes and one exclamation such as "Honoria, you *don't* believe this lie, do you?" would almost settle the entire business at once. Still, such a tax upon wifely credulity could not safely be levied more than two or three times, and he began to feel that it was just as well Cora had kept silence.

There was something that smelt of miracle in the way this man contrived to keep his actual character hidden from wifely eyes. His dissipations, it is true, were concealed with care, and he would have blamed himself as the most arrant of dolts if by any chance a stray scrap of compromising note-paper had fallen into Honoria's hands. He had never before behaved so imprudently as in the case of his recent interview with Cora. Of course his wife might have popped into her room at any moment, apart from the whole question of his having chosen his own fireside as the theatre of a possible little sentimental comedy. But, as it was, fortune had not proved so kind to him, after all, in the matter of complete non-discovery. Martha, the chambermaid, had a right to slip nearly everywhere, and she was the sort of woman who could put into excellent accord for eavesdropping purposes her keen ear and cat-like step. There was a little passage-way leading from Mrs. Conover's dressing-room to her bedroom. Martha had happened to enter the latter, and a sound of muffled voices had floated to her. That was enough to set her nerves greedily tingling with curiosity, and no snake in its insidious ventures among the grasses of the field ever moved more noiselessly than could she. It was not far to the keyhole she just then desired to command. What she heard proved, as we know, a matter of great discredit to her employer and of its honorable opposite to his companion. But later she held an important confab with her repentant Joyce, in which they both agreed that close future vigilance of Cora might produce more inculpating results.

One afternoon, not many days later, Conover sought his wife's presence with the statement that their friend, Casper Drummond, had returned from Florida and would dine with them that evening. "Rudie Champny may come, too," Conover added, " though he isn't just sure if he can. But you'd better set a plate for him."

"The disreputable fellows !" exclaimed Honoria, as she rang the bell for Joyce, to bid him prepare two extra places. "What do they say about their goings-on at St. Augustine, Rob?" she continued. "Are they the least bit ashamed?"

"Oh, it all blew over, I believe," said her husband. "I forgot to ask them about it."

"Blew over! There was a column of scandal in the *Town Tattler.*"

" Nobody minds what those libellous little sheets print."

"*Don't* they! Well, I should die of mortification if it attacked *you* in that way. But of course it *couldn't.*"

" I hope you're going to be civil, Hon."

"Civil? oh, of course. You know I'm very fond of Casper. And I like Rudie too. He talks entirely too much, but he's a jolly little soul. I disapprove of them *both*, Rob ; they're so horribly fast. I often wonder why they are fond of you. They and you *can't* be very congenial."

"No, we're not. But I've known them such an age. I suppose it's that."

" How tiresome of Rudie not to be sure whether he could come or no! I hope we won't have an empty chair at the dinner-table. That's always such a kill-joy."

But Rudie came with his friend, Casper Drummond. The pair were both in good spirits and looked healthfully bronzed by their Floridan fishing and shooting. Mrs. Conover gaily told them, as the party sat down to dine, that she did not believe there would be much dinner to speak of, as they had given her so short a notice. But, as it turned out, the dinner was both copious and excellent. There had been two good hours for the preparation of it, and the Conovers' cook knew how to unite skill with expedition. The champagne was like liquid ice, and of a "dry" quality beloved by just such men as the three now assembled. Joyce waited solemnly and faultlessly, but even he had to turn away once or twice for the purpose of hiding a smile at the crisp and buoyant stories of their adventures and escapades told in comic, glaring candor by the two guests. Mrs. Conover sipped her champagne freely, and laughed with a boisterous jollity that seemed to set the pointed flames of the candelabra wavering. Just after the roast was served she proposed that they should send over to the Windsor Hotel and try and get four seats for Daly's.

"I'm crazy to see that new play," she declared, "and Rob hasn't taken me yet. They say Ada Rehan's glorious in it, and Lewis, Drew, Mrs. Gilbert are all simply tremendous. Now, don't look bored, Casper. You're not going to dart off after dinner. We've got you, and we intend to keep you for the whole evening."

"I never dart off after dinner," said Casper, with a twinkle in his pleasant blue eyes. "It's death to digestion."

"Rob seems to have done a good deal of it lately," said Rudie Champny, in his crackling way. "Otherwise what's the meaning of your not yet having seen the new play at Daly's?" He lifted his finger and shook it at his host. "Rob, Rob, we fellows from Florida have to come back and teach you proper manners to your wife!"

Mrs. Conover instantly grew grave.

"Rob's manners to me are always *perfect*," she declared. "It's been my fault. He'd have given up the club if I'd really made it a serious point."

The two friends exchanged a quick glance across the table. They had long ago heard that "club story," and they knew the peculiar ethics of Conover's career in all its audacious developments.

The seats for Daly's were procured, and the gentlemen were permitted only a very few puffs apiece at cigar or cigarette. Mrs. Conover, while upstairs, being assisted

by Cora in putting on her bonnet and mantle, suddenly
exclaimed :

"Oh, Cora, do go into the back room, just behind Mr.
Conover's, and see if the towels and soap and everything
are all right there. Those gentlemen who've been dining with us are going there at once to wash their hands
and brush up a bit before starting for the theatre. Oliver
ought to meet them, by-the-by, as they come upstairs.
Find him and tell him to be ready."

Oliver, a pale young man of patrician appearance but
excellent capacity as a servant, was the valet of Conover.
But his master had just sent him out with a briefly-
scribbled note, which doubtless concerned that part of
the gentleman's life shrouded from vulgar gaze, for a
great confidential understanding existed between Conover
and his man, who was discreet to a striking degree.

Cora went into the room designated by her mistress,
and had just emerged from its lavatory when she came
face to face with Casper and Rudolph, who were entering
from the outer hall. She had no idea, as she lifted her
eyes to their faces, that any recognition would result.
Mrs. Conover, usually loquacious enough, had not told
her who the two dinner-guests were to be.

She crimsoned as she saw Casper Drummond, and then
recoiled. In all her life she had never been so forlornly
abashed.

"By Jove, it's you!" he said. "What—why, what
in God's name are you doing here?"

He had never forgotten her. Indeed, during their
southern trip he had spoken of her again and again to
Rudie, wondering as to her fate and regretting that he
should have been the means, howsoever indirect, of
working her harm.

Of the three, Rudie showed by far the most presence of
mind. "Not so loud, Casper," he said, and glanced
toward the open doorway as he spoke. It seemed to him
as if he saw a bit of dark stuff, that might have been part

of the skirt of a gown, flit out of sight; but in another
instant it struck him that this effect might only have
sprung from a trick wrought with his eyes by the speed
of his own movement. Turning quickly to Cora, he said,
in a voice full of hurry and yet hardly above a whisper :

"You're living here as maid, now ; isn't that about the
size of it ? "

"Yes, sir," said Cora.

Just then Drummond caught her hand. "Bless me,
Cora, how pretty that cap makes you ! Still, I don't
like it."

"Be careful, Casp," reproved his friend. "Somebody
will hear you. Rob may be upstairs after us any minute."

Casper's fingers tightened about Cora's hand. He had
on his evening dress, and it seemed to her that he looked
handsome as a god in it. His eyes were like dizzying
splendors to her; his smile seemed a whole history of
passion in itself. For sheer joy at seeing him again she
could have thrown her arms about his neck. As it was,
she only stood and trembled before him, trying to draw
away the hand that he retained.

"Where did you fly to that night ? " he pursued. "We
hunted all over for you. I wasn't content with that,
either; I hunted for you the next day. That beast of an
Owen Slattery had been dragged off to jail after my friend
here gave him his handsome polishing. I found out his
address and went to search for you there—at his mother's, you know. She pelted you with abuse, but I didn't
believe a word she said ; I saw that the arrest of her son
had made her half crazy. . . After awhile I gave up
looking for you. But I've never ceased to remember
you. Ask *him*" (with a wave of one hand toward Rudolph) "if that's not true. . . And now to find you
here—here, of all places ! It's *too* queer ! it's——"

"Casper ! " broke in his friend.

Immediately afterward Mrs. Conover's voice was heard

calling from the outer hall that they had just five minutes in which to drive to the theatre before the performance began.

"And do please make haste," she added, with all her native shrillness, "for I don't want to miss any more of this piece than we can possibly help."

While she thus spoke, her husband was heard coming upstairs to join his two guests. Cora had slipped from the room at the sound of her mistress's voice, tearing her hand from Casper's, and hastening toward a door that led into a sort of library beyond.

"I should think you'd lost your senses," muttered Rudolph tartly to his friend.

"Why?" queried Casper, in a flurried way, his eyes following the course that Cora had taken.

"Why!" Rudolph echoed. "Pshaw, man, because the chances are that Conover himself has got the girl this place, and your loud talk might have made things devilish awkward!"

Casper stared at his friend. "Conover's got her the place?" he said, as if he were repeating some rank absurdity. "No, no! I don't believe a word of it! Good heavens, I'll *ask* him! Yes, Rudie, I *will!*"

He took one or two steps toward the door that led into the hall.

"In the name of common-sense don't make such a fool of yourself!" said Rudolph.

The next moment Conover came jauntily and unsuspiciously into the room.

XIV.

CASPER did not ask the question. But he passed a most uncomfortable evening. The clear sparkle of Ada Rehan, the terse force of Drew, the dry jocoseness of Lewis, the sapient fun of Mrs. Gilbert, all failed either to lure or distract him. His entire evening had been spoiled, and after the play was over and they had left the theatre he pleaded a headache as his excuse for not going to sup at Delmonico's.

He felt that he had almost offended his hosts, and yet he got away from them at last, and walked up Fifth Avenue in a dismal and irate mood. The headache had, of course, been a myth ; he was far too healthy to have one. Rudie's words were like a thong that lashed him. *Could* Conover, with all his evil, have achieved that special piece of badness ? He was loth to think so, deeply as he distrusted the husband of Honoria. After all, it was not *like* Rob Conover. He behaved with too much caution for that. He was too balefully wise in his generation. No, Rudie must have been wrong.

Then he laughed at himself, as a man of his wealth and comparative status in the world might well do, because of the spell this girl had woven over him. The idea of his meeting any woman at a low Bowery ball and being concerned so about her weeks, months afterward ! It was too nonsensical. And yet the web had somehow been spun for him. Though its toils were of silk they had the strength of iron. Her face had haunted him in Florida. It had beamed on him to-night with a new intoxicating beauty. He felt that he would risk much to see it again. In his own room, at his father's handsome brown-stone mansion in Fifty-Seventh Street, he soon wrote her a note, begging that she would agree to meet him wherever and whenever she might be merciful

enough to decide.   He directed his missive, in a disguised
hand, to Miss Cora Strang, and posted it the next morning.   Then, in a fever of impatience for several days afterward, he awaited results.

None came.   Cora received what he had written and
read it with guilty amazement, with melancholy joy.
But she did not answer it.   Not to do so cost her keen
pangs, but she still kept loyal to her own stanch creeds.
Of what use would it be to encourage a love like this?
He was above her; he might mean her well, but even
allowing that he did, how could his doing so bring happiness to either of them?   As his wife, she would remain
below him.   She had no education to speak of; she was
not a lady in any accepted sense; he would be ashamed
of her though he kept on loving her.

She had gained a terrible shrewdness of wisdom, and
she listened to its monitory voice.   There was no use ot
compromise.   The law of her future conduct must be
written out and obeyed, though the ink that she took to
write it in were drained red and wet from her bleeding
heart.

Besides, liking to think him high-minded and honest,
as all chaste women like to think the men whom they
love, she could not help feeling herself assaulted by a
great and bitter doubt regarding the purity of his real
motives.   There was fine heroism of renunciation in her
silence, but there was also the worldliness of a spirit that
had confronted human turpitude at its nakedest and basest.

"Don't you feel well, Cora?" asked her mistress, one
afternoon.   "It seems to me that you're paler than you
ought to be and that somehow your spirits are low."

"I guess I'm pretty well, ma'am," she answered.
And then, more as a feint of inward embarrassment
than from any better cause, she went on: "It's very
kind of you, I'm sure, ma'am, to think about *how* I happen to be feelin'."

"Kind?" said Mrs. Conover.   "Not a bit, Cora.   I'm

afraid it's selfish ; for you've got to be so sure and quick
with all your work that I should miss you more than
words can tell if your health really gave way. You do
my hair ever so nicely nowadays ; nobody can do it bet-
er. And, by-the-by, you must make me look as fine as
a fiddle for this afternoon at the Estabrookes. I'm to be
one of the ladies that receive with Mrs. Estabrooke.
She's a person that gives herself more *airs !* She was
a factory-girl, they say, before she married her husband,
and later on he squeezed a big fortune out of patent
pickles. Now she's got a house over on Fifth Avenue
and has made a kind of dash at society. Of course
society padlocks its doors. But she's so conceited she
doesn't know it does. She thinks it's let her in as friendly
as you please. She'll have Mrs. Schmitt, the jeweller's
wife, receiving with her in pink satin, and Mrs. Millbank,
the confectioner's wife, in blue silk, and Mrs. Wendelkin,
the eating-house keeper's wife, in—in yellow brocade,
for all *I* know." Here Mrs. Conover gave one of her
most enterprising peals of laughter. "And she acts
just as if they were all the first ladies in the land. It's
so funny. Mr. Conover and I just *roar* over her."

Cora had scarcely caught the last few sentences. "I
never heard of a factory-girl gettin' so high up in the
world as that," she said. "I guess it don't happen often,
ma'am, does it ? "

There were depths of meaning and of delicate wistful-
ness in those final words that wholly escaped Cora's
listener.

"Well, it *is* a little unusual," she replied. "But Mrs.
Estabrooke's husband made his lucky strike after they
were married, you know." She gave a gay turn of her
head toward Cora and scanned the girl's face intently for
a moment, with its winsome traits of coloring and con-
tour. "There's a chance for you," she went on, "if
you'll only be wise in selecting the right sort of a man—
somebody with plenty of push and go in him to work

his own way. With so many girls in your station the great trouble is that they marry foolishly. They leap into marriage as if they were taking an afternoon plunge at Coney Island. They should show more common-sense about that one matter of finding a good husband than about almost any other that affects their lives—and they usually show less !"

"They love too much with their hearts, ma'am, and not enough with their heads, I suppose."

"That's just it."

"And you think," asked Cora, "that they shouldn't let their hearts have much to say, ma'am?"

"Oh, I believe in love, Cora. *I* married for love. But do you imagine that I'd have let it control me unless I'd felt certain Mr. Conover would make me the model husband he *has* made? No, indeed!"

Cora had no answer to this line of reasoning. It seemed to stab her as with a blade of ice. That this woman should so trust the dissolute sensualist whom she had wedded had for her no element of comedy, not even a grim and satiric one. It was all merely tragical and lamentable ; it fitted those darker experiences with which her life had been thus far so replete ; it added another spray of rue to that funereal little nosegay she had gathered in her brief saunterings along the highways of time !

Conover came home earlier than usual, to accompany his wife. She heard him snarling irritably at his valet, Oliver, because the latter had procured him an unsatisfactory bunch of flowers for the lapel of his Prince Albert coat. He was evidently in a bad humor, and his wife, who also heard his harsh voice, gave a few smiling nods at her maid in the long mirror before which she was stationed.

"He detests the Estabrookes, and it's awfully good of him to come home like this and go with me. Some husbands wouldn't be half so obliging."

In the most unexpected way Cora found herself face to
face with Robert Conover a little while afterward. She
had gone into one of the drawing-rooms with the intent
of searching for a certain fan which Mrs. Conover felt
convinced that she had left there on the previous evening,
and which would harmonize with the apparel she had
recently selected. Cora found the fan without having
by any means a long hunt for it, and was about quitting
the apartment when Conover suddenly strolled through
the very doorway she had approached. He looked
smart and spruce in his modish gear. The "button-
hole" which he had made a subject of reprimand with
Oliver gleamed colorful against the dark, speckless broadcloth of its background. He was drawing on a pair of
yellowish gloves, and had drooped his head a little as if
to satisfy himself concerning the neatness of their fit.

"Oh, it's you?" he suddenly broke forth, lifting his
head and coming to an abrupt standstill. "How are
you nowadays, eh? How are you getting on?"

"Very well, sir," said Cora, wanting to glide past him,
but not doing so.

"You never look at me—you never seem to know if
I'm even about when we happen to meet one another.
Haven't you got over your mad fit yet? Do you still
think I'm the worst man in town?"

"Oh, no, sir."

He raised one kid-encased forefinger and shook it at
her with something between a smile and a frown.

"There are worse men than I am, and don't you forget it! I—confound it, I wanted to be a good friend of
yours, but you wouldn't let me." A new mood now
came on him like a flash. He put with great quickness a
hand on each of her shoulders, and peered into her face,
stooping forward. "Look here, girl. Let's make it all
up. Kiss me and say you forgive me. Just one. Now
don't get riled again. Give me only one, and I'll—"

She sprang back, saw a sideway for flight between two

heavy armchairs, and took it with the precipitance of eager haste. . . .

"I'm glad you found the fan, Cora," Mrs. Conover said, three minutes afterward. "But you hurried too much; you're out of breath. Has Mr. Conover gone downstairs yet?"

"Yes, ma'am; he's waitin' for you, I guess."

When her mistress had descended and left her alone, she threw herself into a big, soft chair and gave one or two shudders. This fire that she had hoped was ash had sprung up into flame again. Would her days here always be cursed with the chance of such odious encounters? If these were to be her doom, why not take prompt measures and fly from it? She could coin some tale of illness and get back into the Lodging House for a fortnight or so, saying that the change to former scenes might raise her spirits. Then she would get Mrs. Montrose to ask Mrs. Conover for a recommendation, and advertise with the money she had already saved. It would surely be a much surer and safer course. If any hint of the real truth came to that wary and hostile Martha, her mistress would be told it, and then the air would thrill with dire discords.

'Shall I stay here any longer?' she miserably mused. 'Hadn't I better go right away? Hadn't I better speak to her when she comes back from the reception? She won't think it so queer after what she said to me about not lookin' or actin" well . . . I will, I will! I'll be sorry if I don't. It's the right plan for me to hit on and stick to. I'll just brace myself up to it and get away before worse things happen.'

Her resolve looked clear to her as she sat and brooded in the fading light of the early spring afternoon. But this thought of departure brought with it a dull pain. After all, Mrs. Conover had been very kind to her. *She* had never felt the faintest breath from that temper which had in her hearing been called so hot. And to go away might mean so wretchedly to change for the worse !

Park Avenue, in its noble width of boulevard, began to be bathed in the bluish tints of dusk. Cora was near one of the windows yet not actually gazing from it. She could see the solid roofs of the houses opposite as they rose against a sky filmed with gauzy rose. From below came the mellow roll of carriage-wheels and the clatter of hoofs. People were driving home from receptions, visits, airings in the Park. Those very sounds, common-place enough, grew freighted for Cora, now, with a fresh meaning. They were the voices of prosperity, good repute and comfort, and they seemed calling to her "stay." How did she know if she would ever get another place like this ? Mrs. Conover might refuse to give her a proper recommendation, and her future quarters might be chillingly second-rate—in some household where the daughters did the bedroom work, and they all ate in the basement, and the halls were covered with oil-cloth and smelt of soap-suds on Mondays and of burnt flannel on Tuesdays. Of course, even this would be princely com-pared with what she had seen and been through else-where. But her present surroundings held so much of grace and prettiness ! They would help to ease the ache of the wound love had dealt her—for she had now faced the truth that she loved Casper Drummond greatly, and that living on without his love must always mean irreparable loss, though it might also mean such gain, stern yet sweet, frugal yet appeasing, as comes to courage and self-control.

She told herself that she had plenty of both ; and yet both quailed before the prospect of leaving this new and grateful abode. Oh, how hard fate was to her ! What if she should watch her chance and pray Robert Conover —pray him on her knees—to be pitiful and leave her in peace? Would he turn her appeal into mock and jest? Did his course, after all, spring from any real evil? Was

it not only the saucy and lazy selfishness of a man with masterful whims and abundance of money to sate them?
. . A fresh resolve began to displace the former one. She would make this last trial! Why not? If it failed, she could fall back upon her previous purpose. Perhaps to-morrow or next day she could grasp the occasion to urge her entreaty.

"I will! . . I will!" she said aloud, and rose from the chair in which she had sat for an unexpectedly long time. The room had grown quite dim. She lit one or two of the gas-jets there, and then went into three of the other rooms on the same floor, doing likewise for each. The room which was called the library contained but few books, though its purple cushioned chairs and dark walnut appointments gave it somewhat the look of a study. It adjoined Conover's apartment, and she illumined both. She stood in the library for a moment, casting her eyes here and there upon the sombre, tasteful decorations. These had always especially pleased her, and the love for objects of harmonious hues and shapes belonged as much to her temperament as did the hate of what was coarse and tawdry.

"I might have been so much happier," ran her thought, "if I'd had more of this to feast my eyes on instead of the ugliness and meanness I've seen so much of! And if I'd only been born to it all, as *she* was! Ah, what a strange, unjust world we live in! Good luck's like the lightning, I guess. It strikes just where it pleases, only in a different way! And there's such a monstrous crowd of people that it never pays the least attention to!"

Suddenly, while she stood under the chandelier, two of whose jets by the aid of a chair she had just succeeded in reaching and lighting, a quick, strong, unfamiliar step sounded in her ears. The library had two means of entrance, one from Conover's neighboring room and one from the outside hall. It was there that the step had become audible. She waited, sure that it was approaching the latter door. All at once a figure appeared on the threshold of this door.

"Mr. Drummond!" she said, turning pale.

Casper hurried toward her. "Yes," he replied, in a low voice, with his words coming very fast. "I knew they'd be out this afternoon—I knew where they were going. I've been at the same place myself for a little while, and slipped away. I told the man down below that I wanted to come up here and get a book I'd borrowed the other night and forgotten. I thought I'd find you—anyway, I took my chances. It's awfully lucky."

"Lucky?" she murmured. She had let him seize and hold her hand; she had indeed felt powerless to rebel against the rush of gladness that his mere presence evoked.

"Yes—why not? Oh, did you get my letter? *Did* you? Come, now; don't deny that you did?"

"I got it—yes," she murmured. The tears were gathering, but she choked them back.

"And you wouldn't answer it?"

She forced her hand from his clasp and caught the back of the chair by which she had lately mounted to light the chandelier.

"I—I *wanted* to answer it, but I thought it was better not to."

"Better not to? Why?"

"Oh, don't ask me. You know as well as I do."

"No, I don't. What a queer girl you are!"

"Yes—I'm queer—in one way."

"In all ways," he said, with a light yet insecure laugh.

She raised one hand and waved it toward him flurriedly. "They'll hear us talking!" she warned, with a pained, alarmed look. She had the sense that it would be right and prudent to dart away from him without the exchange of another syllable. But she could not go. A magnetic witchery breathed from him, detaining her. Till that instant she had never realized how she loved

him and what power for good or evil over her that love
gave him.

" *They'll* hear us talking ? " he asked. " Who are they ?
Do you mean the servants ? "

" Yes. There's one—Martha—she doesn't like me
and—and watches me half her time."

He threw back his head and snapped his fingers contemptuously. " Let her go to the devil ! " he said, but
with a voice whose tones betrayed caution. " I've a
perfect right to be here. I've met you by the merest
accident."

" But Martha looks at me lately in the funniest way.
I catch her doin' it. I sometimes think she's heard—"

" Well, heard what ? "

" Oh, nothing."

Casper had been watching her with a smile, but now
his face clouded. ".Do you mean you're afraid she's
heard certain talks between you and the master of this
house ? "

" Talks ? " echoed Cora, with a start. " How did *you*
know there had been any ? "

His smile came back, but with a bitter gleam in it.
" Because I guessed why you were here, as soon as I'd
got over the surprise of seeing you here."

"Why I was here ? " she repeated. " What do you
mean ? I came because Mrs. Conover saw me at the
Lodgin' House and chose to engage me. There wasn't
any other reason but that. Did you think there was any
other ? "

" Yes." He looked at her steadily. " And I'm afraid,"
he added, " that I think so still."

" Why, don't you believe me ? " she questioned, with
wonder but no pique in her voice. She had not considered till now the possibility of having her word
doubted by him. First love is often, with pure spirits
like hers, a very ecstacy of trust. It unconsciously
demands what it finds no difficulty in bestowing.

"I'd like to believe you," he said, with another search ing look. "So you went to a lodging-house, eh? You mean a place of charity, I suppose. And Mrs. Conover brought you here? You're sure it wasn't—*Mr.* Conover?"

"No!" she denied. "No, indeed!" A flash left her eyes. "Ah, you're a friend of his—I know that—I heard them speak of you some time ago—I heard you'd written *him* a letter from—from somewhere you'd been to—I forget where it was."

"Florida?"

"Yes—that was the place. You're *his* friend, and he's told you false things about me."

"He's never spoken a word to me about you in his life."

"Then why do you ask me whether I came here because *he* wanted it? What is *he* to *me?*"

Her indignation pleased him, half banishing suspicion. "You almost as much as told me that you'd had certain talks with Con—with Mr. Conover," he pursued. "Do you mind if I ask what these talks were about?"

He saw her eyes droop, her color deepen. "Oh, never mind, never mind!" she said.

"I see," he retorted, with his voice hard and brusque. "He made love to you. It was just like him. And you, Cora? Tell me, now, honor bright—what did *you* do?"

She met her questioner's eyes frankly then. It was pleasant for her to deal in the plain, fearless truth.

"I begged him to go away from me. The second time he spoke to me I—I *ran* from him. Before that I'd said to him that I wouldn't touch a cent of his except what wages I earned. I—"

She paused here, beset by a sudden doubt lest it were impolitic to make these admissions. He seemed to read the cause of her hesitancy, and nodded briskly several times.

"The cold-blooded scamp!" he muttered. "You did

right, Cora!" he broke out in another moment, with an ardor and geniality that wrought its electric response in his watcher. "I beg your pardon for doubting you. But when I met you here I—I recollected just what that man is. I'm not really his friend. I've known him pretty well as men know one another in big cities like this. But I've never had a grain of respect for him. And I don't see how you can go on living here with such a fellow threatening your peace—no, I'll be hanged if I do!"

"I—I want to go on livin' here," she said, with a tremor as of supplication in her reply. " If I could only get him to promise he'd never bother me any more! I've been thinkin' about that! I've said to myself that if I should try to move his heart in—in pity for me, just as a beggar in the street might try, he'd see what I meant and feel sorry and let me alone."

Her earnestness, her piercing and undeniable sincerity, thrilled Casper.

"If he were anything except a flint, Cora," cried the young man, " he ought to curse himself because you *had* to ask him like that! He ought to feel as if he must crawl away from you and hide his head! . . But, see here, my good girl, don't you expect it from Robert Conover! He's a man that's never stopped yet where it was a case of pleasing his own infernal fancies. He's—"

"Hush," shot in Cora, with sharp tones, lifting one finger and glancing toward the next room. " There's someone *there!*"

"You're right," said a hard, cold, high voice that both recognized. And then Robert Conover joined them.

He faced Casper, without even a glance at Cora. He had been listening in convenient ambush for at least five minutes past.

XV.

MARTHA had been the cause of her master's eavesdropping. She had learned from Joyce of Casper's entrance into the house and his ascent toward the library. Rudolph Champny's fleeting vision of a withdrawn bit of feminine drapery, several evenings ago, had been no phantasm. Stealthy, inaudible, she had heard, that evening, what had both perplexed and pleased her. Perhaps the hate she bore Cora was based on fear lest the restored allegiance of Joyce might at any time lapse again into inconstancy if an atom of encouragement were cast to him. She had already made herself aware that Casper and Cora had met in the library, and when the sound of Conover's key turning in the lock of the front door downstairs had reached her she had hailed his appearance with sinister delight. She knew that trouble for Cora—serious and telling trouble—might now be made to ensue, and she had gone at once to meet her employer with a demurely innocent face and the tidings that Mr. Drummond was then in the house.

" But he's talking with Cora in the library, sir," she had added, and then had broken into an embarrassed sort of laugh that swiftly caused Conover to raise his brows with surprise.

"What's that?" he inquired. "Talking with Cora? How do you mean?" And as he watched Martha a flush stole up into his face.

Martha looked the paragon of sedate shyness while she answered: "Mr. Drummond told Joyce, sir, that he wanted to borrow a book out of the library. I guess he just met Cora there, sir, by chance; but I heard 'em speakin' together as if they'd known one another before."

These were the precise words needed to stir Conover's mind with astonishment and mistrust. "Known one another before!" he muttered, as if to himself. Then he went straight upstairs and did exactly what Martha would have sworn that he meant to do : he played listener, after crossing with great caution the hall-threshold of his own apartment.

Meanwhile his wife had already started from the Estabrookes' in her carriage. Conover had preferred to walk home, as the weather was fine and the walk not far.

Both had had quite as much of the reception as they desired, and unto Mrs. Conover there was fated to be no more social peace henceforth forever. She had heard of the "Four Hundred," as it is nowadays not inaptly named, and she longed to be included among its dainty little multitude. Thus far the scheme of doing so looked a hopeless one, but although the wall that guarded the holy domain was both high and of uncrannied smoothness, yet were there such things as ladders. It may be that she had already planned the making of a ladder entirely out of gold. Now a ladder of gold might be slippery, but about its firmness there can be little question.

She had once liked the Estabrookes, for all we have heard her tell Cora to the contrary. She thought them and their friends common at present, because she had just waked to the idea of what commonness in people rich and prosperous actually meant. Mrs. Schmitt, Mrs. Millbank and Mrs. Wendelkin beamed upon her in a new light— and a very raw and garish one. She had acquired that sudden reverence for the manners and habits of the Amsterdams and Manhattans which is an early symptom of the New York "society craze." She had never known anyone belonging to those august cliques, but she felt convinced that they all had angelic good-breeding and floated where the more usual mortal merely walked. Of old she had been wont to tell herself that she moved in

an "intellectual" set, and to-day, among those gathered
in the Estabrooke drawing-rooms were Viola Benedict
Beverley, who gave readings from Browning where
courage was wed with indiscretion, and Edith Potts
Phipps, who had written a novel which her friends
thought reformatory, but which her public proclaimed as
nasty. Both these ladies were far away from the old
conventional type of the blue-stocking. They wore bon-
nets that no Schenectady or Ten Eyck would have declared incorrect, and their silken draperies trailed with as
much grace as though the scissors of that fashionable
Fate, Worth himself, had irrepealably cut them. But Mrs.
Conover had no longer the least respect for such person-
ages. The newspapers (which are responsible for many
heart-burnings) had taught her to despise them and to
label them contemptuously as "Bohemia." In these
same frescoed drawing-rooms she had acquitted herself,
last season, with much native gayety and good-humor.
But now she felt discontented and fatigued. She had new
worlds that seemed to wait for her conquest. This
wasn't "the right set," and she had made up her mind to
get into the right set or to pave the paths of its approaches
with the bones of her ambitious intentions. As a consequence, her natural geniality affected those whom she met
like its tarnished and yesterday self. She tried to modu-
late her boisterous laugh, to restrain her volubility, to
pose as a lady of the first fashion, who had drifted into
an atmosphere neither native nor sympathetic. But the
result was flatly disastrous. Nobody understood the delicate subtlety of her new-born snobbery, and those who
had formerly enjoyed her opulent animal spirits now felt
inclined to wonder whether she were not under some sort
of congenial cloud. "It can't be that she's out of health,"
whispered Mr. Jott, the journalist, to his friend, Mr. Plauditt, the playwright. "She looks too chipper for that.
I shouldn't be surprised if it were her devilish young rake
of a husband. She married him for love, you know . .

a runaway match . . her old uncle was purple with fury about it for weeks. She married, though, for hot love, and half New York has heard of the pranks he plays with the marriage-tie. He treats it as though it were a shoe-lace—to be undone as he pleases."

"Some day it'll break, however," said Mr. Plauditt, "and then Conover won't find a shoemaker who'll give him another."

Jott laughed. "You can buy shoe-laces anywhere," he returned. "I dare say Conover 'll manage that."

"Shoes are a harder matter, though," said his friend; "especially when you've lost credit with your wife's boot-maker, and haven't one of your own."

This was the sole sort of recognition Mrs. Conover received, as regarded her new state of feelings. Being unconscious that any unpleasant interpretations were given to her altered demeanor, she preserved it, and felt the cold hand of ennui clasp her own. When her husband came up and whispered to her that he was going, she responded that she had done her duty by remaining two hours, and that she would shortly follow him in the carriage.

The whole assemblage had grown an empty babble of voices to her. A year ago she had enjoyed being a babbler in the same throng that now composed it. This chronicle is not concerned with either her social longings or achievements, so little more must be recorded on the subject of what she desired or what she attained. But for a moment to look on her just as she now stands before us —a woman who flings away much innocent pleasure of human intercourse for the fancied ideal of patrician supremacy—how unfortunate seems her lot! Let us say that she will sooner or later succeed in pushing her path where many another plutocrat has pushed it before. Let us imagine that by dint of struggle and strife she gets the Amsterdams and Manhattans, the Schenectadys and Poughkeepsies, to befriend and support her, in spite of that stigma of the Tweed Ring which her husband has

openly confessed his name to be soiled by. Let us suppose that she becomes not merely a member of the "Four
Hundred," but a leader of them, and that some evening
at a Patriarchs' Ball, when the gentleman who is almighty
as a superintendent of such revels finds Mrs. Van Wagenen
absent by reason of a sudden cold and Mrs. Van Corlear
absent by reason of the death of her son, Livingston
Stuyvesant, this gentleman may offer to her—*her*, Mrs.
Robert Conover (once a nobody, now the aristocrat possessor of her dead Uncle Abner's millions), a place at the
Delmoniconian "table of honor" downstairs. Well, the
prestige will be extraordinary; the journals of to-morrow
morning will record it; there will be no more strain and
torment. But her real and genuine pleasure . . . where
may that be found? In the midst of after triumphs will
she not tell herself how few vibrations the nerves of
vanity can give compared with that larger and stronger
system of sensibility which we call pure, gregarious
human nature? Will all the airs and graces, all the artifi-
ciality and snobbery, all the calculation and pretension of
the "Four Hundred" compensate for past hours of simple
enjoyment among friends once prized because they were
companionable in a sweeter and wholesomer sense? Will
she not now and then demand of her own thought,
whether she be at Tuxedo or Newport, at Lenox or at
Richfield, what is the true tangible pleasure won from all
this parade and vacuity?

But to-day she was merely vexed and bored with the
aimless drift of everything. She had lost interest in the
people, and she did not specially care if she offended her
host or not by going away twenty minutes or so before
seven o'clock—the time at which the reception was to
end. Her husband had breathed in her ear that he
couldn't stand it any longer. Conover failed to stand it
because he had seen no woman pretty enough or recep-
tively flirtatious enough to amuse himself with.

Entering the library, he strode into it with a wrath which he panted to govern.

"My fancies, as you call them, may be infernal," he said to Casper, "but you play a mean part in sneaking here like this to say what you've been saying."

Casper's face was mixed war and contempt. "I've said what I've said," he exclaimed. "I won't take back a word of it. 'Sneaking' is a fine term to come from *you!*"

Conover laughed with ringing sarcasm. "I'm glad to find out," he cried, "what opinion you hold of me!"

Casper pointed to Cora. "She can tell you," he replied, "the opinion you ought to hold of yourself!"

"She doesn't know what *you* are," came Conover's answer, blent with a fierce sneer, "or she wouldn't believe your character had a shred of decency left in it."

Cora saw the hostility in either face, and the threat of contest it foretold. She sprang wildly between the two men as they advanced toward one another.

"Oh, don't!" she broke out, with pleading hands raised to right and left. "Stop lookin' at each other like that! You ain't either of you got any reason to do it. Mr. Conover won't ever speak another troublesome word to me after I've begged him not to. He'll leave me alone—he'll see I'm only a poor girl that wants to earn her wages and live quiet. He forgot himself once . . twice, but he ain't goin' to do it any more! I told him I wouldn't tell his wife he'd . . he'd played sweet on me, and I won't! He's goin' to have mercy—ain't you, Mr. Conover? You'll be a gentleman, sir, and remember I'm only a servant; won't you? You'll——"

"Robert!" rang a voice that acted like magic on the trio.

Mrs. Conover had spoken. She had swept through her husband's room into the library.

Casper was the first to regain self-possession. "Ah, you're here!" he said to Mrs. Conover. "I'm sorry you came, but since you *have* come it can't be helped!"

Honoria Conover was livid. "I heard what that—that girl said about my husband!" she burst forth, with a dash of one hand toward Cora. "Casper, if she dares to tell you my husband ever made love to her she lies—she lies horribly and vilely!" The old characteristic shriek was never so potent as now; an anger that justified all the tales about this woman's terrible temper was blended with it.

"Oh, I say nothing . . . nothing!" declared Cora, as she drew backward and burst into tears.

Mrs. Conover turned on her like a pantheress. "But you *have* said something, and I heard you. Martha told me things downstairs that I wouldn't—*couldn't* believe! But I believe now—I see with my own sight—hear with my own ears. You dare to accuse my husband—*you!* What are you? What were you when I took you into my house?"

Her light-blue eyes had grown two dark blots of fire. She tore off her bonnet, dislocating strands of her hair that it had been pinned into, and that now fell dishevelled about her shoulders, while the bonnet itself hung dangling. "You, Cora Strang, I say," she madly went on, "you accuse my husband of this horrible thing! *You!* a castaway that I took, out of charity, from a common lodging-house! *You!* a creature of the streets perhaps—how do *I* know?"

"Stop!" cried Casper. "You shan't say that! You've not a shred of right to say it!"

"I do say it!" she raved. She turned to her husband, who had drawn backward, as if he had given her wrath supremacy and abdicated his own. "Rob! as if I believed it of you! as if I could!" She shook her gloved fist at Cora for an instant, and again turned to her husband. There were purplish blotches on her cheeks; her voice was the yell that Cora had heard in slums. "Rob, you might almost have killed her for what she's just said about you! Why are you so meek, Rob? To think of such a charge from a girl we've raised out of the gutter! Ah! what a lesson!"

"You're like a lunatic," Casper said to her. "You don't know what folly you're talking."

"I know," pealed the answer, "how you're in league with her against the good name of my dear husband! . . . Get out of my house, you liar, you wretch!" she shrieked, the next instant, to Cora.

She flung one arm about her husband's neck and dragged him forward a little, again lifting a clenched fist at the girl who now cowered with locked hands and dilated eyes. It was a rage at once awful and ludicrous; it challenged humor, and yet it teemed with epileptic transport.

Casper faced her now, and with a most resolute look. "The girl *will* go away," he said; "she'll go with me. Please be quiet, and don't raise the neighborhood with your silly shrieks." He paused for a moment, and looked at Conover. "If *you* were half a man," he said, "you wouldn't stand this bullying from any woman, wife or not!"

Conover tore himself free from the arm that wreathed his neck. "I'll show you how much I'm a man!" he said.

He instantly struck a blow at Casper, which was parried. But before he could strike a second one, Mrs. Conover shot in between them and rained stroke after stroke upon Casper's neck, temples and cheeks. He could not help laughing aloud, and yet, in another instant, he saw that it was no matter for laughter. Mrs. Conover, with flushed face and working lips, had fallen senseless to the floor. Absurd as her outbreak had been, its pathos was also frightfully manifest. She had made, in her lurid fanaticism, a miserable fool of herself. But while she lay on the floor, unconscious and as if stricken with apoplexy, an element of piteous horror surrounded her condition.

Conover stooped over her. Casper, however, darted toward Cora. "Get your things," he said, "and leave this house. You must leave it at once. She's only fainted. I wish she was dead, the infernal jade! You *can't* stay here any longer. Don't wait; don't think of waiting. Go away at once. I'll go with you. Do you hear me, Cora?"

"Yes," came the answer, in a forced, wandering way. "I'll go—I'll go, right off . . ."

She sped from the room, and caught sight of Martha in the hall as she darted upstairs. To make herself ready for the street was brief work. Then she sped downstairs and saw Martha again. A hand caught her own as she passed the library door. It was Casper's.

"Come with me, Cora," he said.

She drew back from him a little, and looked at him with her enkindled eyes, feeling as if two jets of flame were scorching their way into her cheeks.

"You don't believe I'm what that woman called me, do you?" she asked.

For answer he caught her arm within his and almost impelled her downstairs.

A short while afterward they were in the street together. The cool air blew refreshingly on her face. It dissipated her faintness. For a few previous seconds it had seemed to her that she must swoon outright.

XVI.

"You're all safe," came Casper's voice to her, as if through dense folds of fog. "Don't tremble so. There's no danger."

"I'm not tremblin' because I'm afraid," she answered.

They walked on together for a block and more. "That woman is a devil," slowly began Casper, "and yet in some ways you might almost call her the complete opposite. She's got a devil's temper; her early life gave it to her; the rich uncle that brought her up never knew how to manage her. She married a man she thought was perfection, and she's never really found out that he doesn't care a fig for her, though she constantly suspects he doesn't. God knows what her reasons are for suspecting. I guess they're because—well, well, I won't talk of that. The way she behaved, just now, was like a page in a dime novel. She simply made a ridiculous idiot of herself. The way she struck *me!* Good God! I'm stinging yet with her infernal strokes. But I forgive her—I forgive her even while I feel the force of her funny little fists. The fact is, she's got so much real good in her, poor Honoria, that I won't *let* myself be angry with her."

"You had good cause to be angry," said Cora, as they walked along. "I think you behaved very well."

"Very well?"

"Yes, you kept your temper; I like people that do that."

He pressed her arm. "Do you? So do I . . . Cora, where are we going together? What on earth shall I do with you?"

"I have money," she said. "I'll go to a hotel. I don't dare go back to Mrs. Montrose at the Lodgin'-

House ; she'd ask me lots o' questions, and— No, I'll go to a hotel for—for to-night, anyway. You just leave me at one—there's Cammoran's in Third Avenue—I've heard of it—I've never been there, but I've heard of it. It isn't far away. Then I'll say good-night to you." She mentioned the address more explicitly, and they walked eastward into Third Avenue.

Soon after this they came to a big brick edifice, and Cora paused, saying, " Well, good-night. I'll go in here. It's a decent place. I'll go in."

"Cora!" he softly cried. "Shan't I ever see you again ?"

"No, no," she said, with her heart feeling as if it would burst.

And then she got away from him and went inside and procured a room from the sleepy clerk, who did not care anything about her, so long as she was of reputable appearance and came unattended by a man.

She went to the room they showed her and sat there half the night in tremulous anguish.

She had left *him !* Yes, and why ? The clasp of his hand burned still on her palm. Had she not been right ? A thousand voices—the voices of her early Christian education—seemed to thunder back " Yes."

After a while she fell asleep, still dressed, or partially so. When she awoke the sun was flaring into her little chamber. She went downstairs not long afterward and swallowed a meagre breakfast in the restaurant. Her heart was terribly heavy. As she walked out into the street a sense of the cruelty and heedlessness of the vast city came over her as it had almost never come before.

"What shall I do ?" she thought. " I'm alone. Effie would be good to me and perhaps let me stay with her for a little while, if I only knew where to find her. Since marryin' she must have gone to live away from her father and mother. But where ? I won't—I daresn't—set foot in Prince Street again, to ask about her."

The morning was pleasant. Even the ugliness and soilure of Third Avenue were endurable, under that clean arch of sky and with that southerly breeze pulsing buoyantly. She had gone about one block when a hand dropped on her arm.

The hand was Casper's. "I've been waiting for you," he said.

"Waitin'?"

"Yes. I got up ever so early—for me, and I've been hanging about here for an age. I was bound to see you when you left the hotel."

How dear the sound of his voice had grown to her! She tried to make hers composed as she answered:

"That ain't right of you. Remember, we—we didn't expect to meet one another again."

"Oh, *I* expected it," he replied coolly. "I knew all the time that I'd see you again, if I had to move heaven and earth."

"But it's wrong, it's wrong," she declared. "You know it as well as I do. If you mean fair by me you'll—you'll let me alone. Yes, if you mean fair you must. There ain't any other way."

"If I didn't mean fair by such a girl as you are," he said, under his breath, "I should deserve to have my throat cut."

She bit her lip, looking straight ahead. "Then there's nothing to do except one thing. You know what that is."

"Never see you again?" he asked.

"Yes."

"But that might not be the only thing to do."

She started. "What do you mean?"

"Can't you guess?" he returned; and then, while she guessed, or thought she did, and grew exquisitely hopeful as to the real meaning of his words, he began to speak again. Between what he had just said and what he said now there was a relevancy that brought Cora no added

cheer. "I'm right under my father's thumb," he told
her, "and have to do pretty much as the old governor
says. He's fond of me, but he don't give me my head in
everything, by a long shot. I have to toe the mark a
good deal more than I'd like. It's worse, lately, than
it's been in years, too. Dad's heard of some larky
things that I did down South, and so he keeps a tighter
rein on me. . . Still, we're on pretty good terms. I've
got him to help you, Cora."

"To help me?" exclaimed the girl. "How's that?
I don't understand you."

"He knows Mr. Pillsbury very well. You recollect
Pillsbury's great emporium, there, on Seventh Avenue.
Pillsbury and my old gentleman have been cronies for
years. I asked him to get you a place there, for I was
sure he could do it by just a stroke of his pen. At first
he refused point-blank ; I suppose he thought I was up
to some deviltry or another. Afterwards, when I swore
to him just what a good girl you were, he knocked under
and gave me a note. Here it is,"

She almost seized it from him as he showed it to her.
"Oh, how good of you !" she exclaimed. "I'm so much
obliged ! It ain't sealed ; I may open it and read it,
mayn't I ?"

"Certainly. It doesn't mean much, but it will be something for you, at least."

"As long as it ain't starvation I shall be thankful ! "

"Starvation ? Oh, I hope it's a good deal better than
that," he said. "It ought to be. Those girls behind the
counter at Pillsbury's get pretty well paid, don't they ? "

"I've heard they don't get very much," said Cora, "but
if it's only enough to live on I shall bless my stars."

"But you'll let me help you along with a little more,
if it isn't enough to live on?" he asked persuasively.
"Come, please say that you will, Cora."

"Let you—help me—along?" she repeated, raising
her eyes from the paper that she had been reading as they

walked onward. "Ah, you've done that already. You did it when you got me *this*." And she began to replace the letter in its envelope.

"Don't browbeat a fellow. I'm sure you know just what I'm driving at. When you're there in Pillsbury's you'll need a friend. This idea of our not seeing one another, Cora, is all stuff and nonsense."

"No, it isn't," she said, as if with the edges of her lips.

He gave a great sigh, that was audible to her above the jingling cars and rattling carts of Third Avenue. "Well," he said, "I suppose I'd better show I've got some sort of manly pride in me."

She turned, shot a pleading look into his eyes, and then instantly withdrew her own. "Show you've got pity," she said, "and forget all about havin' any pride."

"Oh, I've got plenty of pity, and you know it. I've got love, too. The right sort of love."

"The right sort?" he just heard her say, and no more.

"Yes—yes—yes," he insisted, leaning his lips close enough to her ear for their speech to rise keen above the engirding clatter. "It's the right sort, if ever a man had it for a woman. I loved you that night we first met. I felt I did, hundreds of times afterwards, and when I saw you so suddenly at the Conovers' it—it was almost as if the skies opened and showed me one of the angels, wings and all. . . And now, Cora, you want to leave me forever. Well, that shows you don't care for me. . ."

"No," she could not help contradicting.

"No?" he echoed. "You *do* care then?"

"Yes—I do."

"You love me, Cora?"

"Oh, never mind, never mind!"

"You love me? Answer. *Do* you love me?"

She kept silent, with her mouth tightened together and her head a little drooped, as they still walked along.

"You won't answer me, then?" he presently demanded; and his tones were hard, sullen, angry. "I see. It's because you don't want to hurt my feelings. . . My *feelings!* Pah! Much you really care for them! Much you cared for them last night, when you left me as you did!"

At this point Cora paused. She was pale, and a weary melancholy gleamed at the line of her lips. "Here is the street where Pillsbury's is," she said. "I'll strike across into Sixth Avenue. Good-bye. Good-bye, and thank you very, very much for that letter."

The anger died from his face as he looked at hers. "I'll go across with you," he said.

She turned westward without another word, and he walked at her side. It seemed to her a long time before he broke the silence between them again, saying, with what seemed to her an obstinacy both delicious and sublime :

"*Cora!* won't you tell me whether you love me *a little* or no ? I didn't mean to be harsh with you then. I beg you'll forgive me. You must think me a devilishly ill-natured sort of chap. But truly, I'm *not!* It—it was only a little trick I thought I'd play on you. I said to myself that I'd get you to speak right out by making you believe I was furious at you. But the trick didn't work, did it? Good God ! how could I be so mean as to scold you when I know what trouble you're in? All I wanted was to hear from you whether you don't care for me just a little? You see, I've screwed down my conceit several pegs. I understand that you don't love me *much*. That was more than I ought to have expected. But a *little*, Cora? It's going to be such a comfort—if we've got to separate, as you say—for me to recollect that all the love hasn't been on my side—that is, not quite all! "

These murmured platitudes, delivered by a very ordinary young man as she walked with him along a dingy and ill-odored side-street, had for poor Cora the richest eloquence and poetry. She had wanted to escape the confession of her own regard for him ; but now there seemed cowardice and treachery in her doing so, after he had laid bare to her the mysterious pain of his own heart and showed her with such vividness the heat and leap of its flame.

"Oh, I do love you," she broke out. "Not a little, but a great deal. It—it was just the same way with me, too, after I met you.that first time. But I've always tried to keep in mind that there wasn't any use thinkin' the least bit about you. . . ."

"Still you did think!" he said, with great eagerness. "You did, because you couldn't help it. That was the way it caught hold of *me*. And I don't believe in fighting against feelings like that. They're—they're too sacred." Somehow his eyes had forced hers to look up at them several times of late ; and now it seemed to her as if he were only putting one of his glances into correspondent fervor of language as he pursued : "We can't stay separated, Cora ! *I* can't, and I know, now, that you can't ! We've *got* to see one another every once in a while. Why should we care what a few people may say ? "

"I must care !" she softly cried. "I must ! I'm all alone in the world ; I can't afford *not* to care."

"You can't afford to be without a good friend, since you *are* all alone in the world."

"Then it must be a woman friend, not a man. . . Or, at least," she added, as if self-correctingly, "not a gentleman like you."

"Oh, pshaw !" he objected ; " I shouldn't be surprised if you took me for a good deal more of a gentleman than I am. It often seems to me as if I were a terrible loafer —especially when I get a few drinks into me."

"It's like stabbin' me with a knife when I hear you talk that way," she said. "If you'd been brought up as Owen Slattery was there might be some excuse for you. But ain't you had careful schoolin', and everything of the very best right through your life ? " She came to a stand-

still, now, and as the high morning light threw its pale
penetrance upon her face, searching the flawless texture
of her skin and finding new brown-and-gold shadows in
her unique eyes, Casper wondered at the strangely lovely
picture she made. "There's the place," she went on,
"just over yonder in Seventh Avenue. Now before I
leave you I'm goin' to ask a promise of you."

"A promise?" he said, with sudden bitterness. "What
is it? That I won't hang about Pillsbury's as I did about
the hotel?"

"I hope you *won't*, but I wasn't thinkin' of that just yet.
He brightened . "Well, what's the promise, then?"

"That you won't ever drink too much again ; that
you'll recollect me when you're goin' to, and—and *not!*"

"Then you *do* mean we've got to part with one another
for good and all!" he said, falling back from her a little,
his face all sorrowful consternation.

"Yes—won't you promise?"

"No, I won't. I feel more like promising I'll drink
myself dead in a month or two."

He saw the color fly from her cheeks, and the sight
gave him a pang of pity. "Forgive me, Cora," he said.
"Yes, I *will* promise! Whether you leave me now or not,
I'll always try to see that darling face of yours peeping
over the brim of the glass when there's any risk of my
getting too much of a load. You'll keep me, perhaps, from
making a fool or a beast of myself." He got possession
of her hand now, and feigned to be shaking it in simply
the most ordinary fashion of farewell. "But there's one
thing, Cora, you can't keep me from, and that's from
having the sharpest kind of a heart-ache—the kind that
years don't heal, and that sometimes makes us mad
before we've done with it!"

"Oh, don't talk like that!" She had withdrawn her
hand from his clinging hold, and had made a few slight
steps away from him. She looked as pale now as she

had looked under the tirade of Mrs. Conover. "Keep your promise, and—good-bye!"

She was turning away when he sped up to her side. "I want a promise from you in reward for mine. Come, you must give it. Otherwise I won't keep mine. It must be a very solemn one, too."

"What is it?"

"You've enough money to get along on for a week or so, haven't you?"

She smiled sadly. "For a good deal longer, livin' as cheaply as I've learned how to live."

"I'm awfully glad. Still, if you'll only consent to take it—just as the merest loan, say—I could let you have fifty dol—"

"No, no," she broke in. "Has the promise anything to do with that?"

"It hasn't—no. Since you're fixed all right for the present as regards money matters, I've nothing more to say on the subject. But I want your promise that inside of the next five days you'll let me hear from you and make an appointment with me to meet me somewhere— I don't care where. It will have to be in the evening, for you'll have commenced work over there at the big shop, and you can't get away till after dark. But let it be inside the next five days. Now, will you consent to this? It's a compromise between us, Cora. I'll agree never once to disturb you during that time. Perhaps the meeting I'm begging you for may really be our last. If you keep on forever telling me that we mustn't and can't be friends, I suppose you'll win your way in the end. But write me a note, and meet me, and then we'll . . we'll settle it once and for all."

She demurred, rebelled, refused. He pleaded, insisted, and at length he threatened, though with a fierce tenderness that wrought upon her more potently than his entreaties. "I shall watch for you, and find you against your will," ran his menace. "You're certain to get your position here at Pillsbury's, and you won't want to have me waylaying you as if I were a shopkeeper with a dun. You'd better consent to meet me quietly of an evening, and to take a little stroll with me, only for a half hour or so. Not a soul need see us. Such things go on here by the thousands every night in the week . . Now, don't press your lips together and try to look as if you had the heart of a stone."

She gave an abrupt laugh, dreary enough to be a vocal symbol for the flowing of tears.

"Oh, well, I'll write," she said ; and she loved him all the more for the spark of triumph that lit his eyes.

" How handsome and strong he is, and what a will he has ! " she thought ; after they had finally parted, and she was on her way to the front entrance of the huge·emporium that already had begun to swarm with feminine shoppers.

And Casper, watching her light, flexile figure move away from him across the wide, mud-beclogged avenue, thought what a worthy and duteous little wife she would make him, and how right and fine a course it would be for him to speak certain words to his father about the honest love she had roused in him.

XVII.

BUT Casper was not the man to take any such frankly straightforward course. He was far too weak and easy-going. He had yielded to not a few vices in his life of seven-and-twenty years, and the paternal frown had often been very gloomy in consequence. He dreaded that paternal frown. It meant a tightening of the purse-strings, and what was he to do if his allowance were once cruelly cut off? True, he was not merely the only son, but the only child as well. Still, though both his parents worshipped him, their devotion was now tempered by anxiety.

If he had been better reared and educated he might have had a sense of revolt and disgust at the means by which the man whose name he bore had built for himself, a few years ago, that broad-fronted house in Fifty-Seventh Street. Not that there was any particular luxury inside its carven walnut portals. A few glaring frescoes clad the walls, and in the big drawing-rooms were some bad oil-paintings and several painful marble statues. These represented the taste of his wife, who had been a pretty and buxom blonde when Aaron Drummond married her, but was now enormously stout, and with a complexion one deep apoplectic pink. Her husband's money had been a surprise to her from which she had never recovered. It had begun suddenly to flow in, and as the influx augmented she had shown an almost delirious exhilaration about spending her share of it. Casper, as he grew up, tried to check her riotous vulgarity—that pride of purse in her which had set its flamboyance amid the calm of a naturally simple and benevolent soul. Money had literally made her mad. There was a kind of insanity in the kaleidoscopic way she dressed, as much as in the craving she forever showed to tell everybody just how many dollars everything had cost. But Casper's efforts were fruitless, and though she adored him with a fondness even more than maternal, his precepts and reproaches had probably come too late. The leopard, with characteristic stubbornness, retained its spots.

In the case of her husband, Mr. Aaron Drummond, the spots were of a different sort. They were black as sin itself, not merely as the dye of foible. Drummond was a New York alderman, and ever since the days of the " forty thieves " it has been admitted that New York aldermen have taken office to make money by the sale of their votes. The " forty thieves " have long ago passed away ; they belonged as far back as the year 1852, and constituted that board to whom the notorious Jacob Sharp first applied for a franchise to build a Broadway railroad. But among their successors have flourished many rogues ; the dishonors, like handsome traditions, have been handed down from one corrupt council to another ; bribery, as though it were the pestilential purple of a Caracalla, has been made a civic heritage, and coarsely flaunted as one. The group of men among whom Drummond found himself may not have equalled in venality the group that followed it a few years later—one so vile that even our metropolitan torpor at last tingled into life under its brazen wrongs. But for all this, the then body of aldermen were a bad lot, and above his fellow-members the father of Casper had been said to tower with a badness patriarchal and satanic.

He had the vigorous frame of his son, though a face at once stronger and less pleasing. Of what was notable in Casper as good-humor mixed with voluptuousness, he did not possess the slightest vestige. He had not given to his son those black and quick-moving eyes, nor that aquiline arch of the nostrils under each of which grew a tiny dark tuft of hair, like a bit of moss under a ledge of rock. He did not often smile, but when he did it was a smile of great profuseness, and lit his visage too suddenly and too keenly. You felt that it was factitious as a shaft of lime-light would have been—a judgment wholly correct, since this astute man smiled only when he wished to mask the traces of greed or malice. On Wednesday of every week he would meet his brother-aldermen in their smart room in the City Hall building, and there during the session his personality would dominate as much as did his bodily massiveness. He would plainly show himself the leading mind, as business went along in its series of petitions, motions, resolutions, communications, reports from departments or corporation officers, unfinished affairs, special orders of the day and messages from the Mayor. Most of his colleagues were men of an inferior mental type. Their countenances testified to this. Any small act of deceit or even theft might be expected from those on whom nature had set no stamp save one of blended commonplace and meanness. Drummond looked as if born for larger and darker things. He had managed to make himself feared and yet not hated by his associates. They knew him to be unscrupulous as a stroke of lightning and not a whit less cruel than one, but they clung to him notwithstanding, as if some sort of moral dignity had won their allegiance.

Nothing, however, could have proved more divergent from the facts. He it had been who had negotiated that magnificent "divide" for all of them in the granting of that franchise to the Improved Street-Sweeping Company, not long ago. Of course he had received a good deal bigger bonus than any of themselves. But then he had done harder work. He was in with the law-firm of Arbuthnot, Clancey and Tomlinson, a legal house that had stood as the advisers of the litigant company in that well-known suit. He had held secret talks with these gentlemen, all men of the wariest prudence. He knew how to "handle" them. He understood how to approach questions that if not discreetly dealt with made a fellow think of Sing Sing and have a cold feeling at the root of his spine. He was on friendly terms with three or four eminent city-judges. Oh, yes, they all conceded that if such a man as Drummond had been the "boss" of a ring like Tweed's in former days he would have hidden his tracks far too neatly for capture to have overtaken him.

The receiving of the bribes on that occasion had been touched with the red light of drama. A very big sum of money was to find its way quite miraculously, one morning, into the drawer of a certain empty room of the City Hall. A certain man was to bring it at a certain time and to place it there. It was to be a package made up of many minor packages. The man was to flit away after leaving it. Then somebody was to enter the empty room—an alderman, of course—and secure the spoil. The man came—and went. He saw a few more men talking together outside in a lobby, and paying him about as much heed as if he were a nomadic janitor. He saw another knot of men in converse on a stairway. He met still another a little lower down, in the vestibule by which he had entered.

He had performed his task. The package lay there. It was to be secured and distributed. It contained a certain fat wad of bank-notes for every separate alderman. But who was to be the first who should pass inside the room and possess himself of the composite prize? This meant no trivial thing to do. There might be watchers. The Improved Street-Sweeping Company itself could not be trusted. They had made their concession of so many thousands, but might they not mean some treachery in the way of surveillance? The building was very public. Open doors and halls frequented by passers had the hint in them of spies, prowling almost anywhere, nimble and alert.

Be this as it might, the time for prompt and bold action had come. Aaron Drummond tapped a brother-alderman on the breast. "Go in, Farrish," he muttered, "and get what's there. Remember, you've agreed that you would."

Farrish turned pale and drew back a little. There came to his lips a sulky, recalcitrant smile. He looked with dogged defiance at Aaron Drummond.

"I guess I—I can't," he stammered. "I—don't feel equal to it. Why don't *you* go?"

"Me?" said Drummond, with a scowl.

"Yes — you. You've got your other private extra boodle. We all know it. *You're* the man to go."

This was dishonor among thieves with a vengeance. Drummond looked at the backslider for a moment, and two little specks of flame seemed to swim in the dark of his dilated eyes.

"All right," he said, and strolled with a lounging gait into the empty room.

In less than an hour every alderman had his infamous wage safely stowed within the pocket of trousers or waistcoat. Every one, that is, except Farrish. As Drummond was quitting the City Hall, that afternoon, buttoning a heavy overcoat across his broad chest, Farrish, who was a small man, with sparse gray whiskers and a measly complexion, joined him.

"Look here, Drummond," he said, in timid tones, with a furtive look to right and left, "I guess you've got something for me."

"I guess I haven't," said Aaron Drummond, staring straight across the park as his large limbs bore him onward.

Farrish fell back, aghast but understanding. A malignant sneer flared across his face, and then died away. 'You'll be sorry for this,' he thought, as he clenched his small hands and stared after Drummond's burly figure.

But Drummond would not have agreed that he was ever destined to be "sorry." He had punished "little Tom Farrish," as he usually called the refractory alder-

man, and there would be an end. When Tom gave his
word the next time, perhaps he wouldn't back out of it
suddenly, like a poltroon. As for being afraid, what was
there to fear? The fellow might know certain things,
but where were his proofs? Besides, if he struck at a foe
in Drummond, he struck at friends by that very act. But
in any case he was a coward, and cowards are never
dangerous, reasoned his opponent, if they run the least
risk of hurting themselves when they hit back.

Time had passed on. For some little while the
Board had been comparatively spotless in its behavior.
Its President would sometimes look at his remaining
twenty-one constituents, as he presided over them, with
a smile that seemed to ask "Are we not blameless?"
and their multitudinous answering smile would seem to
embody the idea: "We are an assemblage of saints."
For truly the record of recent "grabs" had been creditably slight. Two or three corporations had been worried
into handsome secret settlements, but then one of these
was a gas-company that would certainly swindle its
future patrons, and one was a "bob-tail car" concern that
ought to pay well for the homicidal privilege of doing
without conductors.
And so the government of our great and noble city had
been administered through these months as through
hundreds of others. Aaron Drummond and Tom Farrish
were comparatively the better types of municipal rulers.
Their very personal appearance differed from that of the
coarse, bloated, vicious-eyed beings daily visible at the
City Hall or in any of the various departments. Here
the rowdy swaggered, as he swaggers to-day, with a
morale as dark as his dyed mustache and as much love
for the country he pretends to serve as for the green faro-
table in the gambling-house he haunts o'nights. Indeed,
he loves both in about the same way—for just what they
will "bring him in." His country yields him, in many

cases, a fair annuity.   Perhaps, if he be in Finance or in
Taxes and Assessments, or in Public Works, or in Buildings, or even in Law, he may easily reach from five to
seven thousand dollars a year as regular salary.   But the
"perquisites"—more coldly termed by some realistic
commentators "the pickings and stealings"—net him
thousands besides.   The faro-table, not to speak of the
poker-pack, is less remunerative.   It may now and then
shower gold on him, but it is not trustworthy as a source
of steady emolument ; and so, without the power of cheat-
ing his native land, our patriot would perhaps feel forced
to re-seek the corner grog-shop whence he first found
means to figure as a servant of the state.

Ah, the dreary staleness of all diatribes against this
professional politician and his uncleanly ways !   The
newspapers, when not his sworn allies, have made
him shabbily familiar.   Now and then these newspapers,
that do so much good work mingled with their evil,
have caused him to start in affright from his booty, like
a hunted thief, and drop it as he hies to some haunt of
guilty refuge.   But he soon re-emerges ; the scare is
over almost as briefly as one of those blue, smoky thun-
der-storms of a July midday that come growling and
flashing down upon the tall tower of the *Tribune* edifice
and the gray, many-windowed Post Office.   New York
has sounded a war-cry to her decent citizens—to those
who love the republic they were born in—to those who
set an unsullied life above millions of wage marked by
one least blot of shame—to those who are nature's true
gentlemen far more than caste's trumpery grandees.
And fine spirits, not a few of them, have rallied at the
call.   Primary meetings have been attended in full force.
The villanous machinery of New York politics, whose
momentum is avarice and whose cog-wheels are the
discipline of crime, suffers for a short period calamitous
threat.   "Rings" are on the verge of rupture ; "bosses"
tremble in their boots ; a banner of doughty crusade is

reared by the unsoiled hands of honorable citizens. Then, somehow, the old order is re-established. Disgust and languor—culpable, even criminal, on the part of these transient revolutionists—coldly precludes further action. Once more the old indifference benumbs those very tax-payers who should be most active in charge and foray. The mountain of protest has only brought forth, after all, a meagre mouse of dissension. The "bosses" wink at one another ; the liquor-sellers whisper to their vile clients in the back rooms of saloons that the squall has subsided and calm will soon come again. The calm, they might well add, that is born of stagnance and miasma—the calm that means not peace but sloth, not repose but swoon, not resignation but slavery. It has been well said that to own and control four wards makes the professional politician of New York a leader, that half-dozen such leaders form a "ring," that one such leader may be powerful enough to bring three or four others beneath his yoke and therewith become a "boss," and that a Boss thenceforth wields power no less base than terrible. Who that loves right and justice can question what pregnancy of truth lives in words like these? But alas ! there is never the needful persistence of question, of antagonism, of assailance. There is only the random spurt of either, and then, once again, the pitiable armistice between challenge and concession, between bravery and prudence ! With a shrug of the shoulders probity goes back to its ledger, its counting-house, its fashionable club, its domestic privacy. With a leer fraud takes up the broken thread of its wrong-doing, and hopes there may be a long time between now and the next conscience-twinge of its natural foe. And there will be ; it is always that way in New York. The guillotines used in the old revolutions have become so rusty and effete that they will not serve in the new. Fresh ones are made, only to be thrown aside at the fateful moment, while the Leaders and the Rings and the Bosses chuckle together in triumphant concert.

Aaron Drummond had smelt some bad sort of craft in his son when the latter had asked him for a word or two that would serve Cora at the Seventh-Avenue emporium. He was always sniffing at the manifestations of Casper's character, as though bent on detecting some huge fault. Drummond perfectly understood, in a secret way, his own immoral trend. It had been a part of him since he was a stable-boy in a little New Jersey village. There he had sold, each week, a few pecks of stolen oats that belonged to his employer and should have been given the horses as their regular fodder. What he gained in return was a mere song, and yet he exulted in its acquisition. He used to tell himself afterward that it had been the sole means of helping him to "begin life." He had no sympathy with the knavery that means exposure. There his sense of human crookedness appeared to commence. Being found out was the great unpardonable crime in his topsy-turvy ethics. That he was a scamp it would take the lenient soul of charity herself to doubt ; and yet he had given largely to the poor since his purse grew fat, and had shown a kindliness to struggling applicants that men of thrice his real integrity might have repressed or forgotten. His radical and undermining trouble was perhaps the spite and rancor with which an early youth of effort and privation had taught him to regard society. It was, and from the first had been, for him, an enemy to betray by strategy, to circumvent by chicanery. He had a copious fund of good-will for his kind in all matters of mere individual appeal or desert. But when it came to dealing with men as a multitude, the bitter stings of early environment asserted their baleful stress of reminiscence. He might have been, if born differently, a man of excellent practical worth and honesty. But he did not know this, and no power could now teach it to him. He possessed, so to speak, the makings of a secure morality, though as unconscious of the fact as a bird born caged is unconscious of its capacity to skim tree-tops. He constantly looked to find in his son the same cut-and-slash hostility toward the world at large which had always been his own gift of dollar-getting and vantage-winning. But Casper was forever disappointing him, and he could not understand that the lazy unconcern which this child of his loins evinced for personal supremacy of any sort whatever was in large part owing to his early circumstances of ease. "Casp's all you," he used to say to his wife; and this remark dimly veiled a kind of odd, melancholy contempt.

He had dashed off the note which was to place Cora at Pillsbury's, but after doing so he had put one of his sprawling hands on the coat-sleeve of Casper and very seriously said :

"You think this is a square girl, with no humbug about her. You tell me you ain't a bit fond of her and just want to let her have a chance of earning a virtuous livelihood. All right, Casp. Only, take my advice and don't bother your head any more about deserving cases of the young female kind. They're dangerous. And depend on it, boy, they'll always know just whose son you are, just what a big brown-stone house you live in, and just how much people say your old father, here, may leave you if he should pop across the big divide."

"Why, dad," Casper had answered, "if you could see the girl yourself, I'm dead certain you'd——"

"Oh, I might give her a check for fifty dollars," broke in Aaron Drummond, with a swift, high flourish of one hand. "I've done those infernally foolish things a good many times. I'm not speaking of the *girl*, Casp ; I'm speaking of girls like that *as a class*. There, get along, now, for I've got twenty letters to scribble off this morning, if I've got one, before I can even manage to start for down-town."

Casper was leaving the gaudy-frescoed room where his father sat before a desk that looked as if its glossy and over-carved woodwork must smell of varnish, when the alderman suddenly called out:

"Oh, by the by, boy."

"Yes, sir," said Casper, pausing.

"Did you take passage on the *Aurania*, as you said you'd do?"

"No, dad, I didn't."

Drummond raised his massive head from the sheet of note-paper above which it was bent. "Didn't?" he queried. "Why didn't you?"

Casper scanned the florid scrolls on the carpet beneath him, as he answered slowly:

"I've thought that perhaps I mightn't go across this season at all, dad."

His father did not seem displeased. He began to write, but as he did so he replied in a half-absent fashion:

"Well, if that's your mind, do as you want. But I hope Hilda Stoutenburgh's got something to do with your staying on this side the ocean. You know how much I'd like to see you make up, once and for all, to that girl."

"Yes, I know," murmured Casper, in a blank, colorless way, as he at once left the room.

Casper had in truth begun to hate the very name of Hilda Stoutenburgh. She lived in a handsome new mansion up Fifth Avenue near Seventieth Street, and she was one of the two daughters of Jacob Stoutenburgh, the wide-known millionaire brewer. It was not until many hours after his interview with Cora while they had strolled together in the direction of Pillsbury's that Casper sought his mother, for the purpose of venting some rather spleenful petulance. Mrs. Drummond was upstairs in her bedroom, being served with the cup of tea that she usually took about an hour after dinner. She had clad herself in a yellowish wrapper which was peculiarly unbecoming

to her fat, sanguine-tinted face, and she received her son
with a long, quivering sigh of welcome.

"Oh, Casp ! you didn't eat dinner with us again to-day!
We missed you so ! "

"Did you ? " said Casper, flinging himself into a chair.
"No, no — I never take that slush," he went on, with a
gesture that made his mother drop the tea-pot she had
just lifted. "You know I don't, ma, and yet you —" He
checked himself, as though pricked by a sense of his own
irritability.

"Dear me, how cross you act ! " whined Mrs. Drummond. "Susan," she proceeded, to the waitress at her side,
"you can go, then."

"I'm glad you sent her away," said Casper, soon after
the door had closed upon Susan. " The fact is, ma, I've
been miserable all day."

"Miserable ! " echoed Mrs. Drummond, her obese body
beginning to tremble like an ill-held jelly. "Oh, Casp,
why ? "

"Because dad spoke to me again about Hilda Stoutenburgh. Now, I'm not going to marry that girl. I don't
like her and I won't make up to her. By Jove, I never
heard anything so scandalous in the whole course of my
life ! trying to force a grown man like me into marrying
a girl he doesn't care a cent for ! What the devil, ma, does
dad mean by forever lugging her into his talk ? Why
should *he* care whether I marry her or not ? "

Casper's tones were peevish and querulous. His mother
looked down and shook her head agitatedly as she answered
him :

"I— I'm sure, Casp, I don't know. I — I guess it's because your pa is such a friend of *her* pa's."

" Friend ! fiddlestick ! " scoffed Casper. "They haven't
known one another well for more than a year ! "

XVIII.

WHAT Casper said was quite true. Mr. Jacob Stoutenburgh, brewer, and Mr. Aaron Drummond, alderman, had
but recently been brought into one another's intimate acquaintanceship, and then entirely through the medium of municipal politics. For the purpose of erecting a
new brewery rather far up-town, Mr. Stoutenburgh had
sought the sanction of city authorities, and failed to ob-
tain it. The Board of Aldermen had the right, in this instance, to forbid a certain most necessary invasion of the
so-called stoop-line, and their veto put the brewer into
unhappy straits. He had known Aaron Drummond
slightly for a number of years, and held him in high con-
sideration, he was a man of success ; he knew how to
line his pockets. Jacob Stoutenburgh believed in that sort
of a man. If some youth in his brewery had been caught
with a few theft-gotten dimes, he would have scowled
upon him with ire that might have meant a prison. But
stealing thousands (and not getting a striped suit and a
shaved head in consequence)was a very different affair. It
came vaguely but appreciably under the head of "politics."
Mr. Stoutenburgh admired and esteemed "politics"
greatly as a means to an end. He had felt his late rebuff
with considerable force. His plans for the monstrous
brewery were entirely laid out, and, unless he could get
the sanction desired, heavy loss might ensue. It seemed
to him that he had gone to work in both a liberal and circumspect way. He had not approached the civil mag-
nates with any flourish of lucre, but had let the aroma of
intimation precede him, pungent and insinuating. And
yet all his diplomacy had been futile. His petition had
been quashed, and for the first time in many years he

stood aghast at the discovery that there were objects of eminence and predominance in New York which money could not attain.

"There's something queer about the whole thing," he said to his wife, one day. He said a great many things in a ruminative tone to Mrs. Stoutenburgh, who was expected to hear and digest them without volunteering any opinion in reply. If she did he immediately snubbed her, and she lapsed into silence. She was a small, thin, soft-eyed woman, with two dominating passions—or shall we say prejudices? One was for her husband, as a sort of divine being who had consented to descend earthward and make his fortune in beer, and the second was for her younger daughter, Hilda, whose gifts both of body and mind she held ideally radiant.

Stoutenburgh was a German of the tall, lank and bony type, with big yellow moustaches and an imperial. His blue, lustreless eyes did not betray the intelligence that was behind them, but in the solid mouldings of his lower jaw were signs of a dogged will. He, too, worshipped Hilda, taking Sophia, the elder of the sisters, rather carelessly for granted. There had been a time when he would have confessed that the great longing of his life was to possess a son; but Hilda had caused both himself and his wife to forget that no such blessing had befallen them.

"I guess I'll see Aaron Drummond and try to talk the matter over sensibly," he said, with his gruff voice and sibilant German accent. "There may be some little hitch that can be set aside in that way."

"Oh, yes, there *may* be," said his wife; and was instantly repressed by a cold, glassy look that seemed to remind her she should receive remarks and not originate them.

Stoutenburgh made approaches to Drummond, and before long the alderman and his family dined with the brewer. Casper groaned over the prospect of going, but when he found himself at the Stoutenburgh mansion its

glories pacified him.   Everything was on a scale of sur-
prising luxury.   He had often grumbled to his parents
about the dwelling in **Fifty-Seventh Street**, speaking from
his standpoint of superior culture (such as it was) and telling them that they ought to have upholsterers and other
such fellows come in and "fix things" more tastefully.
The Stoutenburghs, on moving into their present home a
few years before, had accepted the aid of deft and refined
decorators.   There were other signs, too, of the wisdom
which art may sometimes teach wealth.   The three ladies
appeared in gowns of striking beauty, that cast reproach
on the pyrotechnic raiment with which poor Mrs. Drummond waddled into their drawing-rooms.   We may say
what we will on the subject, but nowadays there are few
parvenus who cannot command a perfect outward semblance of "style."   Tailors and modistes have become
for everybody in New York who chooses to open a ple-
thoric pocket-book, the eager purveyors of advice.   None of
our rich citizens, though their dollars be but of yesterday,
need clothe themselves with less elegance than do the
Amsterdams and Manhattans ; or house themselves
either, for that matter, since it is now all an affair of taking
one straight and easy path, to which Plutus is the only
toll-keeper.   With manners, with the right air, the proper
decorum and dignity, it is of course a different question ;
and even a man as little trained in the real civilized
niceties as Casper had not taken many sips of the excellent Stoutenburgh claret or eaten more than a course or
two of the dainty viands that were served him, before he
became aware how sharply the hosts of the entertainment
contrasted with their surroundings.   Not that Hilda, who
sat beside him and talkéd to him most volubly, could be
called actually vulgar.   She was coarse and loud, but a
film of education, of good usage, nearly always overspread her deportment.   He soon saw she was responsible for all that the household contained in the way of distinction and punctilio.   She was evidently its head, as re-

garded all such graceful details. Not that she had yet learned, like Honoria Conover, about a social world with which material beauty and daintiness nicely harmonized. She was yet quite ignorant of the " Four Hundred ; " she seldom glanced at a newspaper ; that sort of reading bored her ; she preferred the novels of Mrs. Southworth, and other fictionists who embellish the hard lines of life with a prismatic edge no less pretty than mendacious. But even these books now and then irked her, and she would sometimes fling them disgustedly aside. " I know they're trash," she told Casper on the evening when he dined in her company, " and it often does me good to order my horse round and ride off the effects of them. We're so near the Park, up here, you know, that I can be right in the thick of it like a flash. Do you ride, Mr. Drummond ? "

" Yes, a little," said Casper, who rode rather well.

"Oh," said Hilda Stoutenburgh, " I should so love to have a gallop with you ! "

This had a provocative sound, truly, but it was nothing to what soon followed. " I know some girls that ride," the young lady continued, " but I don't care a pin to go with them. I don't believe I—I cotton to my own sex very much," she rattled on, seeming to give the touch of slang a swift vocal caress in passing. " Do you ? "

" To your sex ? " inquired Casper. "Yes, very decidedly."

She smote him on the arm, and not with any gentle tap, either. " You know that isn't a bit what I mean." Here she grew quite grave and stared at him so attentively that he was forced either to let her thus hold his eyes with hers or else avert his own almost rudely.

The eyes with which her sudden scrutiny attacked him were of a lucid, crystalline azure. Casper had never cared for such eyes in a woman, nor had he liked such extremely square shoulders as were a feature of Hilda's trim and solid shape.   Her broad, blond, German face was certainly handsome, with golden down lightly fleecing the upper lip and a rich fulness delicately puffing the lower.

"You remind me of some one I've—no, you don't, either— I guess it must be . . . Oh, well, never mind."

After this broken little monologue the girl drooped her gaze, and Casper saw that on the even, pinkish pallor of her cheeks a tinge of color had begun to quicken.   Just then some dish was offered her, and as she turned her head and both uplifted arms away from him he heard her say with a bold yet oddly tender inflection :

"Do you believe we ever meet in the flesh the people we dream about ?"

He hardly knew how to answer her, at first.   Then it occurred to him that he would merely tell the blunt truth. "No," he said ; "I think all that is only flummery ; don't you ?"

"No, indeed," she replied, lowering her voice now in a way that he would have liked better in a woman who attracted him more. "I felt, almost as soon as I saw you, that I—I somehow must have seen you before now... And I remembered it all, after a little while—I've *just* remembered, in fact.   It was in a dream."

"Oh, it was," he said, with a dryness and gelidness that did not at all dispirit her subsequent recital.

She then recounted to him the sort of dream that a girl of just her vigorous, ardent temperament might easily have had.   It was a kind of galliard nightmare, in which her horse had run away with her, and a cavalier whose face she could not discern had come thundering along at her side, anxious to reach the bridle of her own terrified beast.   At last he did so (it all had the sound of something Casper had read in some rubbishy romance), and then, just for one fleet instant before she awoke, the face of her preserver became visible to her.   It had been that of the man to whom she narrated her melodramatic dream, and she now made this declaration to him with a vibrant voice and with stolen looks at his face that struck him as audacious from their very timidity.

He received her little autobiographic burst with matter-of-fact coolness. He thought it "infernal gush," and told himself that she was one of those girls who couldn't be with a man five minutes without wanting to flirt "till everything was blue again"—whatever such a state of everything might be supposed to mean. For his part, he hated flirting, and nearly always had. He wanted either to make downright love to a woman or else leave her alone. There were a good many cases where he preferred the latter course, and he began to feel very certain that this Hilda Stoutenburgh was one of them.

After their guests had gone that evening, Hilda laid down the law to her family in that laconic and imperious way which they all three considered so original and captivating.

"The dinner was very nice," she said, "though Cartier did better in some things last month, when those brewers from Milwaukee dined with us. The *filet* was over-done, the Roman punch had a queer, stalish taste, and there was sand in the lettuce."

"I thought *that*, too," murmured Mrs. Stoutenburgh. "I mean about the sand in the let—" But here a glance from her lord silenced her.

Hilda trailed her splendid skirts toward the open piano, where rested a sheet or two of song-music that for some capricious reason she had refused to sing, though her contralto voice (thought by her parents and Sophia to equal a Scalchi's) was not either poor or ill-trained. She began to pass her begemmed fingers airily over the keys as she now proceeded with her further opinions. A few caustic comments on the guests who had been asked to meet the Drummonds here left her lips, while Sophia and her mother (who were the meek little images of one another) exchanged amused glances, and her father broke into a noiseless laugh.

"Oh, Hilda, how that tongue of yours can trot!" he exclaimed. Here Mrs. Stoutenburgh gave a loud, rippling laugh, in which Sophia at once joined, as though to make such an exhibit of wifely daring more agreeable to ears paternal. "Come, now," Mr. Stoutenburgh went on to his spoiled darling, "what did you think of the three Drummonds? The dinner was given out of compliment to them, as I guess you don't need I should tell you."

Hilda struck a resonant chord, and then wheeled round on the piano-stool, facing her father.

"I think," she broke forth, "that old Mr. Drummond looks and acts like a successful undertaker. When he put those grim eyes on me I felt as if he were considering how long a coffin I'd want. . And as for *Mrs.* Drummond! Well! she made me think of Barnum's fat woman going to a fancy-ball in the costume of a rainbow."

Mrs. Stoutenburgh daringly applauded this, with the boisterous support of Sophia, and her husband leaned back in his chair with one bony hand laid against his yellow moustache and imperial, covertly chuckling.

Hilda was well used to being petted by her kindred as a wit and sage of the aptest quality. "And then," she pursued, "the way that woman *talks!* Why, before I'd been near her ten minutes I knew what wages she gives her coachman, and how much her best stair-carpet cost a yard." In an altered tone the girl soon added: "It was a relief to find one member of the family that you could get on with."

"Ah," said her father, jocosely narrowing his waxy eyelids, "you mean young Mr. Casper, eh? I thought you rather made up to him . . Well, child, you might do worse than marry Casper Drummond."

This was a great concession. Sophia opened her eyes very wide, and Mrs. Stoutenburgh, as if knowing she would be pardoned for any speech that tended to extol the value of their treasure, burst forth rather peevishly:

" Marry *him*, indeed! I guess our Hilda *might* do a great deal *better!* "

But this line of discussion did not seem to please Hilda. She presently went upstairs with an abstracted air, watched by the sister to whom her moods were as important as sky-changes to a mariner. Their two bedrooms adjoined one another; modest and diffident little Sophia could never get used to the luxury of hers, with its costly hangings and silken coverlet and spacious dressing-glass. " Do you know, Hilda," she had once shyly said to her sister, " I think I was a good deal more comfortable, somehow, when we used to live down in East Broadway and things were all on a very much plainer plan than here."

Hilda had replied with the haughty falsehood that she was quite too young in those days to recall how life in East Broadway had been lived. Sophia rarely referred, now, to their childish past. But the sisters would have very intimate talks together, in spite of that spick-and-span gilding with which prosperity had touched up their worldly environments. Now and then Sophia would have lonely or "shivery" feelings as she lay all alone in her big room, and would steal into Hilda's bed, sometimes waking her and sometimes not. The moment she was near her younger sister all Sophia's nervous fears fled. Hilda had no such folly as a single nerve; she slept like a plowboy, ate with the craving of thorough health, could gallop miles in the Park and return thence unfatigued— was the wholesome and sturdy opposite, in almost every personal and physical detail, of her timorous and fragile sister.

For this reason it surprised Sophia when she saw any touch of melancholy or depression in Hilda. To-night the latter came into her sister's room with a brush in one hand and a flossy blond strand of her copious hair looped in the other. She had on only her chemise and underskirts, and the generous moulding of her bust and arms

14

gleamed statuesque in the dubious light. She sat down on the edge of Sophia's bed and began slowly to brush the pliant depths of her hair.

"I wish mother hadn't spoken as she did about Casper Drummond," Hilda began, with lowered eyes and unwontedly brooding mien.

"How *did* she speak?" asked Sophia quickly . . . "Oh, yes, I recollect now." And here Sophia gave her dark, sleek little head a slight toss. "I'm sure," she went on, "you *might* look a good deal higher than he is. You might go to Europe some day and marry a lord, or a prince . . . Why not?"

Hilda sat with drooped head. She had stopped brushing her hair, but the brush still rested in its folds, and as the light struck her bended arm its pink elbow looked like the top of a tight-shut rosebud.

She was used to this sort of encomium from her fond family. It did not always please her nowadays, and sometimes it seemed merely like giving her deficiencies a background to glare against.

"Sophie," she suddenly said, throwing her sister a cloudy and nettled look, "do you think I appeared as if I were making up to Casper Drummond? Father thought so. Come, now, did it strike you that way? Answer truly!"

Sophia gave one of her harmless little laughs and seated herself, half-disrobed as she was, in a rocking-chair near the bedside on which Hilda rested.

"Why, Hilda," she said, "I thought you liked him, yes. I thought you acted as if you liked him—well, quite a good deal."

Hilda flung the brush on the bed, and prying a white strong hand under the heavy hair at both her temples, pushed it backward with an expression of pain and wildness that almost made the sensitive Sophia cry out from alarm.

"I—I don't know what came over me, Sophie," she

began to stammer. "I—I've never felt before as I did to-night—never! There was something about him that dazed me—that made me feel as if I could catch hold of his hand and kiss it—kiss it, till my lips ached!"

"Hilda!"

"Some girls wouldn't tell this, would they, Sophia? They'd keep it hidden even from a second self like you. But I can't. I—I must tell you, or my heart will—will burst with the secret!"

"Oh, *Hilda!*"

"Don't look so shocked. It's nothing really wrong. It's only nature, and how can there be any sin about loving as nature prompts us to love? For I suppose it's —it's my way of falling in love at last. You know I never did do anything by halves. Look how I rushed into horseback-riding—how I went mad over tennis last summer—how I got fads for French, for botany, for rowing, for—oh, Sophie, *don't* stare at me as if you believed I was out of my senses—*don't!*"

Sophia said nothing, but she still kept up her stare; she simply could not help it, for this imperious, love-scoffing, Diana-like sister had so amazed her by the change just betrayed.

"But he doesn't care a feather for me, and never will, Sophie . . never will! It isn't in him to care. I read that he wouldn't and couldn't as I sat there and watched him. He isn't handsome; he hasn't much brains; he's nothing, if you please, except big and strong and ordinary. And yet I—I've somehow *been waiting for him.* I've—"

Sophia, pierced with distress and disgust, sprang up, at this, and caught Hilda by either shoulder with her frail hands.

"Oh, do stop!" she cried. "It's too horrid, Hilda! It's as if you were bewitched—bedevilled!"

"Perhaps I am!" leapt from Hilda; and she flung both arms about her sister's neck and broke into a storm of paroxysmal tears.

XIX.

OVER their cigars, after dinner that evening, Aaron Drummond and his host, Jacob Stoutenburgh, had exchanged a number of rather significant words. They resumed this converse later, during a visit paid by the brewer to the alderman, one morning, in his Beekman Street office.

"It's hard to say just why the vote went against you," admitted Drummond, seated in his wheeling green-morocco chair, with his big legs crossed and his eyes about as lifeless as if they had been black agates. "Yes, I *will* grant that much—it's hard to say why some of my colleagues turned up their noses at your claim. I haven't talked with 'em ; the Board's had a good deal of business lately ; I cast *my* vote as you may—ahem—imagine."

"Yes," nodded Stoutenburgh. "*You're* no enemy of mine, Mr. Drummond ; I know that. Couldn't the petition come up again ? Soon, I mean ?"—here Stoutenburgh coughed, and gave a twist to one of his yellow mustache-points —" under—m'm —yes, under, I may say, as it were, more—favorable circumstances ?"

Drummond pursed his lips judicially and put his large head a little on one side. He let so long a silence ensue that the pendent clock on a wall of the office ticked hysterically, as if resenting this rudeness to a visitor. Then he said, in measured, neutral tones :

"Who are your enemies on the Board ? or—ahem—haven't you got any ?"

"Why, there's Farrish," began Stoutenburgh.

"Farrish ?"

"Yes. He don't like me. We were both in Kansas Consolidated a good deal, about two years ago, and happened to have the same broker. Farrish got the idea that

I served him a bad turn at a rise in the market through
getting our man to give him false advices and then buying the shares he'd let go of in consequence. But it was
all the merest fancy on Farrish's part. He couldn't
prove what he blustered about, you understand, Mr.
Drummond . ."

"Of course not—certainly—so like poor little Tom
Farrish!" mused the alderman, with an air of smileless
diversion.

—"And he just escaped a libel suit for letting himself be
interviewed by the *Weekly Ratcatcher*, a slanderous little
journal, dead and buried now, which you may recollect."

"I do—of course—certainly," said Aaron Drummond,
with sombre yet unctuous affability. He wheeled his
chair round so that his big fleshful knees touched the big
bony knees of Stoutenburgh. He lifted one hand and
snapped thumb and middle-finger so loudly together that
their sound seemed to stop the pretentious tick-tack of
the neighboring clock.

"Farrish!" he exclaimed — "little Tom Farrish!
Bah! he's a very small potato, sir, between you and I."
Here he slapped the hard, wide thigh of his companion
with brief but telling sociality, leaning forward to do it,
while the green-morocco chair seemed to give a faint
corroborative creak. "Yes, sir, a very small po-ta-to,
sir, inside the Board or outside. I'm glad to hear, Mr.
Stoutenburgh, just how the land lays. If *he's* been gab-
bling about (and I'll admit to you that I guess he has),
then it won't take much hard work from me to undo what
nasty work he's hatched."

Aaron Drummond made, there and then, in underrating
the vengeful spite of "little Tom Farrish," his fellow-
alderman, what was perhaps the one most serious mis-
take of his whole shrewd career. Not that he had not
sevenfold the personal influence with the board that his
despised foe possessed there. He had, and presently
used it, and to the glowing triumph of Jacob Stoutenburgh,

who gained the boon of house-front for his brewery
beyond the legal stoop-line, and paid for it, no doubt, in
that mystic way which is known most clearly to the
gossipless linings of aldermanic pockets. But Farrish, for
all his defeat, chose not to die with meekness. He had
been balked of his revenge with respect to Jacob Stoutenburgh, but such frustration seemed to him a trivial injury
now. He transferred his malice to Aaron Drummond,
and he saw his chance of lighting a slow match that
might lead to the latter's final ruin. As it turned out, he
entirely miscalculated the feelings with which Stoutenburgh would receive his advances. Far from behaving
as if he now held the means of steeping the alderman in
disgrace, the brewer smiled, stroked his yellow imperial, and—offered to do nothing whatever. Meanwhile
Farrish had given him two most compromising letters, to
read and return. One day Stoutenburgh returned them
with the simple comment that they appeared to make a
rather shabby showing for Drummond. But when
Farrish tartly inquired if he didn't mean to do something
practical, Stoutenburgh stared at the questioner coldly
with his rayless blue eyes.

"Something practical?" he asked, as if he were repeating two words in Hindostanee, heard now for the first
time.

"Why, yes," blustered Farrish. "Don't you see?
Don't you catch on?"

Stoutenburgh smiled a wintry smile. "I guess I do,"
he said, a trifle boredly. "And if I do—what then?"

"What then?" grimaced Farrish, his little frame giving
a galvanic start. "Why, man, whatever solid cash you
paid for the vote that fixed you all right with the Board,
you can either get handed back to you out of Drummond's
clothes, or else whack him so hard for squeezing it from
you that he'll remember till his dying day."

Stoutenburgh smiled again, and seemed for a moment
to meditate. "And how about that whack you speak of

affecting *you* also, Mr. Farrish?" he calmly inquired.

"Me?" shot out Farrish, quite with a volcanic air.
"*Me!* I never saw a cent of the money—not a cent!"

"Oh, you didn't."

"No. Drummond counts me out, so to speak. I
offended him, and he believes he can squelch me completely in consequence. He can get his two-thirds vote
for almost any measure he chooses to take hold of and
push. He overrides me, snubs me, and thinks I'll come
cringing to him with an apology, some day, and so crawl
back into his good graces. But he's wrong, and I propose to show him he is before we're done with each other.
I—I propose," concluded Farrish, with the droll assumed
majesty of a man who has no native majesty at all, " to
—to print it on his hide!"

" I perceive," said Stoutenburgh, after a slight pause ;
" and you would like to employ me as your printer, eh,
Mr. Farrish?" . . . Before the annoyance caused by this
sarcasm could take an eruptive form the brewer proceeded, in more assertive tones :

"How, then, since you have received none of the
'cash' you accuse me of having paid to get my claim
legally approved, do you dare risk the statement that I
ever paid a dollar?"

Farrish grew livid. This looked like treachery worthy
of Drummond himself. He blurted out something with
respect to the "boodle" distributed by Drummond among
his fellow-aldermen, and the personal confidences which
had made him certain of this fact. Then he strove to
correct himself, and fell into another little gin of his own
imprudence, watched all the while by Stoutenburgh's icy,
impassive eyes. At last he paused, half in irritation, half
in defiance, feeling that he had been fooled with, and yet
not quite sure if this were the case—a pathetic little per-
sonage, with powers of spite that were prodigious, with
principle long ago a wreck, and with worldly tact and

penetration never by any means equal to the sinister forces that so often set them working.

All this while and for many succeeding weeks Jacob Stoutenburgh watched his beloved Hilda with new and alarmed gaze. She was like a girl in a fever, and yet she betrayed no symptoms fit to challenge medical heed. To her trio of adoring watchers it soon transpired that Casper Drummond had ensnared her young spirit in a curious abiding spell. If she had wanted to marry the moon there might have been some discussion among her kindred about the advisability of certain sublunar signals to that effect. Her wanting to marry Casper was an affair of so much easier management that father, mother and sister held it in relative disdain. Of course the young man would fall at her feet as soon as he realized the truth. To shower him with courtesies, however, failed of making him do so. The Stoutenburghs went to a fine semi-suburban villa at Mount Vernon during the summer, and when June came Casper was bidden to run out there from town a good many more times than he found agreeable. He made love to Hilda, in a way. She made love to him with so much hectic impetuosity and directness that not to return her advances would have been almost a denial of the commonest breeding. At this time the Conovers used to joke him upon the "dead set" organized by the whole Stoutenburgh family. Perhaps a few of Honoria's light, keen jibes made him crueller than he might otherwise have shown himself. However this may have been, he certainly dealt in cruelty. Hilda thirsted for his presence at Mount Vernon, and he repeatedly caused her to thirst unsated. Once or twice he took the cars from New York in a reluctant and rather bad humor. Naturally amiable and complaisant, this change sat ill upon him and became him more infelicitously than if his had been a character with niches and crevices for which gloom had an old-time right of tenure. He never, in all their meetings, mentioned marriage to

Hilda, but after the Stoutenburghs came back to town he began to feel that circumstances were drifting them each day more unavoidably together. His father and hers had grown somewhat intimate, though the evening visits which made them so were usually paid by the brewer. If Casper looked into the paternal eyes he seemed to read there a special behest; his mother would startle him by irrelevant laudations of Hilda; the whole atmosphere of the Fifty-Seventh Street abode appeared sown with mandates that he should go and propose to the brewer's daughter, and one or two of the gaudy goddesses on the frescoed walls of his home would now and then affect him as if murmuring some such bit of counsel. All the while he was reluctant, and at intervals fiercely so. That he should finally have grown determined to escape a union which was charmless for him took origin (though he would by no means have admitted the fact) in his first haphazard and rather disreputable meeting with Cora. Perhaps the trip to Florida may have had an avoidance of Hilda as its chief cause. He had said one day to his friend, Rudie Champny, just before they started off in each other's company:

"Upon my soul it will be a relief to get rid of New York, for more reasons than one."

Rudie was never particularly delicate or circumspect with his friend, and just now his response took an almost brutal strain.

"Oh," he said, "you mean that Stoutenburgh girl they're flinging at you so? If I were you, Casp, I'd just take a stand and keep it—that is, provided I'd made up my mind not to marry her. What the devil is the use of compromise in a case like that? You'll have to snub the brewer's whole gang sooner or later. Why don't you do it now, once and for all?"

Casper gave a shrug and a scowl, and then spoke as if between shut teeth: "I'd take a stand quick enough if I could. But if I did, the first thing I knew, dad might kick infernally about money matters. The paternal market, Rude, is a good deal like the Wall Street one ; it gets flurried from the funniest kinds of causes."

After his return from Florida, Casper's relations toward Hilda Stoutenburgh were unsocial in the extreme. He had presented himself several times at her house in a perfunctory and cheerless way. Hilda had received him with a manner that was arctic one instant and tropic the next. The lovesick girl wore her heart so glaringly upon her sleeve that if some sort of temperamental indifference had not swayed her visitor he might have gone away after having let emotion run off with him and land him in irrevocable troth-plight. But thus far no such event had occurred. On the day when he made his little compact with Cora he still stood perfectly free as regarded any engagement to the daughter of his father's new friend. He received, on the following afternoon, an earnest little note from Hilda that begged him to make one of a small theatre-party she would superintend an evening or two later. But he wrote as politely as he could, declining the honor of being her guest. His real feelings baffled all introspection ; he was not a man given to any so subtle a process as self-analysis . . And yet the thought rose savagely paramount with him that to pass half an hour in Hilda's company before he became sure of how Cora was going to treat her promise would be simply a kind of gentle purgatory.

Cora treated her promise with all due loyalty. Before three days had elapsed Casper got his expected and longed-for note, saying just where she would be and at what hour.

The place of tryst was prosaic enough. It was the corner of Seventh Avenue and a street but a short distance beyond Pillsbury's, over which the spell of silence and darkness had now been laid. The hour was half-past eight in the evening, and Casper felt a thrill of strange joy as he saw the lamplight gleam on Cora's face and clasped her hand with an eager tensity.

"Am—am I late?" he asked, in so excited a whisper that his tones pierced her with the same pleasure some act of spontaneous and unconscious homage might have given.

"No," she said; "I've only just got here."

"Take my arm," he replied.

He felt her hand tremble as she slipped it where he longed to have it rest. He turned and looked into her dim face. They walked down the shadowy side street together, leaving the brighter avenue. It was a perfect spring evening; the sky above the house-tops hung cloudless and star-fretted; a delicate and delicious wind was blowing from the south. As they passed a vague stoop they saw two forms that seemed like two lovers holding converse, and the next instant a young man met them with a young woman who leaned on his arm and gazed fondly up into his face. It was a night for lovers to be abroad; love and spring were in the air; below this vernal twilight, fanned by these brisk and exquisite breezes, the harshness and hardness of the city melted into a romantic glamour.

Cora's heart was beating so that she dared not trust herself to speak. She had never been so near to him as this; the contact with his firm frame dizzied her delightfully; she had the surrendering impulse of the woman who loves, and this wrought in her a fright that was both pleasure and pain. With Casper the correlative ardor of sex keenly prevailed. The light burden of her hand and arm was a novel ecstasy for him.

"Here is love at last," flashed through his being, and the virile protective impulse became so forceful within him for a few seconds that he had an insane yearning that some calamity might beset her, some unguessed power of the night itself, from which he could shield her by that very strength in which her treasured physical frailty bade him

exult.   Nature spoke between these two with her mysterious and magnetic methods.   Each was conscious of the
other's thraldom.   To break that by speech was merely to
clothe rapture in commonplace.

"You kept your promise," Casper at length said.   "You
met me—you do love me!"

She made him no answer, and he soon went on: "I
suffered till I got your note, and when I got it I kissed it
a thousand times.   It's nothing but a bit of rumpled
paper, now.   What a good hand you write!"

" Do I ? "

"Oh, yes.   There's many a lady that can't touch it. . .
Cora ? "

"Well?"

"There isn't a soul in sight now. . .   The street's so
dark, too . .   Please."

"No, no!"

"*Please!*"

He had his will, as men in such cases nearly always do.
Her kisses met his lips like blended fire and fragrance, the
one stinging almost to blissful agony, the other intoxicant
and mesmeric.   They had paused and his arms were
stealing about her when she pushed them away.   People
were coming and had already drawn nearer than they had
thought.

"Never mind—forgive me—it's all right now," he said,
in tones remorseful enough for a repentant assassin.
"There; let's go along just as we were going before."

They did, but Cora had a terribly guilty feeling as they
passed the people whose approach had startled her.
These, however, gave no sign that they had witnessed the
stolen caresses, and soon she breathed more freely.

"Now tell me about yourself," began Casper.   "The
note fixed things for you at Pillsbury's ? "

"Yes, it worked like magic.   To-day was my third
day behind the counter."

"Well . . . and how do you get on ? "

"Oh, pretty well."

"Only pretty well, Cora?"

"Oh, I'm new and strange yet." She gave something between a laugh and a sigh. He pressed her arm with his own stouter one, and the mere helpful friendliness of this act made her eyes moisten. "Still, I guess I'll do better soon. There was some trouble among the other girls about my gettin' the place as I did. I could see that easy enough."

"Trouble?"

"You see, there's twenty waitin', for every one that leaves; and my comin' right in over the heads of so many others that must have had friends in the store tryin' to push them—why, it caused lots of surprise and talk. They've put me in the ribbon department. I get six dollars a week.

"Six dollars!" exclaimed Casper. "Good God! is that all?"

She told him more as they continued their walk. She had managed to find a small room in a boarding-house not far from the great shop. The food was not remarkable; it had a mean enough flavor after the excellent fare at Mrs. Conover's. But she thought these quarters would suit. The hours at the store seemed very long—from eight o'clock until six. And yet she would get used to them—oh, she felt certain of it! The great point, just now, was getting used to nearly everything. Some of the girls were nice, but not all. They were a better class of girls, though, than she had expected to meet. One of them, a pretty little blonde named Lily Luttrell, she had got to know quite well already. Lily was close beside her at the ribbon-counter, and had been kinder than anybody else. It was doubtful if Lily were quite as good as she ought to be; she said the boldest things, though they made you laugh at them, they were so funny. She was often saucy to her superiors, too, though nobody seemed to mind what she said or did. She made the soberest girls laugh, and she was always in such merry spirits that it would have taken a very grim person indeed to quarrel with her. She wore better clothes than any of the other girls, and had such a lovely pair of real pearl ear-rings ! She would show them to you, pulling them out of her ears, if you admired them, and tell you, with one of her sweet little laughs, beginning like the coo of a pigeon, that they were a gift from a friend.

"I don't know what I should have done but for Lily, this day or two," Cora went on. "She's been such company, somehow. She's made me feel so much more at home ! Why, her little plump face, with its bright blue eyes, and its dimples, and its smile that shows teeth as white as milk, is a pleasure just to look at. If she ain't good—and I'm afraid she ain't—you forget you've doubted her; and . . . well, it's queer my sayin' so, but you almost don't care what she is, good *or* bad, because she's such a mischief, and so sociable, and so full of kind, pleasant ways."

"I'd like to see Lily," said Casper. "She must be splendid fun. Would she tell you, do you believe, who gave her those pearl ear-rings, if you were to ask her hard enough ?"

"Oh, I guess she'd tell anything," replied Cora. "I don't think she cares a fig what she tells."

But Casper wearied, after a little while, of further talk about the inmates and the doings at Pillsbury's. He wanted to talk of other things, though these were only the devotional nonsense in which Cora scented peril, while she admitted the secret happiness that lurked there.

"It's gettin' on to ten o'clock," she at length said ; "I'm sure it is. I must be in bed by ten. I'll go right straight home, now." And she drew her companion in an opposite direction from the one they were taking along the lonely and dusky boulevard of Tenth Avenue.

"You'll have an oyster or two with me somewhere," began Casper ; but she cut him short at once, with an emphasis that defied further persuasion. When they had reached the Seventh Avenue corner at which she had originally met him she drew her arm from his and said with all the decision she could muster :

" Now, good night. I—I've kept my promise, and—and you mustn't ask me ever to keep another one. We musn't ever see one another again. It can't be—it *can't !* I've thought it all over, and I'm certain I'm right. It's the only way. I've got to take it, and I'm goin' to be brave about takin' it, and not flinch a single bit. But I'm thankful to you—oh, so thankful ! Now, remember *your* promise—I mean the one about not drinkin' too much ; and . . well, I can't say any more . . Good-night, and God bless you ! "

" Cora ! " He had caught her hand and was holding it with a tightness that hurt her. " You shan't go like that—you *shan't.* No, no ! . . *Cora !* "

But she had torn her hand away. " God bless you, Casper ! " shot from her pale lips.

He may or may not have heard the words as she darted off. A jingling car passed at this moment, and a few yards further up the avenue had suddenly occurred a riotous fight between two separate gangs of loafers just emergent from a liquor-shop. People were hurrying toward the scene of turmoil, and sudden oaths rang out raucous in the placid night. All at once a policeman's club made those hollow sounds on the pavement that mean violation of the peace and sharp summons for aid.

Casper heard them, but he did not stir. He stood and stared after Cora's disappearing form. It may have been that the dull, bleak strokes were like symbols to him of his own drear dismay,

XX.

Cora was very tired when she got home, but sleep did not come to her for hours, notwithstanding. She hated and yet rejoiced to think that she might perhaps have irritated Casper into never seeking her presence again. A semi-sleepless night put certain signs of fatigue into her face, which Lily Luttrell noticed and quickly commented upon.

"You don't look very bright this morning," said her new friend, scanning her with a pert air, at once impudent and amiable. "Not that you're any less pretty than usual. Mercy, no! It's only that you've got a kind of drowsy shine in your eyes, as if you hadn't had rest enough. *Had* you?"

"I didn't sleep very well."

Lily gave a musical giggle as she drew the cover from a great square of multicolored ribbons. "Is that *all* it is?" she asked, with a roguish sparkle in her blue eyes. "You're sure you didn't let him keep you up too late over a stew and a bottle or so of beer? Eh, Miss Strang?"

Cora laid her hand on Lily's plump arm. "Please don't talk like that," she said. "I never do those things. I don't believe in them, and I don't do them." Then, seeing the girl's dimples deepen with an expression of comic solemnity, she could not resist a smile at the pursed mouth and puritanical frown.

"Beg your pardon, Miss Strang," said Lily. "Of course you wouldn't speak to any gepman under fifty. Girls with figures, hair, skin and eyes like yours mostly don't. They save 'emselves entirely for the consolation

of the old. I understand that perf'c'ly. I'd do it, too, if I
was anything but a good-for-nothin' little gadabout, with
no more looks than one o' the dolls in the toy-department."

" You've a great deal more 'looks' than a doll," said
Cora, quite seriously ; " and I guess you've got plenty
of real character besides, though you cover it up with
your jokes and jollities."

" Character !" laughed Lily. "I had one once, but
I'm afraid its all gone to grass long ago. Now, see here,"
she proceeded, in her lightsome, jocund way ; "I wasn't
fishin', just then, when I spoke about *looks*. My ! when
I'm near *you* I feel like hidin' my head."

" It's a very pretty head," smiled Cora.

Lily lifted her rounded shoulders and gave a skeptical
scowl which she could not, for the life of her, have made
ugly. "Oh, bosh ! I'll do ; I'll pass in a crowd. That
is, for the next few years. But later on I'll get fat and
be wearin' loose sacques and things to hide it. I know
it's comin'. All the women-folks of our family *do* get
fat. What makes people call me pretty nowadays is only
because I'm young and healthy and have what they call
a contented mind."

" Don't you ever feel blue, Lily ? " said Cora. She
could not resist the familiarity of the dulcet surname, and
her companion at once brightened and smiled her bewitching little smile as she heard it.

" Blue ? Me ? Oh, never. I'm always merry as a
cricket. I can't help but be ; it's *in* me. I just float
right along on the top wave, like a cork. I have to,
somehow ; I can't sink ; I guess it's because I'm so light
—because I'm a born fool. Oh, there's so much in that—
in bein' a real born fool, and not carin' ! You don't
know what a comfort it's been to me ! I've seen lots of
trouble. Yes, indeed !—death and poverty and—oh,
well, no matter . . There ! that's me ! I'm always sayin'
to myself, 'Oh, well, no matter.' If I'd sat down and
brooded I might have gone crazy . . Now you *do* sit down

15

and brood. You needn't tell me you don't, for nobody ever had those eyes and that mouth that didn't. You take things hard and I take 'em easy; there's the difference between us. I don't care a snap for to-morrow as long as I've got a little money in my pocket-book to-day. I *can't* borrow trouble. If I tried with all my might and main I couldn't get Providence, or whatever it is, to lend me a bit. And I ain't good, either. Oh, I don't make any bones about it; I just *ain't*. Some girls here carry on like mad after hours, and come to the store with their eyes red from want of sleep, and yet *talk*—well, they *talk* as if butter wouldn't melt in their mouths. But I ain't any of that kind. Not that I *tell* my affairs, but I don't *lie about 'em*—that's all ! "

The more that Cora saw of Lily Luttrell the less moral weight seemed evident in the girl's volatile and dauntless nature. But she was one of those privileged beings who appear permitted to go as they choose without scandalizing anybody. One might as well have blamed a bacchante for her crown of grape-leaves as Lily for her supposable follies. It seemed appropriate that she should be at the ribbon-counter in Pillsbury's ; her personality, so to speak, was decked with ribbons, and her indiscretions had the effect of being a-flutter with picturesque knots and bows of them. She went dancing through her days, and you felt that she might be dancing to a music that would end, some future time, in a plaintive, sob-like fall. But meanwhile there was a spark of wholesome cheer in her voice, mien, phrase and motion that Cora found in no one else of the great feminine throng at this busy and bustling shop.

A great many of the girls astonished her by their prosperity. They lived "at home," and had been graduated from the various public schools. They were not forced, like herself, to face a kinless and unprotected solitude. Not that they were often content with their lots ; incessant grumbling was the burden of their discourse, and the American "push" flowered gloomily forth in it as a growth of restless desire. They had ample means for observing the contentment created by a well-filled purse; they witnessed the pleasure and freedom of unhampered expenditure. Fashion, in a hundred voices, forever spoke to them; they lived amid an incessant rustle of gowns and tinkle of gew-gaws. Cora began to see how vanity consumed them—how they would spend the last dime of their salaries in tawdry trash like brummagem bracelets, rings, hair-pins, combs or bangles—how they would have imitation French heels fixed to their shoes, threatening health and sometimes dealing secret pain— how there was, in short, no whim or flippancy of self-ornamentation to which they did not pay deference. Reared to feel the influence of false, voluptuous and self-ish aims, they were most of them ripe for the scythe of sin long before its blade cut into their lives. Not a few of them had refused offers from decent men because the unions that would result might not raise them high enough in a worldly sense, or perhaps for reasons in which lazy dislike of household cares and tasks played no inferior part. The newspapers kept them familiar with the deeds (and sometimes the misdeeds) of our nabobs and grandees. The silly novels and story-papers that they read told them too often how "Fanny, the Flower-maker," or "Selina, the Sewing-Machine Girl," had married her tall dark hero, with a drooping silken mustache and four or five millions. The future of their dreams would seem to rumble with the mellow sound of their own carriage-wheels. In almost every case they looked upon this waiting behind a counter as the merest threshold to something more thrifty and luxurious. Luxury was chiefly what they sighed for and craved—that, and the devotion of the male sex. One would lace herself cruelly; another would pinch her feet to such a degree that her walk was only a half-graceful limp; another would take clandestine draughts of vinegar to make herself interestingly pale. It is from womanhood of just this frivolous and idle-minded sort that infamy is most apt to select its victims. Year after year they had drifted away, led downward into the dusk of shame by the crafty hand of temptation. Some had been saved; a lucky marriage had borne its fruit of blessing, perhaps, or parental influence had woven a stronger bond of detention. Those who were ill-looking had stood the best chance of escape, though, as Cora glanced here and there among the multitude of girlish bread-winners, there was hardly a single face that did not wear some touch of attractiveness.

Her own coming had produced a real sensation in their midst. For days criticism was rampant, and opinions hotly differed as to whether she was beautiful or only of moderate loveliness. But in the end she conquered all adverse decision. Her sweet, cordial demeanor may have had much to do with the ultimate verdict. There are some women who will never admit the physical superiority of a sister until they become convinced that she quite fails to pride herself upon it and wears it as negligently as if it were a loose-knotted bit of silk at her throat. So Cora had always worn her gift of beauty, forgetting it constantly in spite of herself, and nowadays only remembering it with a dreary regret that it should have cost her suffering and chagrin. Here, too, she soon found that it flung more thorns than roses in her path. It roused perpetual doubt as to her real blamelessness, and caused more than one skeptic smile to curve the lips of those who heard just where and how she lived. Her associates, in large numbers, would not believe that any girl with such a face and form had resisted all the advances which must have besieged her. A certain sadness began, after a little while, to mark both her manner and countenance. This was construed by the less charitable into an affectation of purity and moral excellence. And yet in the main her unfailing sweet-temper, her quiet aversion to gossip and scandal, her quick sympathy with all troubles and afflictions among her fellows, and her native, unconscious tact in showing neither preference nor antipathy, won their due popular results. Past experience had schooled her bitterly and cogently. She had dealt so much with her own sex under conditions where avoidance might have been savagely resented, that the old discipline, amid these new and politer surroundings, exerted a force born of previous impress. Meanwhile the sadness just mentioned grew upon her as she strove to fling it aside.

Had Casper left her forever? It were better, far better, if he had indeed made the desertion a lasting one. She had done all in her power to bring it about that he should go from her and never willingly look upon her face again. Still, she loved him, she loved him ; and he came to her in the dreams of her tired sleep, his voice sounded in her ears through the commercial babble and clatter of the daily buying and selling at the huge emporium. She was satisfied that she had done wisely, and yet a yearning deep as her love kept that love continuously turbulent. Its waters would not sleep ; they were always tossing and moaning within her spirit, like a sea that some persistent storm holds under the stubborn sway of wrack and blast.

During this time Lily Luttrell appeared to smile and trip before her moral vision as an incarnate mockery of all her steadfast virtuous resolves. Lily was no taintless representative of her chaste-sounding name. Cora had learned with more or less clearness just what an abyss of degradation this merry girl was always peering over. But none of the darkness below ever put a reflected cloud into her blithesome blue eyes.

"I think girls like us make fools of themselves, Cora," she would say, "to fritter away their days tryin' just how good they can be. What's the use of it all? I ain't the kind that can go to church and get set up hearin' sermons

and hymns ; nor from what I've seen of you already you
ain't much in that line, neither. Now, after all, who
cares two pins whether I lark a little or don't? I'd like
to be married decent—of course I would, and so would
any girl that ain't a born goose. But if the kind of feller
I'd take don't ask me and just wants to fool and spree
with me instead, why what can *I* do? Roll my eyes to
heaven, some folks would tell me, and fold my hands in
prayer . . Mercy sakes ! What's heaven ever done for *me?*
And what is it, anyhow? Where is it? *Is* there any?
I hear it said there's people that think no such place ever
was. I don't bother my head much about it, but whenever I do, I always kind o'feel they're right. If there was
any heaven there'd have to be a God, and if there's a
God it seems as though he'd got other things to tend to
besides lookin' after *us*. If he does look after us he don't
show us he does, that's all *I* can say. And since he
hasn't got any concern about me, as far as I can make
out, I ain't goin' to waste my time screechin' or prayin' to
him. I'm goin' to laugh and carry on all I please. I'm
goin' to have as nice a time as I'm able. If there's a hell
I don't believe I'll get into the hottest part of it, because
I never hurt a single soul, if I can help not to, by word
or deed. And I guess the hottest part is for them that
make themselves nuisances to their fellow-creatures. I
think *my* hell, if I've got to go to one, 'll have a draught
in it. When I get *very* thirsty I dare say I can have a *few*
drops of water to cool my tongue with every now and
then—not so wonderful *cold*, but *satisfyin'*, anyhow.
That's the way I *feel*. If I'm disappointed I'll have the
good time here to remember, and if I still keep *me*, when
I'm down there, I'll remember it so hard I reckon it'll
sort of lower the thermometer."

Cora harkened as if under protest to talk like this. At
the time she heard it she told herself that its effect was null
and blank to her. And yet certain audacious, 'defiant
phrases of Lily's would ring in her ears long after she had

listened to them. This girl proved an insidious counsellor for the reason that her half-discovered pranks and misdemeanors were condoned and tolerated by her associates. Nobody ever thought, somehow, of either scolding or reproaching Lily Luttrell, and yet everybody accepted the existence of her gay and dauntless misdeeds. Cora watched her and thought how dreary was her own lot in comparison to the conscienceless abandonment of this little epicurean madcap. No grief seemed to befall her ; she urged her valiant if vicious assault against a ruthless destiny. Anguish and overthrow were the doom declared of her kind, and yet she trifled with fate as if it were a tame lion whose claws had been clipped. The worth and force of womanly purity were made the texts of untold sermons, but here was a little sensuous vixen who curled her red lips at all the moral maxims and polished her pearl ear-rings on the front of her dress as if the whitest chastity lurked below it. This, for Cora, was laxity in a new guise. She had so often seen it invested with either feverish fatigue of self or libidinous challenge to decorum that this new aspect by which it appealed set her brooding and meditating.

Repeatedly she would shake off the subtle effect of example thus produced, and strive to regard it in the light of warning alone. One evening, after she had abandoned all expectation of seeing Casper again, he suddenly appeared to her as she was nearing the obscure little stoop of her residence. He crossed the street from its opposite side and faced her with a smile of welcome that made her heart leap into her throat one instant and then seem to swell and choke her the next.

"Are you sorry I came ?" were his first words.

"N—no," she could not help stammering. "You—you followed me from the store ? "

"Yes."

It was still daylight. Spring had given the town few clement hours of late, and this evening a yellow, watery

glow struggled from the sinking sun between ragged, purplish clouds, while it set over beyond the monastery on
Hoboken heights. As the slant rays fell on Cora's face a
look of sharp anxiety crossed Casper Drummond's.

"You're tired," he said ; "I can tell it by your eyes."

"A little," she said.

"They overwork you at the store?"

"No ; but the hours are long. And this is a busy
season, you know. They say the spring custom has been
pretty large this year."

Unconsciously she had walked perhaps fifty steps with
him, but now she came to a sudden stand still.

"Let's get a little dinner together," he said pleadingly.
"We'll have a glass of wine or so, to brighten you up.
Don't refuse. I know a real nice place across town
It's a *table d'hôte* place, but it's ever so quiet and respect-
able."

"Oh, I can't, I can't," she murmured ; and then, as she
lifted her eyes to the face that had haunted her dreams incessantly since it had last vanished from her sight, she felt
that here was too great a stress of temptation—that she
must yield or break her heart in twain by the very effort
to stay resolute. And so, with an abrupt smile and a
little sighing gasp of "Oh, *well*," she gave consent.

And afterward it all turned out so delightful and yet so
harmless ! The restaurant to which they went was in a
side-street just off Sixth Avenue. The cooking, although
somewhat French, was not superfine, but Cora thought
the food she ate ambrosial and the red wine that Casper
mixed for her with water an enchanted beverage. The
courses appeared innumerable, and for dessert there were
little "bricks" of tricolored ice-cream that melted on
Cora's tongue with a charming relish. Afterward came
coffee, with a mottled slice of cheese that she could not
be persuaded to touch, and some almonds and raisins that
she delighted in, letting her tongue run on heedlessly to
Casper while she cracked the nuts with her white, glisten-

ing teeth.   She told him stories about "the girls," interest-
ing him not because he cared for the subjects of her talk,
but because he loved to watch the smile coming and going on her features and to hear the soft inflections of her
voice.   He said a great many lover-like things, and looked wondrously handsome in her eyes while he said
them.   She thought him, indeed, a star of manly beauty,
and long ago she had made up her mind that many a fine
lady must have yearned for his devotion.   It was toward
the close of the dinner, when the wine had put a rich
lustre into her gold-brown eyes and given her cheeks that
pink which youth alone stores within its magic rouge-pot,
that she ventured to question him about the lures and
sorceries of other women who dwelt in his own world.
She had refused to do more than just sip once or twice
in a bird-like way from her small cup of black coffee,
and when he ordered two tiny glasses of yellow chart-
reuse she hesitated for some time before she would
even taste the viscous golden fluid.   But when she had
tasted it the sweetness of it conquered her, and she gradu-
ally drank it all, though with a dainty air of doing so under protest that her companion thought deliciously droll.
Perhaps the headiness of the cordial emboldened her to
speak with an unwonted freedom.   However this may
have been, something from Casper with regard to the
dullness and tedium of his life and the spot of brightness
which her precious company had given it made her say,
in tones rather piquant and mutinous :

"Oh, that's all very fine, but I guess you've got plenty
of nice young ladies to console yourself with—rich ones
and pretty ones and smart ones, too ! "

He looked at her with a seriousness that struck her as
the most noble and dignified rebuke.

"No, indeed ! " he declared, with low-voiced vehemence.   "There isn't a soul I care a bit for.   On my
word of honor, there isn't ! "

"But those ladies I've seen," she persisted, "—ladies like

the ones that used to call on Mrs. Conover—were so hand-some and so nice. At least some of 'em were, if not all. And haven't you known any like that who got you talkin' pleasant and payin' compliments, and— Well," she broke off, with a laugh full of delicate rippling trebles, "you know what I mean, though I guess you're makin' believe ever so hard that you don't understand a single bit."

"Oh, I understand quite well," he answered, with a solemn little nod. " Before I knew you I got the notion into my head a good many times that I was awfully in love. But I never got it into my heart, Cora, till I *did* know you."

This appealed to her as the most adorable bit of love-making. She could not doubt its perfect sincerity, and perhaps if she had done so she would have been at least moderately wrong. Casper meant most heartily what he said—as he then said it ; and there is reason for asserting that all his former moods and moments of attachment were lukewarm in comparison to the strenuous passion Cora had now wakened. Her tender taunts had the effect of spurring him into expansive confidences, and almost before he knew it he had told her of Hilda Stoutenburgh and of his father's unconcealed preference. Cora listened with a breathless eagerness that she strove to hide. In a very short time she had inwardly told herself that this Hilda must be the boldest and most immodest of young women. After Casper had finished his account she burn-ed to ask him many questions about the lady whom they wished him at home to marry. But she restrained the impulse, and tried not to let him see that a shadow had fallen across the keen and exquisite joy of this their first dinner together.

It was one of an extended series as the spring mellowed into summer. She had yielded to the fascination of being with him, and future renunciation of so rich a boon now became clear impossibility.

XXI.

THE Drummonds had a small cottage at Long Branch, whither they were wont to go about the first of every July. Casper would appear there when he pleased, but this summer his visits were less frequent and regular than they had ever been before. On a certain hot evening toward the close of July he came down in a late train very unexpectedly, and found his father seated on the seaward-fronting piazza, talking to a big man with a dyed black moustache and a diamond shirt-stud almost large enough to have covered one of his capacious thumb-nails.

The visitor had dropped over from a near hotel, where he and many similar gambling politicians loved to assemble. After a little while he took his leave, and Casper, who had gone into the pretty Japanese parlor where his mother sat fanning herself, went forth again as soon as he knew that his father was alone. The room had been newly furnished, and his mother had bored him by telling him the price of nearly every separate article.

Aaron Drummond was inclined to deal curtly with his son.

"I haven't seen you in a week," he said, with some gruffness, as Casper took a seat at his side.

"No," began the heir of the Drummonds. "You see, the city's been rather cool this week—"

"Oh, I don't mean about your coming down *here*," broke in his father." "That's a matter for you and your mother to settle, I s'pose. Of course she feels it, and no wonder . . I referred to your not going near me in the city. I've been there right straight along, through the whole week, as you were pretty well aware." Casper made no answer, and in another moment his father went on, this time with a new sarcastic tang in his tones : " I guess your money must have held out this month better than usual, otherwise I'd have been sure to see you at the office."

Casper stroked his moustache and stared out at the sea, which throbbed and sobbed in the starlight just over beyond the grassy bluff.

" As for it's being cool in the city," pursued his father, " *I* think the heat there has been beastly, and so does everybody else."

"Oh, pshaw!" said Casper; "people read the newspapers and persuade themselves they're broiling."

"What stuff!" muttered his father.   Then, with a roll of his dark eyes toward Casper, who sat impassive and stolid beside him, both hands thrust into his trousers-pockets, while he still preserved his hard stare at the sea, Aaron Drummond resumed, in caustic semitone :   " I guess, if you *staid* in the city, you had some good reason for not feeling how hot it was."

Casper turned quickly at this.   He had a neck-or-nothing sensation as he exclaimed :

"By Jove, dad, you've hit it.   I *did* have a good reason."

His father's lips tightened at their edges for a second, and unless the light that smote one side of his face from the inner hall erred oddly he more or less changed color.

"What do you mean?" he said, shortly and coldly.

"I mean Cora Strang," came the hurrying answer, as though he who gave it had screwed his courage to the now-or-never point.   "Don't you remember the name, dad?   She's the girl, you know, that—"

"I remember.   You've been seeing more of her, eh?"

"Yes, I have.   I couldn't help seeing more of her. It was against her will, though.   That is, at first.   She just begged me to keep away from her.   She's the truest and best and purest little thing that ever lived. We've been meeting one another a good deal in the evenings lately. I take a bite of dinner with her, somewhere, and then, by about nine o' clock or so, I leave her at the stoop of the house where she boards."

"And never go in — of course not," sneered his father. Casper knew now that the storm had gathered to its utmost and might burst at any instant, livid and resonant.

"No, dad, I do *not* ever go in!" he protested. "As I said, Cora Strang is the purest—"

"What's all this to me?" shot in his father. "What do I care for her purity or lack of it? Why have you mentioned her name here to-night? Didn't you tell me, when I gave you that note about her for Pillsbury, that there was nothing—nothing at all—between herself and you?" Aaron Drummond glared more angrily at his son, now, than Casper, in all the idle years of an indulged life, had ever known him to do before. "I ask you again, sir," the elder man continued, rapping his clenched hand on the arm of the bamboo chair in which he sat, "why have you brought up this girl's name to-night?"

Casper made a heavy, dislocating movement of his own chair, and thus faced his father. He leaned forward and put forth his hand, which was refused by a swift repulsing gesture.

"Dad," he faltered, "I—I've spoken about her because I—I'm so fond of her that I want to marry her."

"Marry her!"

Aaron Drummond spoke the words so loudly that it made his wife lift her heavy, obese body from a lounge in the neighboring parlor and move out into the hall, full of anxious tremors.

"Yes," affirmed Casper stoutly, meeting his father's irate eyes. "She's a good, sweet, honest girl, and I want to marry her. I want to give her my name and live with her all my life. She isn't—well, she isn't educated, perhaps, but a year or so would fix that. She's got it in her to be a lady. She's as good as gold. She's—"

"Marry her, then," struck in Aaron Drummond, rising. He did not speak the words in a high voice, but Casper recognized their intense wrath.

He rose, himself, raising both hands, and striving to put them on his father's shoulders. But the alderman receded, and a new effect of light touched his face, showing that it worked with acute agitation.

"Marry her, if you choose," came the hoarse, difficult words. "You'll never get a cent from *me* after you've done it. Never a cent!" His voice grew louder, and he seemed to forget that passers on the great common thoroughfare there by the sea at Long Branch might hear him and be scandalized. "Never a cent!" he repeated, and waved one hand as he passed toward the door that led into the hall. Here his wife met him, her fat form shaking with alarm.

"Oh, Aaron!" she exclaimed, "what's the matter?"

He swept by her into the parlor, and thither she followed him, with Casper not far behind. In the quiet lamplight of the pretty Japanese room these three stood looking at one another.

Casper had already weighed the force of his father's rebuff. He was the first to break silence. He addressed his mother :

"I'm in love with that girl—Cora Strang, you know, mother—the one I got dad to help at Pillsbury's. I want to make her my wife."

Aaron Drummond dropped his heavy frame into a seat, and gave a long sigh.

"Gracious, Casp!" said Mrs. Drummond, staring at her son. Then she seemed to see something in his face, and went quite close to him. Casper turned and looked at her as her hand touched his arm; he had been watching his father.

"Oh, mother!" he cried, and suddenly, strong man as he was, he burst into a flood of tears.

As his mother sought to put her arms about him he repelled her, and flung himself upon the lounge, weeping in a way that told the weakness of his character, yet equally wrung the hearts of both his parents.

Those parents looked at one another. Aaron Drummond stretched out his hands to his wife as she drew near to him where he remained seated. Mrs. Drummond grasped her husband's proferred hands, but turned her tearful face toward the drooped form of Casper.

"Oh, Aaron," she began, " if he *wants* her . . It—"

" No, no," came Aaron Drummond's quick words ; "it can't be. It can't. I won't have it. If he marries like that he quits us. I've said so and I mean it."

Casper rose, dashing the tears—real, wet, heavy tears they were too—from his eyelids. He strode toward his father, and he never showed more piteously in all his life, whether previous or to come, the dolorous feebleness of his natural fibre than when he brokenly cried :

"Oh, damn it all ! I know what you want! You want me to make a blackguard of myself ; and, by God, since you take this course with me, I'll do it if I can !" He sped from the pretty lamplit parlor in another instant.

Several hours elapsed before he re-entered his parents' cottage. He had been over at one of the hotels, where he had met some men whom he knew, and had drunk and smoked with them. His father, after a period of wakefulness, had fallen asleep. But his mother, watchful and starting at every faintest sound, heard his unsteady footsteps as he ascended to the room that all through the summer was kept ready for him.

XXII.

"No, Rudie, you can talk as you please, but I can't do any more than merely listen. I've told you just what's happened."

"Yes," answered Rudolph Champny sedately, as he and Casper sat together in one of the luxurious apartments allotted to his friend at the Fifty-Seventh Street home of the Drummonds. "Oh, yes, certainly, Casp, you've told me just what's happened, and I've given you my advice, friend to friend. Now, if you won't accept it—"

"No," broke in Casper, "I won't accept it, and that ends the story."

Rudie shrugged his shoulders. "As if you wouldn't forget all about her in three months!"

"I would not—nor in three years. No, nor in ten! Nor ever, for that matter."

"Fiddlestick, Casp," said his friend, getting up and beginning to gaze out of a window. "You *know* it is! I'll grant you the girl's nice. But you're as well aware as I am that she's not a lady."

"Oh, pooh! what *is* a lady?" fiercely sneered Casper.

"I haven't the remotest idea," said Rudie lazily; "but she isn't one."

"Very well," fumed Casper; "then she's an honest girl, and that's a thousand times better."

Rudie slowly turned away from the window. His head was drooped, and he had clasped his hands behind him. "If you don't give her up, once and for all," he said, in evident rumination, "and if you're certain (as you say you are) that marriage between you isn't possible, I don't see what the devil you're going to do. It may be that you intend—"

"Oh, never mind *what* I intend," exclaimed Casper, in a wild, random way. "I guess I don't know, myself."

Rudie laughed, and fixed his eyes in grave scrutiny on his friend's face. "I'm afraid you do know what you *intend*," he said measuredly. "But perhaps you're not at all sure whether or no you can carry your project out."

"No, I'm not," returned Casper, doggedly and with averted eyes.

"Look out," warned Rudie, coming up to his companion and clapping him on the shoulder with a brusque, abrupt hand. "New York isn't Paris in those ways. Somehow you can't eat your cake and have it here as you can there. I dare say you know what I mean, Casp."

"I know what you mean," replied Casper, with a queer, fretful laugh. He squared his shoulders and flung open his coat with an air both stern and jocose. "You've given me your advice, Rudie, and I simply say to it that it doesn't suit me. What may happen, God knows—I don't."

Rudie looked at him with a bitter smile. "In the name of all that's decent, Casp," he began, "you don't mean that you'll try——"

But here Casper sprang toward him and placed a hand over his mouth. "Don't say another word!" he cried; and then, while Rudie (who concealed the athlete, as we know, in his trim little frame) lifted his head like a man who feels himself the recipient of something closely bordering on an insult, Casper suddenly threw both arms round his friend's neck and burst forth, in tones full of sorrowing disarray:

"Rudie! Don't be angry with me! I'm a weak fellow. I don't see where I get it from, with that cold-blooded father of mine; but I'm weak as water, and . . and now that things have gone as they have gone, I—I feel as if I might do *almost anything.*"

"That's a funny confession," said Rudie in his throat.

16

He had thrice his friend's nerve and stay when the time of proof brought the time of test. He liked Casper, but he had always thought certain rather contemptuous things about his friend's real pluck and grit. He felt, just now, that his least hopeful judgments were confirmed.

August, that year, treated New York rather salubriously. In the City Hall Park, of a sunshiny afternoon, you found fewer jaded loungers than formerly on the benches ranged for their reception. A persistent breeze blew day after day across the Battery, and with a cool kiss in its wafture that made people wonder it should have got so refreshing a gift from southern sources. Stoutenburgh used to arrive every evening at his Mount Vernon home and declare that town was just as agreeable as the country. He had nearly always gone, at this season, to Saratoga with his wife and the "girls." But Mrs. Stoutenburgh shook her head, nowadays, if Saratoga was mentioned.

"Hilda don't want to go," she had said, more than once, in her usual timid way whenever addressing her husband.

"I guess Hilda don't want to do anything but mope and brood," Stoutenburgh had finally answered, "I never saw such a change come over any girl. She's got thin, too. What *is* the matter?"

He knew—or strongly suspected that he knew—what was the matter. "You don't like the idea of going to Saratoga," he said one day to his pet. "How is that? Your mother says you don't sleep very well. I think you've lost a little flesh, Hilda. Come and kiss me."

Hilda went and sat on the arm of her father's easy-chair and parted his big yellow mustaches with just the old gingerly manner that had always amused him, before she kissed him on the lips—a kiss dearer to him than his wife's—dearer to him, it may have been, than any ever given him by the lips of woman.

"I don't care much about Saratoga this summer," she

said, stroking his rather sparse hair. "I'd just as lief go if you want to go, however. Do you really want Sophie and me to go?"

Stoutenburgh had no more regard for his elder daughter han if she had been a housemaid. All his paternal love was concentrated upon Hilda, whom he thought at once the most lovable and beautiful girl that the world had yet seen. Still, he always tried to conceal his indifference for Sophia. It seemed to him that such hypocrisy was only properly duteous.

"I don't know whether Sophie wants to go or not," he now said, putting one of Hilda's hands to his lips and holding it there. "I guess she don't care much, if you don't. She nearly always wants to do what you do. We all want that—all three of us. You rule the roast with us. We can't help it, you know."

Hilda stooped and left a short, brisk kiss on her father's forehead, while she went on stroking his hair. "Oh, well, then, never mind going this year," she said.

"You say that, Hildegarde, in a kind of tired style. Ain't you well?"

She laughed softly and fleetly. "Whenever you call me 'Hildegarde,' I always feel as if you were going to scold me."

"I've never scolded you in my life."

"No, no; that's true; you never have!"

"But I want to now."

"You want to scold me!" And in her tender tyranny she slapped him gently on one of his cheeks with the hand that he had not placed against his lips.

"Yes," insisted her father, "I want to scold you now. You're forever thinking of one person—a fellow that isn't worthy of you — that doesn't deserve you."

She rose, tossing her blond head and curving her full, red lips offendedly downward. "Who told you that?' she asked, standing at her father's side with folded arms and an imperious look in her light, glacial eyes.

Stoutenburgh fidgeted in his chair. "Oh, never mind," he said. "You care for that chap, Casper Drummond. You know you do, Hilda. Come now . . You don't want to go to Saratoga because you think he won't be there." At this point Stoutenburgh jumped up and took both her unwilling hands, holding them hard while she averted her face. "Hilda!" he cried, and in his voice was a ring of pain and entreaty, "you must get over this! Darling —my sweet one—my daughter—my dear, dear Hilda! It's killing you! You must get over it! You must crush it. You *must!* Do you hear me? I say you must!"

She had fixed her eyes on his and let her hands rest so limply in the clasp retaining them that it was easy for her suddenly to draw them away and throw both arms round her father's neck.

"Oh, I can't, I can't!" she began to sob. "I love him —I love him! I know it's horrible—its unmaidenly, un-womanly, and all that! But to be without him is to be in misery! I think it's to die! I *believe* it's to die! That is so silly, so absurd! Oh, father, father!" and she buried her head in the breast of him to whom she had made this passionate confession, while he felt her frame throb and quiver in his embrace.

"To die, Hilda!" he cried. Her hysteric words had stabbed him. He took her head between his hands and lifted it, raining kisses on her face. "He isn't worthy of you, child, child!" he broke forth. "But you shall have him if you feel like that. You shall! I swear it to you, Hilda, my sweet treasure, my little pet, my angel, my only one, my dear, dear love—I swear it to you! Re-member that I do! Hear me—it's all right—I promise! I promise! And you know I never yet promised you any-thing that I didn't keep my word!"

XXIII.

ALL through these latter weeks Cora had been exaltedly happy. The dulness of Pillsbury's commercial interior had become transfigured for her. She had spent hours with Casper that left their musical echoes ringing through the rest of her nights and days. On two or three red-letter Sundays they had made little excursions into the suburbs. Once they had gone to Fort Lee and dined there on one of the piazzas of the monstrous hotel. Again they had taken a trip to Glen Island, and this Cora had enjoyed with a distinctive zest, perhaps because the weather was especially lovely. Dinner was served in a high sort of balcony whence they could watch, lying just below them, the rocky and weed-fringed shores of the island, with the glorious blue water sweeping beyond. Their dinner was exquisite, and the evening light mellowed about them while they ate. Casper lit a cigar, and the merry breeze from over the summer water blew its fragrance in Cora's nostrils. The west became a drowsy pomegranate haze, and in the sky overhead stars loitered forth like shining-robed guests in some imperial pavilion where each hates too early an arrival. Returning on the boat afterward was inexpressibly pleasant. She could let Casper put his arm round her waist and keep her hand in his without a soul being one whit the wiser, there amid the darkness of the deck. Above them the heavens had grown like a celestial meadow thick-thronged with daisies of light, and beneath them the supple and silken waves went gliding off into the gloom like mystic couriers and pursuivants.

That homeward sail was many a time lived over again in Cora's memory. Casper was so tender and shielding in his ways ; he made her tie his cambric handkerchief about her throat, lest the night air should prove too fresh here on the Sound. How soft its folds were, and how that scent of cologne on it brought back the first time she had ever met him! Repeatedly he leaned his lips to her face in the dimness, and she let him cover it with silent kisses. There seemed less harm in having him kiss her, nowadays. Only a little while ago she had shrunk from it ; there was a change in her—something that resembled the beginning of a surrender and that she could have found no words to explain. As they sat together, that evening, and were swept cityward through the starlight, a cause-less eager longing had taken hold of her. Of course she was not worthy to be his wife—oh, no, no! And yet men *had* married below them—gentlemen like him *had* done so ! (It never occurred to her, in these happy times, to suspect that he was not a gentleman of the very first grade and status, for compared with those of his sex whom she had known in former days he appeared the fine flower of nicety and cultivation.) Ah, if he should ask her, what a delight it would be ! All that furtive pain which lurked behind her joy would die on the instant then ! . . She realized that their present relations could continue like this. They were nearing a certain end, and what would that end be? Just as they could not dart along in the way they were doing now without at last coming to a terminus, giving up this dear, blended motion and repose for the discomfort of a dock and a noisy, hot city, so they could not always keep on telling one another that each was all the world to each. A change of some sort was inevitable, irreversible. And what would that change prove? Must it not of necessity be saddened by the piercing pangs of severance? Surely, yes, if the one sweet consummation were a futile desire ! Not long ago she had believed that there would be sin of a very selfish kind in marrying him, even if he should wish her for his wife. But now that, too, looked different.

How could she drag him down when she loved him so devotedly? With all her woman's heart she would strive to place herself on his own level of refinement. Alas, poor Cora! The height that she deemed almost mountainous, in her fond humility, was only a small enough hill, after all!

"I sometimes wonder," she said, that evening, when a little silence of a minute or so had passed between them—"I sometimes wonder, Casper, that you shouldn't see more than you appear to what an ignorant girl I am. I—I don't know hardly *anything*. But I guess you *do* see it, though, pretty plain . . Still" (and here a faint, excited break jarred her low voice) "I could learn quick—real quick; I most always have learnt things that way." Her next words had a daring ring as she uttered them : "I—I could soon get so that you wouldn't feel much ashamed of me, if you felt ashamed at all. That is, I guess I could!"

She waited with intense covert eagerness for him to speak, but his answer seemed very tardy in coming. It disappointed her too when it did come.

"I shouldn't ever feel ashamed of you, Cora. Don't even think of such a thing!"

This disappointed her, and she told herself afterward that he had quite failed to catch the drift of those few bold yet shy sentences. Here, however, she was quite wrong. Casper had understood her meaning, or rather he had half clairvoyantly divined it.

That evening gave him an added reason for appealing to his father as we have already heard him do. The paternal rebuff did not show itself in his manner to Cora when they met again after his return from Long Branch. A desperate resolve had now entered into his feeble, sensual, if amiable nature. He dared not face a moneyless marriage. At the same time he either dared not or would not front the cold course of renunciation that Rudie Champny had already proposed to him. And yet it

cannot be said that the thought of effecting Cora's ruin
brought to him any other sort of thrill than one of sharp
repugnance. Still, Casper had his anodyne for conscience
whenever he let his fancy picture a possible companionship of that guiltful nature. Say Cora took up her abode
with him, just as if they had sworn vows to one another
in a church. He had a little brick house in the neighborhood of Thirty-Fourth Street, between Eighth and
Ninth Avenues. It was a tiny little box of an affair, and
his father had given it to him on his twenty-first birthday,
rather grimly telling him even then that perhaps the rent
might keep him in his yearly cigars. It had scarcely done
more than this, and of late its two or three trusty tenants
had left it vacant. What, Casper would muse, if some
day he should take down the bill on that little house and
make it a pretty nest for Cora? Hardly a soul need know
that she lived there. His father was tough, but he had
reached an age when men who have done a good deal of
work are apt to sink into their graves before one has fairly
seen their forces ebb. And if his father went he would
be free to marry Cora when he chose. He would choose
'immediately' for his time—ah, *that* he would! His reparation should be prompt, swift, thorough. The whole matter
would merely turn out as if it were a kind of advance pay-
ment on his note. Cora should suffer no real disgrace.
All her after-life would be like a healed wound that does
not leave the least trace of a scar behind it. Of course,
he might die before his father did. Oh, yes, thousands of
such things *might* happen, but the risk in this instance was
a small enough one for him to feel no dread of her taking it.

With sophistry thus pitiful he strove to befool himself.
Still, justice should in one way at least be done him. He
saw in his future love for Cora no chance of satiety or
fatigue. It may be that here he judged his own heart
with entire fairness; in any case he did so with deep
sincerity. He could not tire of the sun in heaven, and to
grow weary of this enchanting girl would be to quarrel

with brightness itself. If he wronged her he would one day right the wrong, and always rank her claim upon him as not simply a sacred duty but a unique pleasure in its fulfilment.

"I'm glad we've never met any of our girls when we've been off on those little jaunts together," she told him, during a walk, one evening. "It wouldn't be a bit nice for me if we had. They've somehow got the idea about me that I'm a sort of a prude—or at least some of 'em have. I don't talk about men, men, men, the whole live-long day, as Lily Luttrell and a lot of others do; and because I keep my mouth shut on such subjects they suspect I'm either a hypocrite or else that . . . well, that I wouldn't frolic of a Sunday for anything!"

"I hope you haven't played pious with them," said Casper.

"Me! Gracious, no! I don't say much, anyhow, about what I am or what I do. But I guess that sets them thinkin'. They're accustomed to hear each other go rat-tlin' on about parties and balls and picnics and—"

"Oh, that reminds me," broke in Casper. "There's going to be such a pleasant picnic up at Jones's Wood next Saturday. I never was there but once; I went on a kind of lark three or four years ago with Rudie Champny. We used to explore the town, as we called it, in those days; we were younger then than we are now. It's a devilish jolly sort of place, Jones's Wood. It's left alto-gether to the big common crowd, but it doesn't deserve to be. Not that the building is anything much to look at, but then it's so handsomely situated—right on the bank of the East River, you know. How would you like to go with me next Thursday, Cora? We could dine together, and—"

"Oh, no, no," she said.

But her refusal had not the decisiveness it had shown at similar proposals in the recent past. Casper went on persuading her for a little while, and spoke in a sprightly descriptive vein of the funny-looking people they should meet, of how they might laugh together over them, of the airiness and freedom which belonged to the place, of the few chances they would run of stumbling against anyone they knew in so big a metropolitan crowd, and of the little cosy, dark tables on the great esplanade overlooking the river, where they might sit and have some refreshment quite unobserved, Cora taking a small bottle of the claret, perhaps, that she had lately confessed to him cheered her up without making her half so queer in the head as it used to do. . . Finally he dropped the subject altogether, and talked of other things. The rest of that evening walk was filled with a poignant unrest for Cora. Casper had never mentioned marriage to her, and he did not mention it now. But he told her (as if under the witching mesmerism wrought by her soft arm laid just above his heart) that he had had a terrible talk down there at Long Branch with his father, and that Hilda Stoutenburgh's name had come up between them, and that he had answered by a much dearer and sweeter name than that—her own.

"Mine!" faltered Cora; "oh, what did you tell him about me?"

"I told him I loved you," returned Casper, who had already half convinced himself that he had given a creditably truthful account of the domestic interview.

"You *did*, Casp? You *did?* And what did *he* say? Wasn't be awful mad? *Wasn't* he?"

"M—yes," replied Casper. "But I didn't care—and I don't now. When he's able to get a bill passed in the board of aldermen calling this town Kalamazoo instead of New York, then I'll marry that Hilda Stoutenburgh, and not before."

"Marry," shot through Cora's mind. "He says the word about her, but he never says it about me—not even to tell me that such a thing can't ever possibly happen!"

Aloud, however, she responded, with a little secret

gasp or two, which she was sure he did not notice, because she choked it down so valiantly :

" But when you told him you—you liked *me !*—what
did he say then ? "

Casper made no reply for a brief interval, though one
that seemed to her a tiny eternity.

" Oh, he blustered and carried on. Of course,
though, darling, he doesn't know you—he's never even
seen you."

Here Casper pressed her arm, but there was no reci-
procal pressure. Doubtless he understood what she was
waiting for. But in a little while he showed that he had
no wish to pursue this topic any further. And Cora had
already discovered that if he did not want to talk of a
thing he nearly always managed, in a cool, stubborn
way, that the thing shouldn't be talked of . . . Soon he
made another reference to the picnic at Jones's Wood,
and she listened with a tacit apathy.

That night she slept only by fitful half-hours or so, and
had bad dreams. Curiously enough, she was back in
the country, among the people whom she had known
since her childhood, but none of them would speak to
her, or if they did they called hard names that made her
start out of sleep with indignant words on her lips, as
from a kind of nightmare.

She did not look like her usual sweetly blooming self
the next morning when she came among the girls at the
store. Her fresh personal graces were so rarely shadowed by the least hint of blight that many eyes (and
some of them jealous eyes as well) interchanged glances
filled with subtle feminine doubt. Thus far, by some
accident of luck, no inmate at Pillsbury's had crossed her
in those nocturnal strolls with Casper.

" She looks kind o' forlorn, don't she ? " whispered to
Lily Luttrell a freckled girl with cheek-bones almost high
enough for the handles of an amphora, and with her hair
a complexity of ringlets and bandeaux. " I wonder what

she's been doin' over night. I s'pose it couldn't a been
beer, could it?" And the freckled girl giggled.

"You better ask her," said Lily, with an unaccustomed
brusqueness. "She *might* tell you to mind your own
business, though, Leonora. Folks do sometimes get
their spunk up when they're asked impudent questions."

Whatever Lily may have suspected, she did not intend
to show any of her comrades that she could think a soiling thought of Cora without weighty proof. "I sometimes feel just certain," Lily would muse, "that they're
all of 'em ate up with envy on the sly." This was probably fallacious, but, like many statements of a similar
breadth and sweep, it contained enough truth to give it
the air of having more.

By the time that Saturday evening came round, Cora
had consented to go to the picnic. They would only see
the ending of it, Casper had explained ; they would miss
all the afternoon games, the Scotch sword-dances, the
wrestling-matches, the foot-races, and the funny race
between three or four men, each tied up in a sack. But it
would be very enjoyable, nevertheless, just to walk about
and watch the dancing, provided the evening proved a
fine one.

It proved magnificent. Our New York August seldom
sees a more perfect evening than that special Saturday.
As Casper and his companion left the Elevated at Sixty-
Fifth Street and walked eastward a rhythmic breeze
blew toward them from the golden cloud-lair of the great
rising moon, which presently left it below her in shadowed splendor, like some glorious cast-off chrysalis, and
slowly kept looming loftier in a heaven that was wholly
cloudless.

On the outside, Jones's Wood building is an affair of
brown-painted boards, in every way commonplace. Its
interior, however, has an individuality. Not that this is
an important one, but that it bears a very homeliness
and gracelessness hard to describe, everything is so

dull, so ordinary, so unadorned — and yet somehow so frankly companionable. Round a large grassy tract run roofed galleries, where revellers can drink their beer at common wooden tables and witness whatever sports the particular rout to which they assemble as guests may furnish forth. All is plain and crude enough, yet the sense of spacious convenience attracts and cheers. Upstairs are galleries as well, and beyond, toward the river, broadens a great ball-room, where many a belle of Eighth Avenue or Avenue A has danced with her favored gallants till dawn paled the lamplight amid the rafters above. Still beyond this ball-room sweeps a wide, open structure of wood, with rows of benches, and with contiguous tables where countless gay feasts have been consumed and mugs of foaming wassail quaffed, through summer nights that are now but fading memories to those who once felt their charms. Jones's Wood! Ah, what a store of reminiscences it retains! Delmonico's ball-room has no more—indeed it has not so many; for the gusto of the gayety there has been different. The patrician beauty, in her pearls and laces, never thrilled, under blazing chandeliers and amid the perfume of costly blossoms, with half the spontaneous mirth, with half the holiday fervor and freedom, that some girl of the people has known here in the rude edifice where no dapper fops flutter languid eyelids and where the brightest of spangles flaunted by caste might not find a minion to cringe at their glitter. Humanity has laughed and frowned, lived and loved, below these obscure yet expansive roofs. History is not all the record of how royal people meandered through the minuet, snubbed their dearest friends, or took snuff with an ambitious commoner. The world runs away, but its passage is like that of a centipede; it moves upon innumerable feet. There is, after all, just as much life worth analysis and study in a place like Jones's Wood as in a saloon crowded with the Washington senators who make laws or the New York

stock-brokers who make speculations.   Progress is not
the enlightenment of the select few, retrogression is not
the backsliding of the refined minority, tragedy is not
the sob of the aristocrat, comedy is not the laugh of the
dandy.   If Mrs. Amsterdam dies from an overdose of
chloral the newspapers give a column to her demise, yet
they deign only a paragraph for Mary O'Shea, who flings
herself from a ferry-boat with a bastard babe clutched
against her breast.   But to chronicle what is prominent
simply means to infer the great subjacent forces that
render it so.   In the monstrous tale of civilization, that
seems to be and perhaps is so meaningless, distinction
and egotism are only a scum of society ; they rise to the
top, and hence win a fleeting evidence, a transient repute.
Between the festivities of Jones's Wood and those at Delmonico's there is but a faint dissimilar grade.   Some being from another planet would perhaps be incapable of
discerning any—just as we, with a foot poised above
some little swarming round of ants, could trace no signs
of greater or less in their conglomerate mass of brown
and tiny bodies.

To Cora the action and buoyancy of the whole entertainment were stimulantly welcome.   Merry things had
been done at the picnic throughout the day, but now a
bacchanal atmosphere at least scatteredly prevailed.   She
and Casper passed, as they traversed the galleries, a few
throngs of noisy drinkers.   In the big ball-room it told
far less of inebriety.   Here a quadrille was being played,
and the numberless couples were going through it with
steps and gestures that rarely betokened any intemperate
disarray.   All seemed continent and decent enough.
There was plenty of awkwardness and even uncouthness,
and Cora's murmurs to her companion of ''Oh, just look
at him !'' or ''Do see her !'' were gigglingly frequent.
After the quadrille music stopped a waltz was struck up,
and in a part of the adjacent gallery three or four couples
made a fiddler double the time of the orchestra with a

screeching and petulant defiance of it, while they scraped their soles against the floor in a break-down. One woman had grown ghastly pale, but she still danced on in her jerky, shuffling way, with a hand at either hip and a smile that might have clad the white mouth of a corpse. They were saying of her that she had already danced five men into a state of collapse and was prepared to do the same with five more. Her present partner had begun to prance convulsively, as though from expiring strength. "Give it to 'im, Bridget," guffawed someone. "Keep it up, Larry," blurted out someone else.

Casper thought all this a deadly bore, and soon drew Cora away from it. "I haven't seen a living soul here that I know," he said. "The waltz they're playing isn't bad. Would you care if we slip into the crowd and take a turn?"

Would she care! Her nerves were in a tremble of longing. Like everybody who dances well she loved to dance, and while they now mingled with the moving multitude it seemed to her as if her ankles were fledged with wings.

Again and again they danced. He saw how she delighted in it, and felt his own pleasure quicken because of hers. It made him proud, too, as he marked the heed that she evoked from both women and men. He knew that her lovely flushed face, with its eyes of tawny radiance, gave to many that watched it a most bewitching vision. As she stood during one of their pauses and fanned herself with her hat, she heard a male voice close at her side say in tones of contradictory scorn: "The prettiest girl *here*? You better believe it! She's the prettiest girl, I should say, that's ever been here since the place was built!"

Other tributes of admiration had floated to her ears. They filled her with an elixir-like stimulus. It was so pleasant to have him hear them, also, and to catch, by a side-glance at his face, evidence of the satisfaction they wakened.

The wine of success went to her head. She exulted in her beauty that night as she had never in all her life exulted before. Casper seemed to her surprisingly handsome compared with every other man on whom her gaze rested. The women must envy her his cavaliership ; she was sure they did. How good to have him her devoted protector like this ! How tall he was ! how comely and virile of bearing ! True, he did not dance well, but then with what a firm, aidful arm he upheld her ! Through her mind was creeping a perilous thought which is at certain hours likely to assail even the woman best guarded by all the wary sentinels of decorum. It concerned that sort of worship which makes love feminine the opposite of love masculine, and it spoke to her of the delight lurking in complete sacrifice, though self-abasement should mark the limit of such obeisance. A new light seemed to shine in her eyes as Casper searched them. It was on' the verge of his lips to whisper, "You're excited, Cora,' but he restrained the words ; they might tranquillize her, and he loved to see in her this delicate wildness, like that with which myth vestures a wood-nymph among kindred trees. Health, nature and the strong, mute speech of sex gave to her excitement a splendid justification. He who had never cared for what is poetic, dimly felt her to be, as he noted her flashing looks and her brisk motions, a live human poem, with its melodies made from sentient flesh. Such a passion stirred him that he would almost have been capable of kissing her before the throngs which engirt them, and taking their ridicule as the price of the privilege.

"You're tired," he at last said, while a polka was sending its farewell staccatos from the band. "You must rest, now. We'll find a seat, if we can, out where it's cool."

"I ain't *tired*," she answered, catching her breath a little ; "but still I guess it *would* be better if we didn't dance much more, just yet awhile."

He gave her his arm, and they went toward the spacious dusky esplanade. As they passed from the ball-room and were about to enter the domain of shadow beyond it, a small figure shot up to Cora.

"Lily!" she exclaimed. In another second she had taken her arm from Casper's, and the two girls stood facing each other, here in this vaguer light.

"Oh, Cora," sped Lily Luttrell, "I've been watchin' you! How elegant you dance!" She was pressing Cora's hand now, in her own plump and restless one. "Don't look so scared!"

"I ain't scared," said Cora, under her breath.

"*I* won't say a word. But it does me good to see you here. And he's perf'c'ly enchantin'.. Don't blush.. he *is*, and you know it. I ain't been here but a few minutes. But there's three or four hours yet, and I'm goin' to have a good time. Why shouldn't I? and why shouldn't *you*?" Here Lily gave an ebullient laugh, and seized the arm of a dark-mustached young man, temporarily deserted. "Let's both enjoy ourselves while we can!" came her soft and merry cry as she drew her escort, saucily masterful, toward the ball-room. "I'm ever so glad, Cora! It's just what I wanted; it's just what you need to brighten you up."

Cora's eyes followed her buxom, tripping form. For a brief while the sense of Lily's presence clouded her own soul. The girl, with her cheap fineries and her jocund gratulations, had swept up and merrily vanished again like some beauteous and dangerous embodiment of Vice. Her red, smiling lips had seemed to exhale temptation. She had struck a note of sympathy with Cora's mood, catching conscience off its guard. But the revulsion had been sharp, and Cora's cheeks burned with something hotter than the heat of her recent dancing as she replied to Casper's immediate questions.

"So that's Lily Luttrell, is it?" he said. "What a jovial little thing she seems to be!—just as you described her— Here are two nice seats. Oh, this is glorious! How good the breeze feels, doesn't it?"

"Delicious," replied Cora.

They could just see one another now, across the table at which they were seated. The ball-room, yards away, had an unreal, visionary look, with its lights and moving shapes. Two or three bats, out here on the esplanade, were making their dizzy zigzags in the white glare of the electric lights. The music crashed more melodiously at this distance, and the sweet, wild wind seemed in some sort of tricksy league with its echoes. Their table was close against a wooden railing, which might have been marble or porphyry in the beautifying dusk, and if they had chosen to glance a little sharply over its edge they could have seen how the earth broke down in a rocky bluff toward the river, whose waters a full moon had bediamonded. This romantic dazzlement suited the clicking of beer-glasses and the odor of beer as well. No flight of fancy was needful to make these luminous waters Rhenish or to turn the big, sad Blackwell's Island prison on the opposite bank into a semblance of baronial halls. Cora's previous buoyancy quickly returned. In the low talk that ensued she forgot Lily as if the gay creature's presence had been a mere transit of some disturbing shadow.

"What did you tell the waiter to bring?" she asked of Casper.

"Why? are you hungry?" he answered.

"No ; but I'm thirsty—very. Still, I don't want any wine. A little sass'p'rilla, or lemon-soda, or something like that."

"Why, won't you take a few sips of wine?" he asked.

She shook her head. "Oh, I'm queer enough already."

"Queer? Why, you don't mean that the claret you took before we came here has—"

"Oh, no ; not that."

"What makes you queer, then ?" he inquired, as they peered at each other fascinatedly in the dimness.

"Oh, I don't know. I guess it was the dancin'; I'm so fond of it."

"Ah—then it's only the dancing you're fond of, eh? I thought perhaps—but never mind."

She laughed, throwing back her head for an instant. "Well, what did you think? Tell me."

"I thought dancing *with me* might have set you up a little. I'm only judging you by myself, though. I know how dancing with you has affected *me!*"

"How?" she murmured.

"Take hold of my hand, and I'll tell you."

"Not here—not here."

"Only for a second. It's so dark that we needn't mind a bit. And, anyway, what if we *are* seen ? . . ."

Cora reached out her hand, but she suddenly withdrew it just as his fingers were closing about it. A waiter had seemed to resolve himself from shadow, close behind Casper. Glasses were soon furnished them, and in another moment or so Cora said rather anxiously :

"What's in that big bottle? I--I didn't want wine. I told you that I—"

"Oh, just taste how nice this is," returned Casper . . . Then the yellow, foaming fluid began delicately to foam and hiss in their glasses. "I hope it's cold," Casper went on. "Oh, yes, it's like new-melted ice," he pursued, after taking a gulp of it. "There, now ; that will quench your thirst as nothing else can. Just you try it, and see if I'm not right."

Cora raised one of the glasses to her lips. She was very thirsty. The sense of refreshment was unspeakable.

"No, I won't take a drop more," she said, after about three-quarters of an hour had passed, seeming to her scarcely longer than ten minutes.

"Oh, well, you needn't if you don't want," lightly exclaimed Casper. "It's done you good, Cora. I can see how your eyes are sparkling."

As he spoke he filled her glass again. She turned from it and leaned a moment against the wooden railing. How divine looked the moon-mantled river! The music still floated to them from the ball-room. Voices and laughter rose and fell among the dim throngs gathered on the espanade. "I am so happy, so happy," she thought. She tried to explain why she was happy, but the answer of emotion came so quickly it drowned all reasoning. Oh, yes, the cause lay only in his love, his nearness, the full conception of how he cared for her.

She turned to him again. Her own words rang strangely to her as she spoke them, but their tones were quite soft and very clear.

"This ought to be our last night together."

"Cora! Why?"

"Oh, because—you know why. What's the use of my tellin' why? There's something you should say—and do as well. It's more a thing of doin', though, than of sayin'. Casper Drummond, you know what I mean. You needn't try to make me believe you don't."

A silence followed. "Perhaps I do know," he presently said.

And then she heard a great sigh leave him. Would he speak again? Would he speak what she was waiting to hear? Surely she had never before loved him like this. How her head spun! how her blood tingled! And yet it was pleasant; there was no faintness or weakness about it; there was only strength—a strength and a daring that surprised but did not frighten her. Was this what champagne did to you? Where had she heard that it was a treacherous wine for women to take?—women who were girls like herself?.. No matter! It gave her courage; it had made her bold enough to almost ask him if he would not marry her. Perhaps if she drank a little more she would gain a power over him that he could not resist. She began to sip from the glass that he had lately replenished.

"Cora," he now said, suddenly bringing his chair round to her side so that he faced the river, and the moonlight struck full on his face, "listen to me, darling. I would marry you to-morrow—to-night, if—"

She put her hand on his shoulder. "Marry me to-night!" she said. "Don't wait till to-morrow. You've told me a hundred times that you love me. We—we can't go on like this. If you say you ain't willin', all right; I'll leave you and never speak to you again as long as I live!"

"I'd marry you to-night if I didn't care for you so much," he said. "It's because I do that I'm a coward, Cora, and don't dare. Yes, that's the God-honest truth!" .. And then his voice broke into her swimming brain with sentences that seemed to her the richest eloquence. He painted the sternness of his father; he lied (and with a lie that his burning selfishness made almost an unconscious one) about the probability of that father's brief future life. He swore marriage to her, but with a provisional meaning that did not there and then appear repulsive to the ears which drank in his words. Like many another man who plays a part reeking with rascality he mixed his bad, insidious plea with elements of vivid feeling and relative truth. He was genuine, judged by paradox from the standpoint of his primal falsity.

"And, oh, Cora, dear, dear girl," he said at last, "if you'd only cling to me and believe in me till I'm free, I'd fix everything between us right in the end!—right as marriage could make it! .. the marriage that would give us a long, happy life together, with—with money that's sure to come to me, and with no shame for you, but only peace and comfort and good-standing in the eyes of the world!"

As they rose to go she wished she had not taken that last glass. It had somehow a headier effect than the others. They were out in the moonlight now, and yet

she had no clear remembrance of leaving the great pavilion. Going down-town in the Elevated afterward was
like a whirl and a blur.

"This isn't my street," she at length grew plainly
aware that she was telling him. She had talked and
laughed during their little journey, but she could not
recall anything she had said.

"No," he answered ; "but it isn't far away from your
street." Then, very soon, he paused, and laid a hand on
the stoop-railing of a small brick house.

After that he spoke a few soft words, filled with great
persuasive eagerness.

"Oh, no, no," she faltered ; but she did not try to
rush away from him when he caught both her hands and
began again to speak.

"Just come in for a few minutes and see how pretty it
all is," he pleaded. "I've told you about it before, you
know. It's my own little house that I haven't been able
to rent for some time. We'll slip out again the instant
you say so. I've my latch-key with me here. Come in
and see how you like the little parlor. Nobody 'll know.
Come!"

He drew her up the steps. A great nervous sob sounded
in her throat as he thrust his key into the lock of the door
. . A few more seconds and the door had closed behind
them both, and the little stoop gleamed vacant again.

In a great marine city like New York there are always
at night those weird cries of steam-whistles from boats on
the neighboring rivers. Even when the weather is clear
they occasionally peal forth, lonely and lugubrious as
fabled screams of the damned.

Such a sound rang out on the stillness now. It had a
peculiar, lingering melancholy ; and to anyone aware
that a new act in the tragedy of a life had been begun by
this commonplace closing of a door it must have appealed through terms of analogy dismal and terrible.

XXIV.

AFTER we have struck certain boldly sinful bargains with fate it often happens that the pleasure of our purchase clothes us for weeks in a kind of brazen armor against remorse. It was this way with Cora. The first few days lapsed along for her in a pathetic hurry of happiness, and at their end she found that she had performed certain tasks which exhilaration had not permitted her to dread. She had pulled up her roots permanently, so to speak, from the Pillsbury soil, and had met, with excellent coolness, all questions from the girls as to whether she would soon be married or no— and especially from the roguish and more inquisitive lips of Lily Luttrell. At her boarding-house she had rather carelessly told the smooth little falsehood which Casper invented for her, and directed that her trunk be sent to the address given as her new one. She felt it fortunate that this was in a street unsuggestive of the least luxury, though if the contrary had been the case she would per- haps have paid such a circumstance hardly any heed. Her indifference was not born of the least bravado. She simply found herself unconcerned by ordinary events because the mesmeric magnitude of her love enthralled both spirit and sense. It was difficult for her to realize anything with very great clarity, nowadays. A mist curled from the swinging censer of passion, and through its folds reality seemed remote, almost profitless.

Her only regular companion in the house where she had come to live was a woman of middle-age named Lydia, who easily took all the requisite work on her shoulders. They were broad shoulders, for Lydia had both the face and frame of some Carlovingian woman, and with her long, large limbs, heavy bust, square jaws, and brooding eyes, towered at once majestic and grotesque. Sadness, too, clung about her like a grayish nimbus ; but it would not have been so depressing a gloom if the woman had not seemed so to hate speech. She dealt, as might be said, in dissipations of silence ; her taciturnity was gigantic, like herself. For whole days Cora would get no answer from her more expanded than "Yes, ma'am" and "No, ma'am." And yet she looked as if capable of saying a great deal more than that ; or, at least, she gave signs of possessing enough mental power to have bowed in other times beneath some burdensome sorrow.

"I wonder if she's always been so dumb and strange," Cora said to Casper. "Sometimes it's almost like havin' a ghost movin' 'round, though she is so big and solid."

"I don't know anything about her," he replied, "except that she was here when my last tenants left, and I asked her to stay and take care of the house. I guess she's solid, Cora, in more ways than one," he added.

"You mean honest ? Oh, yes ; I guess she is, too."

"But if she troubles you with that glum style of hers I'll send her away and get somebody else."

"Oh, no," objected Cora. "I wouldn't have you do that for anything."

Still, there were times when she would have liked a more companionable servant. Casper could not always be there with her ; indeed, his absences were often somewhat prolonged, for politic reasons that concerned his father's daily trips to town or both his parents' temporary sojourn at Long Branch. Cora told herself that she would have preferred an associate of her own sex in whom she might, to a certain degree, confide, instead of this grim creature who doubtless *knew the whole truth* and yet never sought by one social sign to abate her own loneliness.

The next few Sundays Casper spent at Long Branch,

but during several evenings of week-days they made visits together to suburban places. Now, however, a spell of curious change had set in, distinct as it was indefinable. They did not enjoy their bohemian rambles with half the keenness of other times. Not that they wearied of one another's company. Far from this ; yet the old spice of novelty had somehow died out of their mutual converse. These meetings were no longer flavored with the delicious charm of stolen opportunity. They ate their forbidden fruit, at present, within the precincts of their own garden. To roam abroad showed them no fruit of a more tempting taste on the boughs of other trees.

For the first time in her life, too, Cora felt the tedium of idleness. She did not care to go out much during the day, half because the weather was now nearly always hot and often insufferably so, and half because the open-air sun had another kind of glare for her, not explainable by thermometric results. Work had became a second nature to her, and the sewing and mending that she now and then was called on to do barely deserved such a name. Casper had scoffed at the idea of her making her own clothes. Buying her some pretty gowns and hats and street-costumes had been one of the few earthly joys that could add to his contentment while it took from the weight of his purse. But a little serious dressmaking would have relieved matters wonderfully with Cora. There were books in the house,—novels that seemed to tell of tears and passion and intrigue,—but long ago she had lost the art of reading, and now was no period in which to train faculties that events had fevered and pre-occupied.

One day, however, a chance word or two from Casper made her bitterly reflect on her own uneducated state. She began to crave tuition, and felt within her a capacity for the most ardent study.

" I want to learn how to talk just right," she told Casper ; "I want to say things just as you say 'em, and not with a kind of a hop and jerk and stumble, as *I* say 'em. I'd like to feel that when we get married and you introduce me to folks as your wife, I'm goin' to appear quite nice and proper."

But Casper shook his head in gentle negation. "There's time enough," he said. "What's the use of bothering about the matter yet awhile? Besides," he added, "you're not half as ignorant as you suppose."

One day he said to her : "To-morrow'll be Saturday, won't it ? Well, I shall have to go up and pass Sunday at Mount Vernon. I'd rather be thrashed, but still I'll have to go."

"Mount Vernon ?" she said. "Why, you don't mean you'll leave me all Sunday, Casper ?"

"I hate to think about it—especially when I recollect who I'm going to see."

"Who *are* you going to see ?" came her question. She had believed herself so perfectly conversant with all his affairs that it seemed odd indeed to address him in such terms.

"Why, can't you guess ?" he returned ; and then she saw that his manner somehow was not his own, and that perhaps he was intensifying the blithe look about his eyes to conceal an embarrassment there.

"Guess ?" was her wondering answer. The color slipped from her cheeks. "That girl lives at Mount Vernon ! I remember you told me ! You can't mean, Casper, that you're goin' to see *her* ! "

"I'm going to see the whole Stoutenburgh tribe," he said. "I'm obliged to."

"Obliged ! "

"Oh, look here ! " he exclaimed. "Do you mean to repeat, like that, every confounded word I say ? " He did not speak with the least anger. He went up to her the next instant, and put both hands on her shoulders, while he looked smiling into her eyes.

" But it ain't right for you to go there ! " cried Cora.
" You know why. That young lady is fond of you—she
loves you dearly—she wants you to be—." Here a
look of terror spread over the girl's face. "No, no," she
went on, and caught his hands with clinging wildness.
"Casp ! You gave her up when—when you took *me*,
once for all ! Oh, you *did* do that, didn't you, Casp ?
You *haven't* been foolin' me, have you? When—when
you're free you'll make it all right for me, won't you ?
Oh, remember how I've loved you, and how much I've
given up because of my love—and yours as well ! For
I ain't really doubtin', you know. It may seem so, but it
ain't true. I believe in you just as much as I did *that
night.* Only, promise me you'll stay away from *her !*
Promise—only promise ! "

He put his arms about her and spoke many comforting
words while she wept with violence on his breast. He
was deeply sorry for her, and his pity had begun to tell
him that he would be false in the most hideous of fash-
ions if **he** did not pay her jealous outburst all loyalty of
respect.

" There, there," he said, in the soothing voice with
which we appease a terrified child. " You've my full
promise not to go. I nearly swore to my father, the
other day, that I would spend Sunday with the Stoutenburghs, but since you feel as you do I'll fix up some excuse—yes, even if it's the worst fib that I ever told him,
and I *have* told him some pretty respectable whoppers in
my time ! "

He said a great deal more than this, and lulled her
fears if he did not entirely calm them. But it was never
the same with her after that hour. Dread was forever
assailing her at odd and unforeseen moments ; it came like
a cloud-shadow that suddenly sweeps across the sunshine.
Now and then, while alone, she would make up her mind
to fall on her knees the next time they were together and
implore him that he would at once enter into a secret

marriage with her. But the dislike of wounding and
irritating him would afterward reassert its power, while,
blended with such feeling, was a reluctance to push his
love past the bounds of its present tolerating fondness.

In one sense the folly of calling marriage a failure was
amply shown between these two mated yet still separate
beings. The surrender of the woman had brought with
it that sort of distrust which a language of policy best
describes as the burning of your bridges or ships. Cora
was like one who sojourns in a land where he dares not
tell his true nationality, and hence has no redress in case
of seizure or imprisonment. To enforce by law the act of
matrimony from Casper would have been to loathe such
terms of rehabilitation, and to loathe herself, as well, for
having demanded them. Hence regret had begun to
gnaw at her heart with a fang that each new day sharpened and strengthened. All now depended on the choice
of a man who had not scrupled to dip her innocence in mire. Would such a man save her when the
time came? Dared she to hope so? Occasionally an
impulse would visit her to fly from him and never let him
look on her face again. All the rest of her life should be
both a prayer for his weal and a stern resolve to avoid
further sin! She would prove it untrue that the first step
in wrong-doing counts with a woman so fatally. But to
plan a desertion of him was easier than to carry it out ;
for the merely physical spell he exerted over her was
potency itself, and her eyes would thirst for his face if
only a few hours kept them deprived of it.

Meanwhile Aaron Drummond had come very near
having an open rupture with his son. "I don't know
what queer pull Stoutenburgh has got upon you," Casper
had said to his father one day, "but it certainly looks
very much as if you were a good deal afraid of him."
These words had not been spoken very meaningly, but
their effect upon Drummond was to make him turn pale
and dart a wrathful look into Casper's face.

"I'm afraid of no man, you scamp!" he cried, with savagery.

The assertion was perhaps at this moment quite true. And yet a few days later it ceased to be true. Jacob Stoutenburgh dropped into the office of his so-called friend, and for some little time a most cordial conversation took place betwen them.

"You're down from Mount Vernon for good, then, with all your folks?" Aaron Drummond at length inquired.

"Yes; we got back three days ago."

"All the family well, I hope."

"Pretty well, thank you, Drummond—pretty well—" Stoutenburgh had begun to rub his yellow moustache into the curved palm of one big hand—"that is," he proceeded, "my second daughter, Hilda, feels . . I s'pose low-spirited's the word."

"Low-spirited, eh?"

"One thing appears to suit her about as well as another. That's a bad sign in a young girl, you know. Ain't it, now?"

"I guess it ain't a very good sign. Let me see—Hilda was the lightest of the two?—of course—yes."

"She's the one I had a fancy, not very long ago, that your son might—a—be going to—take a liking to."

Stoutenburgh had been looking down as he spoke these words, but he now lifted his cold blue eyes. Drummond's cold black ones met them.

"I'm afraid," the latter said, in a sullen, spiritless way, "that Casper never means to marry anybody."

The brewer shrugged his shoulders and smiled. "That's his own business. But I think any young man that behaves so is . . well, he is—"

"A fool," broke in the alderman bluntly—"an infernal fool—provided he might get such a wife as your daughter'd make him."

Jacob Stoutenburgh nodded slowly, and appeared to relish this compliment, bluff though its delivery had been.

He had come here to the office of Aaron Drummond in order to effect a certain purpose. It was founded on something in him excessively human—the deep, admiring love that he bore his daughter. But he was prepared, nevertheless, to be inhuman in carrying it out. He held, as might be said, a dagger, but he would somehow have liked to show his weapon without taking it from a sheath palpably silken. If this could be done he meant to try and do it. Otherwise he would reveal himself as that man of iron firmness who had built up a great business out of nothing by sheer force of competitive energy. And so he now said, in a voice that was not far from being one of suavity :

" I guess Hilda *would* make him a good wife. She's a good girl, and a handsome one, too. At least *I* think her handsome. And your Casper's a fine-looking fellow. They'd make a very pretty pair ; don't you agree with me that they would ? "

" Certainly I do. I've told you as much before. But now I've got tired."

There was a kind of hopeless curtness in these words of Drummond's. It was easy for the brewer to perceive, however, that they veiled no personal rebuff.

"Your boy hasn't the steadiest habits," gently pursued Stoutenburgh. "Still, he's young yet. I'd trust him ; I like him, and I'd trust him. . . But you're of the belief that he doesn't ever want to be my girl's husband? Isn't that so?"

"What's the use of my disguising the truth?" said Drummond. "He doesn't want to marry anybody, as you've just heard me say."

Stoutenburgh scanned the floor, and kept silent for so long a time while he did so that his companion at length fell to watching him with a stealthy, sidelong glance.

"Ah—yes," murmured Stoutenburgh, when the silence had become painful. . . "Can't you do anything?" he abruptly asked, lifting his head again.

Drummond now spoke with irritation. "Good heavens!" he shot out, "how can I make my son marry if he doesn't want to? Could you make your daughter do it if she were bound to stay single?"

"I might," came the quiet answer.

"You might?" Here Drummond laughed, a little mockingly. "Upon my soul, I'd like to know how you'd go to work."

"You're getting angry, Drummond."

"No I'm not. But if I should get so, I—I'd have some sort of provocation."

"Why?"

"Because you're so devilish obstinate." Drummond's black eyes flashed, and his lips took a slight sneer. "After all, Stoutenburgh," he went on, in the hard tones whose imperiousness had been heard by not a few of his constituents, "my son isn't the only young man in New York whose father will leave him a pot of money when he dies!"

The brewer's eyes faintly sparkled. "Look here," he said; "I wouldn't have your son marry my daughter only on his prospects; understand that."

The alderman stared. "Oh, you wouldn't! Then you want—?"

"I want him to marry Hilda, but I want three hundred thousand dollars to be settled on him when he does so."

"When he does so!" Here Drummond sprang from his chair, pale and indignant.

The brewer rose, but without haste. "When he does so —yes. And he must."

"Must!"

"Yes. You must bring it round."

"Have you lost your wits, man?"

"I guess I've got 'em just where I want 'em," coolly replied Stoutenburgh. "Don't lose yours; I advise you not to. You did once. It was some time ago. You and little Tom Farrish had a correspondence together about a certain matter—the Improved Street-Cleaning 'deal.' Do you remember it?"

Drummond made no answer. His new pallor was one, however, in its mute way.

"Farrish once brought me two letters," pursued Stoutenburgh, with the sparkle in his eyes getting a little keener. "Farrish hated you, and he let me see those two letters because of his hate. I took the letters and studied them over. I've always been rather a long-headed person, as perhaps you'll agree. The letters were what any court would call damning to you; they weren't like you a bit; you gave yourself away in them pretty bad; I should say you'd always before been twice as prudent."

There was a silence. "You've got those letters now?" asked Drummond, more brokenly and hoarsely than he had almost ever spoken in his life.

"Farrish thinks I haven't," replied Stoutenburgh. He took out a cigar from his waistcoat-pocket and slowly bit off its end. "I gave back *two letters* to your brother-alderman. . oh, yes; certainly I did. But they were not those."

"Not—those?"

"Not a bit of it. I happened to know a fellow that was wonderful at imitating people's handwriting. I gave him the letters Farrish had given me. 'Could you get me up fac-similes of those?' I asked him. I let him understand that I didn't merely want the writing copied, but the color and size of the paper, with every least little speck or spot or mark on its surface. The man seemed doubtful, at first, of his own skill. But he was needy, and I guess that fact made him work all the harder. What he showed me, in a day or two, almost took my breath away. Farrish pocketed the bogus letters without a suspicion. I kept the real ones. There's the whole story. It's very simple—but it means a good deal."

Aaron Drummond gnawed his lower lip. "It means

you want three hundred thousand dollars," he muttered, " as their price."

The brewer gazed at his unlit cigar and appeared to be making a personal remark as he said :

" I want your son *and* the money. I want it to go along *with* him. I'll give my girl the same sum the day she's Mrs. Casper."

Drummond slowly folded his arms as the two men now stood and faced one another. All ire seemed to have left him, but he looked like a man under the lash of some acute worriment.

" That's a fair enough bargain," he said ; " but it's a strange one for you to wish to strike with me."

"True ; it is a strange one."

" Marry your daughter to the father of the man you can prove dishonest ! " The laugh with which Drummond spoke these words had a ghastly harshness. " Did anybody ever hear of such a thing before ? "

Stoutenburgh gave one or two quick nods. " Perhaps not," he said, in dogged semitone. " But what you've done scores of other men have done too. I don't blame you so much. Politics are politics. I'm not squeamish, myself, about the sort of things those letters make plain. To the victors belong the spoils. I dare say that if I'd been in your place I'd have turned out just as hot a spoils- man. As for this proposal I'm putting to you now, it's all a matter that concerns my girl, Hilda. Women have freaks ; and when one of 'em is the child you'd lay down your own life for twenty times over, why, then, putting pride in your pocket seems like a very easy thing. It seems so to me now, anyway. I'm thought a pretty cold-blooded man, Aaron Drummond, but nobody that ever saw much of me when I was in the company of Hilda could say I wasn't an affectionate father. If she asked for the earth I'd try and get it for her. Well, your son ain't exactly the earth, is he ? . . And on their wed- ding-day—two minutes after they're married, if you

18

please—I'll give you those letters. There, now ; do you want to shake hands on it ? "

Stoutenburg held out his hand, approaching three or four steps nearer to the alderman.

Drummond did not stir. His arms remained folded.

"Would your Hilda agree, then, to marry a man," he said, "who'd been bought for her as you want to buy my Casper ? "

The brewer's face clouded fiercely, and the hand he had put forth fell at his side, knotting itself.

"No !" he burst forth. "By heavens, no ! And if you let her hear a hint of these terms I'm offering you'll have the screws put on you so terribly tight that you'll feel sorry for it till the last hour you live ! "

Aaron Drummond had no answer but silence. Except for his paleness no outward sign told of the forlorn heart-failure those last defiant words had caused. For he was thinking, with that speed of reflection that mingled fright and despair understand :

"Does Casper love me enough, after all, to save me ? This man's threat is not based on a lie. Well, if Casper would let me go to the dogs as a poor father, perhaps he'll keep me from them as one that can bribe him with a three-hundred-thousand-dollar bribe. "

After another second or two he went quite close to Stoutenburgh. He did not extend his hand, but there was the sort of change on his face that made it seem as if he would not have been disinclined to do so.

"See here," he said, with a tone of evident conciliatory import ; "there's no use getting so riled for nothing. Let's both sit down again and talk this thing over. Let's talk it over quietly, I mean, without any more foolish heat. "

They sat down, and they did talk the thing over. It should be recorded, too, that the rest of their converse was in every way more placid than the previous part.

XXV.

THE early weeks of autumn brought no new shock to Cora. She was keenly anxious and unhappy, but she tried to conceal from Casper that any trouble weighed on her mind. It was not long, however, before she perceived in him a gloom that he palpably sought to hide from her. There was no lack of the old loving treatment, but the sunshine that had been so wont to gild it had faded into a sickly glimmer. It seemed as if he *could* not smile as he used to do when he looked into her eyes; but more distressing, more terrifying than that he could not was that he so resolutely tried. What was he struggling to keep back from her? Had his father found out the real truth? and was he loth to make her aware of all the agony this must mean for each of them?

He did not arrive at his appointed time one afternoon, and on his coming between nine and ten o'clock that same evening he found her piteously excited. She clung to him, trembling and wordless, with her head drooped against his breast.

"Why, what on earth makes you act this way?" he said, while he stroked her head. "Did you expect not to see me till to-morrow?"

"I—I ain't sure *what* I expected, Casp," she quivered: and then she burst into profuse tears.

But the truth soon transpired. In answer to one or two of his kind-spoken questions came the admission that she had been very fearful of his not appearing at all. "And oh, Casp!" she broke out passionately, "there's times when I'm afraid you may desert me altogether!"

He started, and looked fixedly, for a brief while, at her

flushed cheeks and glistening eyes. "You're getting to be horribly timid," he returned, as he lowered his head a little.

It was not the reply that she had craved or waited for.

"Casper," she said, after a little pause, during which she searched his face with troublous, avid stare, "has —has your father found out that I'm livin' here ? "

" I think he suspects you do, Cora," was the plainly reluctant answer.

" Has—has he spoke, Casp, any more to you about marryin' that —that other girl ? "

Again her lover started ; and this time he bit his lip after doing so and gave a quick, impatient frown. " Yes, he has ! The devil take it all, he's trying to drag me into the match."

"And you, Casp ? you're. . . you're not. . . goin' to let yourself. . . be dragged ? "

He looked down, and smothered an oath.

"What's a poor chap to do ? " he muttered.

"Casp ! "

"Circumstances are sometimes too strong for men with twice my nerve and character."

"Oh, Casp ! you're not goin'—"

"Cora, look here. There never was whiter truth meant to a girl than I meant to you."

She caught his hands and fell on her knees before him. Her face had grown marble, and from it blazed with passionate pleading the gold-brown eyes that had so tempted him to lay on her the curse of his love.

"You mean it now !" she gasped. "Yes, you do ! you do ! " She swung herself back and forth on his hands while she clutched them, her entire mien one ardor of supplication, deprecation, prayer. " You ain't goin' to tell me you'll play me false after all ! You couldn't be like that ! It ain't *in* you, Casp, no matter what your father wants ! I'll work my fingers to the bone for you if you'll only marry me ! We can live, no matter what *he* does ! Yes, we can live ! I'll teach you how to work if you don't know how ! I'll make you so happy ! You're strong, and ever so much smarter than you think ! "

" Cora ! " he cried, " it isn't that I wouldn't stick by you through thick and thin. But my father's in the power of *her* father. He—he'll be ruined, Cora, unless I. . . Oh ! for God's sake don't look so horrible ! What can I do? You wouldn't have me see my own father branded, shamed, disgraced—you don't want me to desert him in the hour of his need for me—for me, who can save him when nobody else in the whole world can. You'll be generous, Cora, and let me prove to him that the same blood runs in our veins. Come, now, use your reason. Though I'm her husband in the law I'll always be yours in love—in . . My God ! Cora ! What is it? Cora ! "

He stooped down, catching her as she sank in a dead swoon at his feet.

For a second or two he covered her face with kisses. Then he lifted her bodily in his strong arms and bore her to a near sofa.

'It's only a faint !' flashed through his thoughts. He drew a large roll of bank-notes from one of his pockets and thrust it into her breast. 'Better leave her like this once and forever,' ran his fleet musings. 'When she comes to herself she'll find *that*. What I've been a coward about saying for so long I can say this way. And then I'll write to her as well—I'll write to her very soon. And she can stay here for months yet. Only I won't come back until it's over. I won't—for there'd be no use. I've given dad my promise. . . '

He turned away, and while he did so the tears that are wept by just such weak dastards as himself gushed from his eyes. He had passed along the tiny outer hall and was about to descend the little staircase leading into the hall below it when a figure confronted him. It was that of Lydia, the large-moulded, melancholy, silent woman.

" You will find Mrs. Strang in yonder," he said, pointing toward the room in which he had left Cora, and using the name some time ago decided upon as that by which she should be called. "She isn't well—I think she has fainted. Go to her, will you, please?"

He saw no sign of surprise in the servant's broad, sad, placid face. Just as Lydia began to move toward the threshold of the room where Cora was lying, he hastened downstairs, opened the small front door, and passed forth into the street.

A little while later, when Cora unclosed her eyes, the first thing they rested on was the rugged, composed face of Lydia, who was chafing one of her hands.

"Do you feel better, ma'am?" the woman presently asked. Her words had somehow the effect of a stone statue speaking.

"Yes—I don't know . . . Lydia?"

"Well, ma'am."

"Did Cas—did Mr. Drummond leave the house?"

"Yes, ma'am ; nearly ten minutes ago."

Just then Cora felt something weigh against her chest, and drew forth, with trembling hands, the package of bank-notes that Casper had thrust into the bosom of her dress. Some impulse made her swiftly try to conceal her discovery from Lydia.

"He left you that," said the woman, with a slight solemn bending of her large head.

"How do you know?" sharply asked Cora.

"They most always do."

Cora shuddered. This creature, with her immobility and her pensiveness, was like a humanized Fate. "What do you mean?" said Cora, looking from the money to Lydia's face with her dazed, glittering, woe-begone eyes. "'They most always do?' Then you know what—what he is to me?"

"Oh, yes ; I know." The woman smiled, and there was something in her smile that struck its observer as both unfathomably wise and weary. "Did you think I didn't ?" And then she laughed; and her laugh seemed to have half the weariness and wisdom of all the world in its fleeting, dismal tones. "He's left you now, and I don't believe you'll ever see him again. But you ought to punish him. You ought, and you can." Here Lydia's broad brows drew themselves together in a frown of scathing sternness. "*I* didn't. I was a fool, and just didn't. But the law makes your case a clear one, or at least I'll swear it does, after the way I've watched you."

Cora feebly rose into a sitting posture on the lounge. "The law!" she murmured. "As if it could help such as I am! As if it could put together the two pieces of a broken heart."

"Don't you care a fig about whether he's broke your heart or not," austerely counselled Lydia. "Throw away those two pieces; you'll find you can get on all right enough without 'em—never just the same as before, perhaps, but a good deal better than you expected. Concern yourself with damages of a very different sort; you can guess those I mean."

Cora dimly felt that she could guess . . . After Lydia had left her she tried to count the money that Casper had put in the front of her robe—and to think. The sum would keep her for a considerable time yet. But she could not stop here beneath his roof after what he had said to her. She would go—but whither? She did not know; she was too mentally tortured to decide. Anyway, she would leave *his* house before another hour passed. He wanted her to stay there and have him come to her after he had married Hilda Stoutenburgh. He wanted her to be. . No! rather the dregs of infamy than that! After all, what was much lower than the degradation into which she had fallen? He had betrayed her. He had made the vestment of self-contempt that covered her one thick-woven and impossible of escape.

In a little while she had decided just what to do. It

would all be very simple. The same trunk which had held her possessions when she quitted the boarding-house should hold these and a few more when she returned to it. Many things that he had given her she would leave behind, taking only those that would prove of actual use hereafter . . . And yet she had hardly begun the process of packing before certain souvenirs of the immediate or more recent past thrilled her to tempestuous tears.

"Oh, I cannot go! I cannot leave him, after all!" she sobbed, while kneeling beside her open trunk. Then, suddenly, she would try to steel her nerves and swallow her tears, not succeeding so very ill, either, in the doleful little effort . . Nearly all her preparations were ended by the time that the early autumn dusk had begun. And then Lydia came into the room where she stood pale, disconsolate, and handed her a letter.

It was from Casper. In a certain sense it was eloquent. It sought to veil the enormity of his desertion by professions of undying love. It pleaded of her to remain where she now was until after his marriage. He would send her more money in another month or so. It would be a new torment to him if she did not thus consent to remain. That very afternoon he had had a most stormy interview with his father, who had forced from him a promise not to see her again until the wedding was over. What he did was hateful to him, and yet it was done, as he had told her, as he would like to tell her a thousand times over and over again, simply because his father's name must be snatched from the clutches of a frightful scandal. But such a love as theirs ought not to suffer the misery of mutual separation on this account. She would forgive him! She was so much more capable than he of all noble deeds like that. Perhaps for several days her heart would rebel against forgiveness, but in the end she would surely conquer even the rightful anger that she felt, and show herself the sweet saint nature had made her.

Meanwhile, so far as concerned his devoted, adoring fondness, that would last in spite of every obstacle a cruel fate might raise between them. . . .

"It *has* lasted already!" she moaned aloud, in the despairing sarcasm of her tortured spirit. "Oh, it's lasted ever so long, ever so splendid!" She crushed the letter wildly between both hands, and then she smoothed it out again with a feverish care and re-read every word of it for at least the tenth time. Then, spurred by an altered impulse, she tore it into many fragments and cast them into the black, fireless grate, where they lay and glared at her like so many hueless yet vivid fragments of her shattered happiness.

That night she slept—or rather lay awake, with throbs and tremors of anguish—in one of the rooms of the boarding-house at which she had dwelt during her term of service as a shop-girl. The landlady had eyed her suspiciously when she reapplied for lodgment there, and had coolly told her that only a single room in the house was vacant, and that this would be more than double the price she had formerly paid. Offering no objection to the amount required, she had paid a week's board in advance. Afterward came the ordeal of facing certain people in the house whom she had known of old. She passed through this trial, wondering if they would not find her changed to a striking degree, even after these few hours that had followed the advent of her misfortune. They did find her changed, and gossiped about her with a diffusion of subtle personality that loaded the air she and they were equally compelled to breathe, as though it had been the taint of some repellent odor.

Still, she scarcely heeded their scrutiny enough to make it a real discomfort. For days it seemed to her as if she were living the most apathetic life as regarded all note or interest connected with her surroundings. It would hardly have been different if some one had given her a drug that made the environing world a sort of partial

nullity, yet left loss and grief to freight with pain every
new pulsation of her heart.

Weeks had multiplied before she woke from her trance
to a realization that she must procure some sort of work
—that she could not spend her existence like this, in
silence, in exclusion from human society, in aimless rambles through obscure parts of the town, in hours of dull,
sombre reverie behind locked doors. A great deal of her
money had gone ; the sum left must be fed by fresh
funds or that too would soon disappear. A surliness
tempered by appreciation of prompt payments had shown
itself in her landlady. That she should wear better clothes
than formerly and yet possess no patent means of support had become a source of fiery though repressed curiosity among her fellow-boarders. Without caring, without
specially noticing, she had nevertheless grown aware
that malice was at work in the treatment of her name.
Once or twice it even occurred to her that she was followed
in her walks abroad, though she never could be really
sure of this. For her own part, a curious indifference
concerning either praise or blame seemed to have taken
hold of her. She felt that she should dread the future, yet
failed to do so. A dreamy languor would often enthrall
her at the same time. Repeatedly she started forth with
the intention of seeking some sort of work, and came
home again only to remember how complete forgetful-
ness had mastered her. And yet this preoccupation was
not a mere blankness and vacuity ; behind it was consciousness of the real truth ; it held within it the delicate
sting of a real pleasure also, though one vague and mysterious. . . Her silences had long ceased to astonish the
other inmates of the house. She would seat herself at the
big, common table in the dining-room and eat her food
without doing more than just answer the occasional word
which someone might address to her. And yet there was
nothing unamiable in this reticence. Whatever harsh
verdicts may have been passed upon her, they did not

spring from any personal annoyance at her coldness. The reserve which clad her could not be called, indeed, by so severe a name; it was an absorption guiltless of the least uncivil element. Week after week it had slowly increased, and with its coming Cora's beauty had taken a more ethereal look, while into her eyes there had crept a glimmering, wistful light, tenderer than before and yet somehow stronger.

Of late she had eaten but little, yet seemed unconscious that her appetite had waned. "I don't think you're a bit well, Miss Strang," said the landlady to her one evening at dinner. Mrs. Keames was a portly woman with a rather acid mouth and little eyes whose pupils were like quicksilver. She did not specially pride herself upon the good repute of her house, but that house contained several boarders whose fastidiousness must not be rashly dealt with. "You've lost most of your color and you seem kind of languid, somehow. *Ain't* you well?"

"Oh, yes," Cora replied, with a drowsy yet affable air. "At least I think I'm about the same as I always was."

Mrs. Keames gave her a doubtful stare, and shortly afterward whispered something to a lady who was seated at her elbow. Cora then recalled that she had had a weak and nervous feeling once or twice during the day; and not many minutes afterward a strange dread of observation so keenly beset her that she thought seriously of leaving the table before the meal was ended. Soon, however, this desire was succeeded by distressing sensations of dizziness and faintness that made her cast a piteous look toward Mrs. Keames and exclaim: "Oh, I—I'm so light and funny in the head! I—I must be goin' to faint or something—I can't hardly *see!*"

She rose, staggering, from her chair, and, although two or three of the male boarders rose also and hurried toward her, the stout body and arms of Mrs. Keames were first in their proffer of assistance.

The next that Cora knew, everything was a misty blur,

and Mrs. Keames was saying in what sounded like a
voice of wild shrillness, "Lean on me—so—it's all right.
I'll get you upstairs to your room and you can lay
down there."

From the basement-floor to Cora's room would indeed
have been a long journey in these painful circumstances.
But Mrs. Keames's own room was just off the two shabby
parlors on the next floor.   Hither a pair of stronger arms
than those of the landlady carried Cora, and laid her, now
quite unconscious, upon the bed.   Her swoon did not
last long, and when she woke from it the male boarder
who had performed his little humanely muscular act had
departed from the chamber.   No one was in the room
except Mrs. Keames and Cora herself.   The landlady wore
a most uncompanionable smile during those few further
offices of aid which it now became needful to perform.

"I'm very much obliged to you," at length faltered
Cora, with her face almost as pale as the pillow on which
it rested.   "I guess I'll soon be well enough, though, to
get upstairs into my own room."

Mrs. Keames made no reply.

Cora's prophecy regarding her own condition proved a
correct one.   "I'll go upstairs with you," announced Mrs.
Keames as Cora walked feebly toward the door.   "Here—
take my arm.   I'm strong, you know, and you can lean
on me all you like."

The outer halls were vacant.   Cora panted a little after
the ascent, but showed no further signs of prostration.   A
look of great trouble had come into her face, however, and
each time that her eyes had met the austere expression on
Mrs. Keames's features her mixed bewilderment and anxiety had seemed to deepen.

"I—I guess I can get along pretty well," she presently
said, with a new timid quaver in her voice.   "If I should
want you again I'll—I'll ring the bell, Mrs. Keames.   It's
very kind of you—very kind, I'm sure to—"

"Oh, don't call it kind," broke in Mrs. Keames chillingly. She fixed her bright, acute eyes on Cora's for a second, and then withdrew them. In that one penetrant glance Cora read discovery, and, with the sense that her secret had been found out, all her old unconcern fled.

She clasped her hands together and reeled backward into a chair. "Oh," she burst forth, "you know, then, you know!"

Mrs. Keames went close up to her and spoke several quick sentences.

"Oh, what shall I say?" Cora moaned, hiding her face.

"I'm sorry," came Mrs. Keames's next words, icily spoken and not at all as if she were sorry, "I'm very sorry indeed, but you can't stay here after to-night. Any one in my position has got to draw a line, Miss Strang. You seem to be well-supplied with money; you can go to—"

"I've got only a little money left," shivered Cora," and —and if I can't work any more what *shall* I do?" She flung out her hands in a gesture of the most helpless anguish. "If you turn me away from here, where shall I go?"

Mrs. Keames pressed her lips together in that merciless manner of which virtue would seem alone to have learned the trick.

"I don't know, I'm sure," she said haughtily. "I presume, though, that one of the hospitals would take you in. I think I've heard that they do, in such cases."

XXVI.

A LITTLE while afterward Cora found herself alone. Mrs. Keames had withdrawn, in that disgust which is supposed to paralyze even rebuke. The small room seemed strangely still. Cora went to the glass and looked steadily for some time at her own image. Its lips appeared to part and speak to her, though she well understood that this was the merest freak of her own fancy.

"You see," said the reflection, "it has been this for days past, and you've known it, but something has somehow kept you from realizing, or caring. Life has been horribly cruel to you, as it has been to so many others like you. After all your struggles, one little hope of happiness was allowed you. And what has it turned into? A curse and a horror. There was so much you were willing to give up, just that you might stay good. But everything was asked of you—the last drop of blood must be drained out of your veins. This you could not or would not give, and you have been struck down with the thousands of others. Ah! how many are ever spared? You fought so hard, you conquered so often! And yet all the while you felt that in the end you might fail, and in the end you did fail, wretchedly, dismally. Oh, what is the mystery of it all? Why are you, and such as you, born into a world where all the odds are against you, where the battle is already waged beforehand, and yourselves are beaten in it, where sin so often means the mere getting of bread, and yet is sternly punished *as* sin, notwithstanding?"

So seemed her own image to address Cora—not perhaps in words like these, but in others of a similar import. She drew back from the mirror; her face was pale as death, her lips were twitching. She thought of the future and asked herself if she were going mad. All her old pride about being hereafter dependent upon her own efforts for support had suddenly vanished. In its place was a desire to see *him* and fling herself before him with abandonment of supplication. If he married her now it would not be too late, and it would take from her this intolerable burden of shame that was crushing her soul to earth.

What if she should steal out of the house now and try to find him? She knew his home—he had often told her just where it was, and once, at night, they had walked past it and he had pointed out to her the very windows of his room. It was night now, but still not late, and . . . yes, yes! she remembered the very number there in Fifty-Seventh Street. She would write him a note—she had pencil and paper and need only scrawl it hastily, as well as she could. In it she would put a request for him to meet her at once on the corner of his street and Sixth or Fifth avenues . . . well, let it be Sixth. There she would wait for at least an hour, after leaving the note at his door with her own hands, taking her chances of his getting it and coming to her inside that time.

"I must see him—I must see him to-night," she murmured, while beginning her note; and a wild, plaintive, half-incoherent screed it proved. But he would understand, she impetuously told herself, after striving to direct the envelope in as legible a hand as her tremulous fingers could control. Oh, yes, he would understand and come to her. No matter what he had done before, this news that she had to impart would thrill his conscience and perhaps work in him the most pitying kind of change. Even saving his father might seem a small affair to him beside the sudden entreaty to save *her!* Why should not this prove true of him? She had never known him to be hard-hearted. And he *had* still gone on loving her—he had wanted her to stay there in his own little house with

Lydia—to stay on after his marriage and accept his support as of old.

His marriage !

She had just begun to put on her hat and wraps when that word "marriage," entering her mind with a new significance, made her pause and gasp.

What if he were already married ? She had not thought of that. Indeed, she had hardly thought at all for weeks ! And yet it might be true ! The writing of her note had made her feel giddy and jaded ; this fresh terror fed her agitation.

But no ; she forced herself to shun such a belief. She had enough torture—why borrow more? By the time that she was dressed for the street her limbs were one nerveless tremor and her head burned with a strange, confusing heat. She was feeble—too feeble for the journey that she had purposed, and she realized this while thrusting into her pocket the roll of bills—a meagre one, indeed—which made the residue of what Casper had given her. At the same time she was buoyed up by a fierce and eager determination.

"I will go," she said to herself; "I *will* go, if I fall dead while I'm tryin' to get there ! "

She turned down the gas in her room and slipped quietly out into the hall. Her light feet made scarcely a sound on the first staircase. All the doors of the different boarders' rooms were shut, as usual. In the next hall it was the same ; but while she descended the second staircase she caught sounds of voices and laughter from the near parlors. The doors of these apartments were open, and in hurrying past them toward the front entrance she was aware that someone had seen her and had come forth on doing so.

" Miss Strang ! " called a voice that she recognized as Mrs. Keames's. " Why, you're not going *out !* Is it possible you can be so—?"

But that was the last she heard of her landlady's flurried

protestation.   In another minute she was speeding down
the stoop, and the sharp air of a chill, starry night was
blowing against her face.

She must take the Elevated to Fifty-Seventh Street if
she wished to go quickly, and there were two blocks to
walk before she reached Sixth Avenue and gained it.
They were long blocks, and they tired her.   More than
this, there was a numbness in her hands and feet and a
sinking sensation had begun to assail her heart.   The
lights of a large corner liquor-saloon presently came into
view, and somehow with them came a memory of the
cold day, months ago, when she had gone into that
Prince Street tavern and sought stimulant against the
nipping cold.

She would get a drink of brandy here ; it might revive
her and make the rest of her progress comparatively easy.
The side-door meant for women soon broke on her sight.
She entered.   The little room in which she found herself
was appointed in glossy auburn woods, and looked not
unlike the antechamber of some prosperous merchant
or lawyer.

The potion she asked for was soon handed her.   Till
now she had scarcely noticed a stout woman standing in
shadow and holding a glass of some sort of liquor.   But
now the woman began to speak, and with tones whose
whining shrillness gave them a quality of insistence.

"Are you takin' a little drop, dear, just to keep the
chill off ? " she queried, in her nasal, insinuating way.
"Well, it *is* a comfort, now and then, ain't it ? "

"I s'pose so," said Cora, sipping her drink and seeming to win from it on the instant a strength which filled
her with keen secret gladness — "that is, if a person
don't take too much, you know."

After paying the barkeeper she had laid her pocket-
book on the sill of the little window-like opening through
which feminine customers were served.   It still rested
there, the elastic not being yet re-clasped about its Russia

leather folds, and an edge or two of the greenbacks within
it gleaming from the loose pouches.

"Oh, of course, my dear, it's dreadful to take *too
much*," whimpered the woman; and she came nearer to
Cora. She had a bland face, in spite of her plaintive
voice; and though her eyes held that watery kind ot
twinkle which few confirmed tipplers are without, there
seemed to Cora a genuine sympathy in her bearing.
"I'm sure *you* never take too much, dear. You wouldn't
have that lovely skin if you did."

"I seldom drink anything at all," said Cora. "But I
was tired to-night, and—"

"Tired? Ah, yes, dear. I see it in your pretty face
now that I look at you a little closer." Here the
woman patted Cora's cheek with gentle audacity and a
hand of masculine size, cased in a drab thread glove.
"And what a pretty face it is! I used to be nice-lookin'
when I was a girl, but never so nice-lookin' as you are."

Cora finished her drink, and then suddenly recollected
her pocket-book. She took it up with one hand as she
set down her emptied glass with the other. It had a
light, thin feeling, and she peered eagerly into it, making
a little pinching movement with forefinger and thumb as
she searched for the bills. But they were gone, and the
amiable lady with the melancholy voice had slipped away
as well.

She was on the verge of raising a loud alarm, when
she perceived that a certain amount in change yet remained within the pocket-book. After all, though the
theft made her a pauper, she yet had means wherewith
to reach Casper. That accomplishment seemed to her
the sole meaning of life, now. But, as it quickly proved,
the liquor that abruptly had given her hope and courage
had in no manner aided her physical peril. For just as
she was about to leave the saloon a more fearful pang of
pain beset her than any she had ever known. Even
yet she had clung to some thought of setting pursuers on

the track of the woman who had stolen her money. But now all such intent deserted her, and she staggered out into the street with a dire and blood-curdling sense of personal exposure and helplessness, while the pain threatened every instant to fling her upon the pavement in utter collapse. For some little distance she walked on with passably steady steps ; then to move at all became added anguish, and with a despairful cry she sank down.

The avenue was full of people, and a crowd at once gathered about her, while overhead thundered the Elevated, speeding whither she had so longed to go, and leaving its wreaths of lamplit smoke to curl as if in mockery behind it.

XXVII.

SOME of the wayfarers hardly paused at all. It was such a common thing, they told themselves, to see a crowd collect about some one who had fallen. Others not only paused, put peered over the shoulders of fellow-gazers. Then came the inevitable questions, "Is she drunk?" and the inevitable replies in various terms of hazarding or sarcastic affirmative.

Cora felt as if she had sunk into a sweep of water and the dark forms pressing round her were waves that might close at any moment over her head. Then the pain, returning in a series of unspeakable throes, made her powerless to answer certain kind inquiries concerning her ailment and its cause. All she could do was to stare up at those who leaned toward her and to moan forlornly between set, hueless lips. This presentment of agony resembled, in such a place and among such surroundings, the maudlin torpor of drunkenness. In a little while all immediate gazers had grown certain that drink was the reason of her overthrow ; and when two policemen at length pushed their way through the throng, they were met on several sides by the announcement for which experience had already drearily prepared them.

"Lift her up," said one officer to the other.

"Lord, ain't she handsome though!" burst from his mate. "Look here," he muttered a moment afterward ; "I guess she's only sick. I—"

"Sick be damned!" shot the sneering retort. "She's drunk as a loon. 'Tain't the first time we've seen 'em good-lookin' and drunk both to once," came the added statement, fraught with that untold worldliness of tone which might almost be called unique amid the phraseology of the metropolitan police.

They lifted Cora with a certain deference to her slenderness and comeliness, but the next instant so wild a shriek of suffering rang from her that these men, who both had wives and children at home, gazed at each other with their hard, shrewd eyes almost moistening from sheer pity, half sure of the truth and yet not thoroughly so. As it now chanced, a young man who was a physician freed himself from the thick of the engirding ranks. He was hardly past one-and-twenty, by his looks ; he had a pale, sensitive, kindly face. " Put her down for a second," he said to the policemen ; " I may be able to tell you what's the trouble." His voice and speech were of the kind that elicit respect. The two men obeyed him, but as they did so the form which they held became quite unresistant. Cora had not fainted ; there had merely come a surcease of her pain, with a sensation of the most dragging feebleness. The young man knelt down beside her and remained thus for several minutes. When he suddenly sprang to his feet again there was a light of humanity and commiseration in his look that soon translated itself into words.

" Here's no case for the station-house," he began, low-voiced and with intense eagerness. "It's one for the ambulance and the hospital. I'm connected with Bellevue. She's. . ." Many ears were strained to hear what he now said, but only the two policemen caught his next words.

Cora just retained consciousness and no more during a full hour. When the cling-clang of the coming ambulance arrived, it smote on her ears with the weirdness of elfin bells rung in a partial dream. Her physical torments had completely stopped, as if through some benign intervention of fate. But they returned later, and with a stress more wrenching and drastic than any she had yet known.

By this time she was in a ward of Bellevue Hospital, where her moans and shrieks rang with a certain ghastly familiarity to many if not all of the ears which they met. Her misery, with recurrent paroxysms, lasted well on into the day. Physicians, young and old, grouped about her bed and drank professional knowledge from pangs which they could not quell and which they agreed sapiently to call the manifestations of a most unusual case. Surgery came into play at last, with its cruel mercies, and with a threat of death in its wake. For some time it was so doubtful whether she would live or die that destiny itself seemed to vacillate. Toward afternoon of that next day, while she lay quite freed from suffering, a nurse bent over her and soothingly said :

" I guess you're going to be pretty comfortable now, right on. The doctors think you are. They've all gone, and that's a good sign."

Cora looked fixedly into the nurse's face for a moment, and then dropped her eyes. " I'm so glad," she whispered.

"Glad?" questioned the nurse. "Glad you're out of your pain?"

"Yes—oh, yes. But I didn't mean that. I meant I was glad because I—I shall never see my child—never, never!—" The last word broke into a sob, but no weeping followed it. You would almost have said, seeing her lie there like a white, wilted lily, that she was too weak to shed even a single tear.

During the next hour or so she rallied notably, and then a long term of convalescence ensued. For many days she did not leave her bed, and the first time that she left it a relapse of her old trouble menaced her and she was obliged to lie quiet again for another protracted interval. The treatment that she received was no better and no worse than is usually accorded a charity patient in any of our public hospitals. People died on all sides of her ; she used to lie awake and count the number of deaths that had occurred since she had begun to take notice of what went on in the surrounding ward. As she grew stronger neglect showed itself in place of previous care. The doctors were civil and genial enough—some of the younger ones a trifle too suggestively so. But the nurses nearly all went through their needful offices with that cold, perfunctory air that seemed to hint of the absence of her wedding-ring. They appeared to say through the very medium of their silence : " We are here to help your body all that we can, but you must not expect from us the social cheer we might give you if shame had not set upon you so plain a seal."

Her sleep, during the earlier days of her recovery, was most fitful and precarious. They refused her the anodynes which had been so delicious a boon of oblivion not long before. Stern periods of insomnia would result from this deprivation, and it was then that the remembrance of how both the nurses and some of the other patients had made their repugnance manifest would cloud her soul with a desperate despondency. She thought of the future and passionately regretted that death had not made such an outlook impossible.

She had no philosophy, no aidful optimism born of culture, no courage of the sort that is nurtured by an educated view of just how much self-blame may be one's rightful desert. She had, and still possessed, a fair share of religious awe and reverence ; but this endowment, in so far as it served her at all, served her ill, since it pierced her with a recognition of her own repulsive sin, and deepened her forlorn realization that the coming scourge and contumely of society would be wreaked only through the just consequences of her merited wrong-doing. When a woman has lost her purity before the eyes of the world she is like some delicate piece of porcelain from which the limned charm of fruit or flower has been rudely scratched. It needs the most careful and skilled craft to re-enamel that injured surface, and for poor Cora, as she lay and mused upon her own moral defection, there was no such deft-fingered artisanship. She had tried very hard to be good; and she had failed hopelessly. This became the incessant haunting formula of her reflections; and week after week many a bitter evidence of how life teemed with sorrow and guilt not unlike her own turned the dreary hospital into a school of despair.

True, it was an edifice consecrated to pity; she perceived that most clearly, and often blessed it for the succor it had conferred upon her. But while it taught her that humanity is not wholly callous to the woes of its fellow-creatures, a subtler lesson was learned from it of the pitfalls into which those fellow-creatures are forever being plunged by the savage forces of birth, heredity and poverty. Hers was doubtless not the trained mind to perceive it, but she had striven to strike a pact of amity with the world, and the world had spit in her face and caught her by the throat as a return for the overture. A sentimental scream at "pessimism" is forever being raised against any cumulative view of instances like these; but it is none the less true that life shouts them to us from the housetops while we stuff our ears with the cotton of individual dollar-getting, and turn even the divine selfishness of family love into an egotistic indifference that either soothes conscience-qualms by lazy almsgiving or quite murders philanthropy by a dull-blooded sloth.

There came at last the time when Cora felt that her discharge from the hospital was closely imminent. In spite of the ban under which she lived she had won a few friends there. Her former beauty was returning to her with a daily augment of sweet reparation and resuscitation. She would snatch glances at herself in the mirror and almost hate herself for "gettin' so pretty again." The restored curves and tintings of her face seemed to bruit throughout the establishment a winsome explanation of her shame. Rumors had reached her that the superintendents would, on the occasion of her discharge, gain her

admission into some Magdalen Asylum or similar home
for friendless women.   But in her heart festered a secret
revolt against any plan like this.   Already she was weary
of system, discipline, coercion.   She longed as much for
liberty as a bird whose broken wing has at last knit together longs for its old gay empire of the air.   Some
peculiar levity had come into her nature, giving her demeanor a jauntiness, even a mild laxity and recklessness,
that had never formerly marked it.   Perhaps a new cynic
impulse lay at the root of all this, for she had in a measure lost the equable temper of other times, and now and
then would greet the ears of her associates with a sentiment full of irony no less novel than caustic.   Her spirit-
ual fatigue had begun subtly to show itself in a light,
defiant waywardness.   The immense problem of the
world had ceased to affect her as of old ; there was not so
much to be thrilled by, after all, in that cold eternal smile
of the sphinx.   It might be that there was more comedy
than tragedy in the woof and warp of things, and no
mean comminglement, either, of real, raw farce.   But anyhow (to put her meditations more in the positive form
which her everyday mind made them take), whatever the
whole big business amounted to, there didn't seem to be
the least chance there for *her*.   It wasn't so much that
the sun would rise to-morrow, if she were dead, just as
it had risen yesterday—there never yet was anybody so
great of whose death *that* couldn't be said.   But it was
rather that the sun was rising and setting all the time precisely as if she weren't there at all !   Of myriads like her
the same might be averred.   Nobody really cared whether
she lived or died.   Yes, however ; perhaps a few people
would care a little about her dying, for that made matters
a trifle easier—it was one more out of the way.   Your
being of no earthly importance here, they liked to tell
you, wouldn't interfere with your being ever so important
when you got to heaven !   There were times when Cora
found herself getting angry as she thought of the people who,

talked about heaven with the confidence they assumed.
' Hearin' em,' she mused, ' is like listenin' to someone
that's only been to Boston, but comes back makin' believe
he's been livin' in Paris or London.'

Her love for Casper was rapidly growing a memory,
and a very bitter one at that. His image rose out of her
past black with blame for her downfall. She held him
more than half responsible, though fully granting her
own faultiness. It was impossible for her to hate
him, and yet, to recollect the part he had played toward her would often stir feelings of severe resentment. He must have clearly foreseen the calamity that
she had been made blind to by the very newness
of her passion ! She no longer put faith in the excuses
which he had presented to her for his desertion. She
doubted him with a sullen, smoldering fierceness, and
pictured him as standing before the world at the side of
an honored wife, himself unsuspected of the crime for
which she (culpable though her copartnership in it may
have been) must reap the single harvest of degradation.

While her discharge from the hospital was yet pending,
she was allowed to walk out alone when the weather
happened to be specially fine. No longer in any sense
an invalid, the late extremity of her illness permitted her,
so to speak, a broad indulgent margin of convalescence.
Any day the fiat of expulsion might fall, and she knew
it ; and meanwhile the freedom which these outings
expressed for her was tinctured, in consequence, with the
dole of omen.

One brilliant winter morning, when the dark stonework
of Bellevue gleamed sharp against the blue river that
verged its lawns, she took her way westward with the
heaviest heart that had thus far weighed her spirits down
since the languor of malady had left them. If she refused
to accept the aid held out by the hospital, what chance
had she to begin again as a self-supporting struggler?
With no endorsements, no recommendations, how could

she gain an inch of foothold? Who would trust her, apart from employing her? Drearily she remembered that she had gone one Sunday to High Bridge with Casper, and that while they had looked together from the mighty span of masonry a thought had come to her of how easy death might be wooed and won by a single leap into that quiet river-bed. If only she had some decent little amount of money to help her in commencing the battle, it would be so different. She knew how to grapple with privation; penury and herself were old contestants. But to start with nothing, and to seek something through that futile means—it was like striving to walk on water, to climb a sheer wall of polished marble, to spring across a chasm that measured ten times her own stature.

In this gloomy mood she crossed several of the large East thoroughfares, and came at length upon the smarter and more populous expanse of Third Avenue. The weather, though wintry, was still mild for the season, and even this ugly boulevard, with its lines of vulgar shop-windows and its crowded, jingling, coarse-painted cars, held an element of contrasted freshness and sparkle. Cora knew that it was almost time for her to return to the hospital, and was on the point of denying herself more than a few fleet glimpses of the activity and bustle everywhere manifest, when a figure suddenly veered from the lines of passers and came hurrying up to her with a brisk exclamation:

" Oh, it can't be! But yes, it *is!* Why, *Cora!* You're thinner, though not much, and just as pretty as you always was!"

"So are you," replied Cora; and then, in another moment, she saw that this had been too hasty a judgment; for though it was the same Lily Luttrell as of old it was somehow a tarnished and faintly faded lily. And then the girl's dress! How violently modish it looked, here among these tawdry or shabby encompassments.

Instantly Cora suspected the truth, and Lily at once appeared to perceive that she did so ; for she tossed her blond head, clad in a fashionable little beflowered bonnet, and promptly cried :

" Oh, I've left Pillsbury's long ago.   I've got something a good deal better than that drudgery. . ."   Here a look of sympathy crossed her face, so vivid that Cora could have kissed her for it then and there.   "And do tell me about yourself ! " she pursued, clasping her companion's hand in both her own, which were clad with long gloves of unblemished kid.

" I'll tell you," said Cora, biting her lips to keep back the tears.   " I'll tell you, Lily.   Only, walk along with me for a little while, please.   People are looking at us."

XXVIII.

THEY walked side-by-side for several blocks. Cora somehow felt a positive delight in making a full confession—in not leaving a detail of her unfortunate past concealed from her attentive listener. Lily at last turned to her with parted lips and flashing eyes.

"I *knew* there was something like this, Cora, when you dropped Pillsbury's as you did. And then you remember that night I met you up at Jones's Wood?"

"Oh, yes," said Cora; "I remember."

"You poor thing! What you must have been through!" lamented Lily. "And *he*, Cora! You say he told you he had to be mar— Oh, the wretch! But you haven't said what his name is. Don't you want me to know?"

"I guess you'd better not know, Lily. I guess I'd better keep it to myself."

"Oh, Cora, you *care* for him *still*, after he's treated you so! I don't see how you can."

"Perhaps I don't care. . . it's hard to find out just how I feel about him. . . I charge from time to time. . . Every now and then I hate him with all my heart. . . Afterward I'll get a little softer, somehow. But I guess I'll end in hatin' him for good and all."

"I should think you might!" said Lily. "Look here, Cora," she went on, with a sudden excited ring in her voice. "You could sue him for thousands and thousands of dollars; do you know that? And you could *get* 'em, too!"

Cora smiled. "I don't hate him enough yet to do it, Lily."

"Oh, pshaw! You let *me* manage it! I know one or two gepmen that would just railroad the thing right through if I asked 'em hard enough. . . Here we are at my street. I'm just in the middle of the block, there." They had paused by this time, and Lily again caught Cora's hand. "You'll come in and sit with me for a little while, won't you, Cora ? "

"No, thank you, Lily. It's time I was back at the hospital."

"Oh, never mind a few minutes' difference. They won't care. Besides, you must be tired after your walk."

"No ; I feel as *strong !* It's funny how my strength has come back to me ! "

"All of a sudden . . . Yes. That's most always the way. Why, good Lord ! you've got fifty years yet, if you only take care of yourself." Here Lily gave one of her old jocund little laughs. "I don't do half as much of that as I might. I s'pose you've noticed that my skin ain't just what it was."

"Oh, no," said Cora. "You look a . . . a little tired."

"I feel like a milk-punch," said Lily, with merry bluntness. "You come along home with me, now, and we'll each have one." Here she slipped an arm into Cora's and drew her over the crossing. "You needn't stay more 'n a few minutes if you don't want to. I'll show you how comf'table I'm settled."

"You don't do any work nowadays, do you ? " asked Cora, as they walked along.

"N . . . no." Now came another leaping little laugh. "Do I look as if I did ? "

"No ; you don't."

"Oh, I've been shoppin' all the mornin' ; that's what's made me feel like a pick-me-up. For mercy sakes don't think I shop in Third Avenue, though. I struck up-town this way from Tenth Street ; I'd been at Dennin's. I got a heap of pretty things there."

Cora said nothing for several seconds. "Is this a boarding-house, Lily ? " she asked, as they stopped before a neat, plain, ordinary brick dwelling.

" M. . . yes. I've got two rooms here. They're fixed up real swell, too, Cora, *I* can tell you."

Lily soon opened the front door with a latch-key. Cora, as she passed the threshold, somehow thought of an evening when she had passed another threshold of a house not markedly different from this, though of more modest dimensions.

They went inside. The hall was papered showily but tastefully, and the drawing-rooms, into which Lily darted as though they had been her own private chambers, were by no means decorated or appointed ill.

"Oh !" exclaimed Lily, stopping short as she came into the presence of two figures that were seated near a table, whose cloth was of some handsome besilvered stuff, with a rich-shaded lamp rising from its center. "Excuse me," she went on ; "I didn't know anybody was here."

"Oh, that's all right," said one of the persons whom Lily had intruded upon. ·

The speaker was a young woman with an olive face, a curled, infantine mouth and dancing black eyes. Her companion was a man of perhaps her own age, apparelled in a flowered waistcoat and gaiters the color of unused cork. He seemed bored by the advent of Lily and Cora, and stared at the brunette, who sat loungingly in front of him.

Lily turned toward Cora, pointing to a chair near one of the lace-curtained windows. "Just take a seat there," she whispered ; "I'll be back in three seconds. I only want to see if my rooms are decently fixed to receive you in. Sometimes the chambermaid doesn't do them up as quick as she ought to, and—well, I had a little supper-party there last night and I'm 'fraid things mayn't be quite as I'd like to have you see 'em."

Away dashed Lily, and Cora took the designated seat. The young man and young woman evidently felt their previous converse to be interrupted, though Cora tried not to appear as if she were the possible auditor of anything they might say.

"So you really think you *will!*" presently said the lady.

"I guess I must," returned the gentleman.

The lady burst into a wildly hilarious laugh. "Oh, well," she cried, "I ain't goin' to meddle in your affairs. You can do as you like. But you'll get yourself into trouble, Jack, if you ain't more careful. You'll—"

She paused, here, for Jack had given her a nervous look, fraught with dread, as it seemed, of some indiscreet divulgence. Cora saw the brunette fling a side-glance toward herself. Then she drooped her eyes and tried, in her mild embarrassment, to imitate complete unconsciousness of all that might be passing a few yards away.

"She *is*!" at length broke from the lady, in tones just loud enough to be audible.

"Nonsense!" said the gentleman.

"I tell you she *is*," came the reply. "Just *look!*"

Cora, still feigning total unconcern, felt rather than saw that the gentleman was looking.

She knew so well what it meant. They were talking of her beauty—her beauty that had been her curse!

At last she concluded that some tell-tale change in her face had made them speak of other things; for presently, in a tone that had the effect of intentional loudness, the gentleman said, having ostensibly taken from the table a book which had lain there :

"How can you read this sort of stuff?"

"That!" sped the astonished answer. "Why, it isn't stuff a bit! Jack, you can't have read 'The Evil that Men Do,' or you wouldn't talk so of it!"

"I haven't read it," replied Jack, "but I've heard it's pretty bad."

"Bad! *How*, bad?"

"Oh, well. . immoral."

The brunette bridled, throwing back her dark, shapely

head a little as she straightened herself in her chair. "It's the plain truth—every line and every word of it !" she declared. "*We* oughtn't to call it immoral," she went on excitedly, with the manner of one who has a treasured cause to defend. "But that's always the way ! The very people that know how true such a book is are always the first ones to stamp on it and shout it down. It ought to do a great deal more good than harm, and I believe it will ! I—"

Just then Lily came bustlingly into the room and told Cora that everything was in splendid order upstairs, and that she had ordered the two milk-punches to be served them immediately.

"Oh, I guess I'd better not take anything like that," murmured Cora, as they ascended together into Lily's apartments.

"Nonsense !" came the retort; "it will brace you splendid."

Lily's quarters—as far as concerned the one room which Cora soon entered—were commodious, luxurious, delightful. In a little while the milk-punches were served them. Lily drank hers with an evident gusto, and rattled on expansively, daringly, about the jollity and ease of her new life.

Cora soon felt the effects of what she drank. Lily's words failed to shock her as they might once have done. Indeed, they suited the animus of many a recent meditation. At length she looked round, admiring the rugs, hangings, cushions, or statuettes with eyes that had begun to sparkle and cheeks that were stamped with two vivid spots of rose.

"It's ever so nice here," she murmured.

Lily got up from her chair and went and stood near her friend. She rested one hand on Cora's lovely cinnamon-colored hair. "Don't go back to the hospital," she said, in a low voice ; "stay here."

"Stay here?" echoed Cora, starting. "How can I ?"

"Oh, easily enough."

"But you—you said it was a boarding-house, and I—I've hardly got a cent in the world."

"Oh, you little goose!" cried Lily. And then she threw both arms round Cora's neck and stooped her vivid, laughing mouth close to the other's ear. She whispered a few words, and then sprang backward. "*Do* stay!" she exclaimed, quite loudly, the next instant.

The spots of rose deepened and grew larger on Cora's cheeks. Her eyes burned like stars.

"Oh, Cora," persisted Lily, brusquely and yet with great kindness; "do, *do* stay. Don't be a fool!"

Cora sat wholly immovable for several seconds. It was just as though she were silently making up her mind that Lily's counsel was altogether right and that she would not be a fool any longer. . . .

As it turned out, she did not go back to the hospital, either on that day or any day afterward.

Most human souls are lax in their receptivity to sin proportionately as they have once been fierce in their resistance of it. Cora did not satisfy herself with half-measures. The ruin was complete. Every moral beam and rafter tumbled, every clamp and stanchion gave way. The intimacy with Lily Luttrell did not last long. Friendship in an atmosphere such as these two women now breathed can no more thrive healthfully than if it were a field-daisy blown upon by the blast of a furnace. They did not openly quarrel; new interests drove them apart. Cora changed her residence. For a time she dwelt in luxury; her delicate and graceful figure trailed silks and glittered with gems. A certain kind of adoration grovelled before her. The next summer went by for her in a whirl of spurious pomp and splendor. She might have held her own through many seasons with a malignant magnificence, but for one cause—conscience.

That cried to her in every brilliant she strung about
her throat, every crimson or purple in which she clad
her shape. Her outraged moral sense demanded some
sort of narcotic; love had no part in her new mode of
life, or, if its influence entered there, the effect was one of
reminded massacre and onslaught. She had murdered
sentiment, but she could not lay its haunting ghost.
Wine brought her peace, and the hands that paid her the
wage of self-abasement lifted to her lips the cup that
deadened remorse. For months her career became one
of mad rashness. She felt herself harden, ossify. Her
beauty lasted, though it became dulled and coarsened,
gaining perhaps in an exuberance prophetic of decay,
like that of a rose forced by chemic heat from bud to
bloom, and baring its fragrant heart at the price of langor-
ous petals. Pleasure thrummed its viol in her ears, and
vice dragged her by the waist into its rompish dance.
The town blushed voluptuously before her sight; it had
no more hints of want or toil in the hectic joys its days
and nights proffered. Experience had flung aside its old
austerities like the worn garments of a beggar suddenly
dowered with millions. Time smothered his scythe in
flowers, though the blade gleamed through their heavy
tangles. Her clock ticked music, but there were hoarse
notes in its cadence now and then, as harsh as when a
grain of sand grits on the teeth in food cooked by the
skill of deftest kitchens. Horrible moments of fatigue
and self-disgust would be banished with draughts of
stimulant that made existence abnormally jocund.
Hope and courage were forced unnaturally from those
lairs which they never quit, so summoned, except at the
cost of fatal future depression. She drew great drafts on
her nervous energy, regardless of that bankruptcy which
awaits all such physical folly. There were times when
she felt like shrinking from the very ardors that she
aroused, as though they had been leprous and pestilent.
Again she would be spurred by a fierce exultation in her

own worst errors, and seem to taunt the very greed of fate, that it should have denied her so much, and yet left her these permitted funds and fonts of indulgence. There was then a bacchanal revolt in her words and mien that carried with it a terrible and poignant charm. You might almost have fancied that she exhaled some odor at once delicious and deadly, like a blossom whose gaudy grace is akin to baleful creatures beamed on by the same tropic sun. "She'd be glorious if she were educated," a certain man of a better class than she often met, once said of her. "She has a beauty that's positively harrowing ; her hair and her dimples and her coloring and those gold lights that swim in her brown eyes make her seem like a sorceress that has glided alive from the mists of song and story. But the minute she opens her lips the spell's broken. She has no more grammar than a lawyer's brief, and I don't believe she knows what's the capital of New York. Besides, she's going at a killing gallop. In a year, at this rate, she'll be on the common streets."

Never was truer prophecy spoken. The summer went by, and in the autumn began those first signs of physical wreck which must prove the haggard harvest of what dissipation had wildly sown. Already a good deal of its flimsy and ephemeral luxury had fallen away from her life. The habit of drink was chiefly a cause of this change. Intemperate women are tolerable only to the lowest of men. All semblance of refined companionship soon ceased with Cora. Her beauty died hard, but a moral death had steeped her in morbid influences before fleshly blights had well asserted their gross claim. During the next winter she made several efforts at reform, which ended, each one, in pathetic disaster. A colder nature than hers would have found it easier to abstain from excesses. In her ears there were always whispers that waited to be dulled ; in her memory there were always pictures that challenged effacement. By February she knew no longer the comradeship, bad as it had been, which once had evilly sustained her. She had broken ties that were strong with the strength of hangman's ropes, and sundered intimacies that were close as the intertwinings of serpents. This part of the transgressor was one that she played ill; she had too much native nobility and chastity for it; she had gone to the devil ungracefully. Deceit, and the facile lie that leaves the lips ambuscaded by a smile, were foreign to her disposition. Often drink would loosen her tongue so audaciously that it betrayed her into candors from which auditors rebelled, as being in their infelicity no less hateful than skulls at banquets. If she had her grudge against men and things, it was her business, they declared, to keep such cheerless announcements decently aloof from the midnight feast or the noonday breakfast. Former associates deserted her; she had reached the pass of being only blithesome in her cups, and at a moment's warning some sort of angry melancholia would prick through the conventional garments of jollity like moth-holes in a mantle of satin.

The tragedy of her life was now dreadful. Her exquisite face had become lined and furrowed by the desperations of her daily routine. It would not be hard to dwell upon the details of her forlorn disarray; the chronicler would not find it difficult to record this or that miserable instance of how she forsook those cleanly and godly ideals which had once lifted her as distinctly above the soilure of past environments as a water-lily is lifted above the bog from which it blooms immaculate. But our concern is not with the filth wherein this unhappy girl waded. The sadness of her career now transcends its criminality. There is a commonplace in lewdness that no nicest art of transcript can render readable.

She would often wander the streets at night. She had a home, such as it was. She had become wholly lost and abandoned. Now and then she thought of Casper, but always, when any recollection of him floated into her be-clouded brain, with a hatred alike hot and impotent. He was married, she would tell herself, and had forgotten if she were either living or dead. He deserved the sternest punishment, and yet he would receive nothing except the softest pardon. It was shameful, it was damnable that he should go free like this, while she must plod along to her grave for a few more months, maimed, shattered, old before her time !

But at last a most unexpected turn of affairs wakened her from this lethargy of condemnation. Leaving her quarters, one noon, after a night whose rashness returned to recollection only as a lurid blur, she entered a certain cheap restaurant in Sixth Avenue and called for food and stimulant. Striving to eat the first and thirstily quaffing the second, she took no note of what other occupants the place might contain. She was alone at her special table, and carelessly raised her eyes as a woman drifted into a seat just opposite her own. In another moment, however, the woman leaned toward her and said :

"Don't you know me ? I can still see that you're Cora Strang, though you're awfully changed from what you used to be."

"You needn't remind me of that," said Cora sullenly. "I'm sure I know it well enough without you tellin' me."

"And you recollect *me* ?" pursued the woman, staring with intent eyes at the ravaged young face that fronted her.

"Of course I do ? 'Tain't such a terrible long time to remember, is it ? You're Lydia—the woman that was forever holdin' her tongue. I never did see anybody that could keep her mouth shut as you could !" And here Cora threw back her head, laughing.

"My God, what a change !" murmured Lydia, below her breath. But the words were loud enough for Cora to catch them.

"Oh, come, now !" she broke out, with a roughness

and brusqueness wholly unlike her in the past ; "I guess I ain't so very much more changed, after all, than *you* are. You always used to be both large and thin, but now you're like a great big skeleton."

A smile flickered across Lydia's broad, bony face, and then died wearily away. "Life changes all of us," she said, "and I've had a heap of trouble since I last saw you. I'd had enough before that, the Lord knows, but more came to me, and this time it was sickness. "

Cora's manner instantly softened. "Sickness, Lydia !" she said. " I'm very sorry to hear it. And so you left his house ? "

"Oh, long ago."

" Because you were taken sick ?"

" Yes."

" You—you didn't stay there much of a while, then, after I left ? "

"About two months . . He used to come there again and again in the hope he'd hear some news of you."

"Of me ? " breathed Cora.

" Gracious sakes ! he acted half out of his wits, at first. He used to talk as if he meant to kill himself. Of course that was only humbug. He didn't gammon *me*."

Cora leaned both elbows on the table, dropping her face between the palms of either hand. "Oh, well," she said, as if between shut teeth, " I guess he's forgotten all the suffering *I* ever gave him. He treated me like a blackguard, Lydia. I loved that man so that I'd have got down on the ground and let him walk over me. You know I did ! "

"Yes, I do know it. I saw it. You *did* let him walk over you, too. He drove the heels of his boots into your face, Cora Strang. God help you, child, I see the marks of 'em there now !"

Cora's eyes flashed ; then a mist seemed to overspread them. She put out her hand and clasped Lydia's. "You're right," she said—"you're as right as you can be. I—I wasn't sure," she added, in another moment, "whether or no you'd *take* my hand like that."

"Not sure?" said Lydia. "Why?"

"Oh, because . . " Cora's beautiful underlip, still so delicate of outline, quivered as she bowed her head. "I dare say you don't need bein' told how—how I've gone right to the dogs this last year or so."

"*He* sent you there," frowned Lydia; "he's ten times more to blame than you've been! Oh, I watched it all; I could have sworn just how it was all bound to turn out! I'd rather take your hand and kiss it than get fifty dollars from his, poor as I am this minute! Once I went through pretty much the same thing—you remember how I said so that day he gave you the money and left you there in a dead faint on the sofa."

"Yes—I remember."

"But what else did I say?" Lydia proceeded, with her face and her tone alike one gloomy rebuke. "Didn't I tell you the law would give you satisfaction—revenge? You could have got both then. I'd have helped you. Ain't you sorry you threw up your chances? Ain't you sorry you didn't hit back instead of flingin' yourself to the dogs, as you've just called it?"

Cora nodded, staring down at the table. "Yes," she muttered, "I *am* sorry. I'm sorry *now*. I'm sorry, now that I hate him."

"Oh, you hate him at last, do you?"

"Yes." One hand, as it rested on the table clenched itself, perhaps automatically. "I sometimes feel as if I could shoot him or stab him as those women in the newspapers do."

"The newspapers," murmured Lydia. She drew from her lap under the table a half-crumpled copy of one of the cheaper morning journals. "It's funny I should have met you to-day of all days. And yet I don't know if it is so funny, after all. Things often happen just in this way, for all that some people say they don't. Look here." And she handed the paper over to Cora, with one finger pressed against a certain paragraph.

Cora took the journal and bent her gaze upon it.

"Married to-day!" she presently said, in a voice full of doubt and bewilderment. "Why, no; that can't be. It's—it's goin' on two years since he——"

"Since you saw the last of him," shot in Lydia. "Oh, yes; of course it is. But there's been some reason why the marriage was put off. I keep an eye on the papers, and I saw, five or six months ago, that his mother—the alderman's wife—had gone off very sudden with heart-disease, or something like that. I guess the reason's there. Anyhow, the wedding's hung fire till to-day."

"To-day!" repeated Cora.

She laid the newspaper down. It seemed to Lydia that she had lost every trace of her old beauty; the pallor that had come into her face made it look prematurely jaded and wrinkled.

"You see," Lydia went on, "that the number of the house is given and the name of the church they're to be married at. There's to be six bridesmaids, too. You'd make a good seventh. Don't stare at me like that, as if you'd like to kill me. *I* ain't the one that ought to be killed."

Cora relaxed her stare. "No, you ain't," she muttered, and began to drum on the table. Then she tossed her head and straightened herself in her chair. "Oh, thank God," she went on, "that kind of a fiend isn't in me, for all he's brought me to! I couldn't kill him—I couldn't even harm him. Bad as I am I ain't one to sink *that* low. I can't forget that I was born with brains in my head and that it takes two people to make a bargain, however vile the bargain may be. . . But I would like to—well, I don't know what I'd like to do!" she broke off, between a sob and a gasp. The next moment she had motioned to a waiter, and was saying to Lydia with a voice full of bluff, coarse notes :

"I came in here to brace up in a mild way on beer. But I guess I'll have a little hard stuff; I feel I've got to take some or else just drop." Then, to the waiter: "Bring me whiskey." And to Lydia: "Have what you please."

Lydia chose beer. But she was not ill-pleased that her companion had ordered a headier draught.

Disappointed, embittered, racked by illness, tortured by poverty, it would have been a malignant delight to this sombre and implacable woman if Cora, in an hour or two from now, could have grown so maddened by a thirst for vengeance on her betrayer that Casper Drummond's wedding-day might sink in the most tragic tinges. Her own lost opportunities would thus have been vicariously redeemed for her, and she would have slaked by proxy the thirst of an ancient hatred which neither time nor perhaps even death had succeeded in quelling.

XXIX.

"ARE you sure my train's all right. Sophie? It somehow doesn't seem to flow quite full enough, but that may be only fancy. . . What time is it? Half past twelve! Well, there's a good hour yet. Besides, I'm going to be about twenty minutes late at the church. A bride always goes up the aisle with better effect when she's about twenty minutes late. People are bored to death waiting for her, and then, when she appears, they're all the more grateful that she's concluded not to disappoint them. . . You can put my necklace on, now, Marie. Be careful not to let it catch in my hair, behind. What a beauty it is! Mamma, do stop staring so; I'm afraid you'll put on that queer, dumfounded look in church, and then everybody'll whisper ridiculing little things to everybody else. Act as if you'd married off two or three daughters before, in necklaces just as handsome as this one. How sweet it was of papa to pick out such glorious diamonds! Has the bouquet come? . . you're *sure*, Sophie? No, I'm not getting excited a bit. That is, I *am* excited, of course, but my nerves feel just like iron. Break down, mamma? What perfect nonsense! Catch *me* breaking down! I never knew a bride that did; they always carry things through with a grand air; it's the groom that . . I wonder how *he* feels now. He said last night he expected to be nervous. I told him that if he dropped the ring I'd begin suing for a divorce as soon as we got out of church. . . . Now, get my veil, Marie; Susan, you help her. . . . Who's that? Bessie Bostwick wants to come in? No, no, *no!* I'm awfully sorry, tell Bessie, but I'd rather none of my bridesmaids should see me till I'm entirely dressed.

Then I'll dawn on them downstairs, all together, like a dazzling vision of—ugliness."

Thus babbled away Hilda Stoutenburgh on the morning of her marriage to Casper Drummond. The reason for the delay in their marriage had been chiefly the one on which Lydia had hit. The death of Mrs. Drummond (who had died almost instantaneously, one morning, from fatty degeneration of the heart, after having passed through more than ten years of burdensome obesity) cast a gloom over the prospective glories of Hilda's wedding-day. To be married quietly because of the bridegroom's bereavement did not suit Hilda the least in the world. She had already named her bridesmaids and brooded creatively over the cut and make of her nuptial gown. Passionate as was her love for Casper, it co-existed with her eager wish for a brilliant bridal. The proudest moment of her life was to be that in which she walked away from the altar as his wife, leaning on his adored arm ; and she desired to invest this moment with all the grace, taste and pomp that wealth could summon. Her dress should be sumptuous, her jewels should be royal. Poor, plain little Sophia should be one of her bridesmaids, and they must all wear raiment that would suit a bevy of princesses. It was true that the assemblage would not be patrician. The newspapers had begun to tell Hilda of another social world beyond her own, very much as they had told Honoria Conover. Still, there would gather a good many rich people both at the church and at the house ; and what real American aristocracy ever was or ever could be except one based on the doughtiness of the dollar ?

But in spite of these feelings Hilda had once or twice been on the point of deciding that the ceremony should take place with all such sober accompaniments as Casper's late loss demanded. She was never quite confident that his love was much deeper than lip-service. He had come to her one day, when she was ill,—when her parents and her sister were nearly frightened to death lest the illness should turn into something fatal,—and he had told her that he loved her and wanted her for his wife. No medicine, no course of waters, no change of climate could have acted so curatively as that one rather brief yet pregnant interview. She had rallied almost immediately after its occurrence, though disappointment soon followed. It is not easy for even a man like Casper Drummond to feed an intelligent young woman on one continuous diet of palatable lies. Now and then bursts of doubt would assail Hilda, and a sense of the fragile tenure by which she held her alleged sweetheart. Occasionally Casper neglected her, not entering her presence for two or three days at a time, or deigning to inform her of his whereabouts. When he did re-visit her and met the tears and reproaches of which her store was plenteous, he endured them with a surly kind of intolerance. In any case he was never more than a lukewarm lover—which at least set some sort of decent limit to his powers of hypocrisy.

Another cause that came very near making Hilda forego her luxurious dreams and insist on a plain yet prompt wedding was a vulgar all-night escapade, quite as public as the Florida scandal, in which Casper and his friend, Rudie Champny, figured roysteringly with their deputy-sheriff's badges, and were talked about by all their friends for a week afterward. Jacob Stoutenburgh scowled darkly over this incident. He thought it a most offensive one, and deplored the notoriety in which it steeped his future son-in-law. Casper bore his reprimand haughtily, and a quarrel ensued, though it was behind closed doors and inaudible to Hilda. She guessed much of what her father had said, and took such vehement sides with Casper that he almost loved her for the fervor of her partisanship. Stoutenburgh was in his daughter's bad books for a fortnight afterward. She found a hundred excuses wherewith to gloze over the ribald behavior of her idol and a hundred sarcasms wherewith to assail her father's past belligerence. The recent death of his mother had made Casper's folly all the less pardonable, but she would not hear a sentence in his disfavor, no matter what may have been her own covert opinions. Jacob Stoutenburgh had nothing to do except sigh and hold his tongue; he was a yoked creature as far as Hilda went, and it is no exaggeration to say that he found positive joy in his bondage. If she had fallen ill again he would have felt like the most miserable of culprits. Hilda existed only to be admired and petted, just as his wife existed only to be discountenanced and repressed.

There was a very savagery about his younger child's love for the man she had chosen that bade the brewer watch her with a new strength of interest. Hilda, meanwhile, was telling herself that perhaps a prompt marriage would be best. She was capable of bearing any indifference from Casper, but she recoiled with inward terror before the prospect of an irreparable rupture. He was to be hers; the stars had said it; her domineering wilfulness had never since childhood set itself so stubbornly upon the attainment of an object. All through her spoiled girlhood she had been demanding and receiving, but now it seemed as if every former force of contumacy and rebellion had embodied an earlier stage in the development of this one commandant mood.

The way in which she took possession of him and marked him for her own began slowly to fascinate Casper. He was weak, vacillant; she was strong and unswerving. It was possibly the freshened gallantry of court-paying with which he now half-unconsciously approached Hilda that caused her to regard coming events with less anxiety and to let the project of a festal and modish wedding once more enchain her desires and her hopes.

And so, after many months, the marriage was at last imminent. Before Hilda went downstairs a little expectant company had gathered in the drawing-rooms. She looked handsomer than even most brides look, for

the magnificence of her dress, the splendor of her jewels,
and the delicately obscuring glamour of her veil, all softened or detracted from the large, blond accentuation of
her usual presence. Her bridesmaids greeted her with
little cries of girlish enthusiasm. They were a pretty lot
of damsels, and she had selected them because of their
faces and statures. The only one who struck an inhar-
monious note among them was her sister Sophia, who
was neither tall enough nor pretty enough for so choice
an assemblage. But the wedding-party, as it left the
house for the church, pleased Hilda, whose critical eye,
under its veil, scanned every costume with an acute sur-
vey. Papa was very good indeed; his Prince-Albert coat
became him, and the bunch of violets in his button-hole
had just the right size and air. Mamma's violet satin and
point-lace trimmings were perfect; they made her look
as if she had been wearing such gear for at least half a
century. Poor Sophie was a failure, but then she always
was and always would be, though it didn't matter a bit,
because she would lose herself, as it were, among the five
other blooming and stately bridesmaids.

Thus ran Hilda's nimble mental commentary, as she entered the carriage which her father and herself were alone
to occupy. Her talk flowed on with great glibness during the drive to church, which was one of considerable
length, as the Stoutenburgh home lay far up-town and the
ceremony was to be held many blocks below it.

"I do believe, papa, that you've got one of your feet
on my train. No? Very well, then; sit just as you are
and I'll have faith in you; but if you budge a single inch
I shall believe you've evil designs on me. Isn't my dress
nice? Yes? you do think so, really? And doesn't mamma
look well? You didn't notice? You horrid fellow! *why*
didn't you? Mr. Drummond is to receive us at the door?
you're *sure?* How old he seemed the night we rehearsed
for the wedding! I never saw a man age so in such a
short time. I shall feel nervous till Casper pops out of

that place in the back. I don't know why, but these modern weddings are such jack-in-the-box performances as far as the groom is concerned; don't you think they are? I am sorry Rudie Champny's going to be his best man, for I never liked Rudie, and I think he has a bad influence over Casper, But then it had to be, for he's really the oldest friend Casper has . . And about Aunt Louisa, papa, and Uncle Franz. It's ever so much better they should be at the church and mix in with the crowd there. I'm glad you didn't oppose me in that plan." (As if he had ever yet opposed her in any plan, since her pinafores !) "For Aunt Louisa, you know, is dowdy and queer, and will wear her hair twisted into that little knob of braids at the back of her head, like a German emigrant that's just landed. And uncle Franz would rather die than go to a decent tailor, and couldn't be bribed to wear such a thing as a glove. No, papa ; they'll pass in the crowd, but they'd both have been horrible in the wedding-party. Then those cousins, Fritz and Louis and Augusta and Margaret ! They're better, of course, but they couldn't have come without their parents—and, besides, you can't be sure just how they're going to look. The girls might get themselves up in magenta-and-green, or something like that, and the young men might come with swallow-tails at half-past one in the day-time. We're such a funny family, papa dear. We're only half civilized yet. I'm the highest point of our civilization, Sophia comes next, and you're third."

Stoutenburgh laughed a little at this last piece of impudence, but not so heartily as he might have wished. The truth was, he felt a dreary dread regarding his daughter's future, hard though he had striven to bring the present marriage about.

The church, as it soon proved, was fairly thronged, and the objectionable aunt, uncle and cousins became safely inconspicuous on this account. Casper looked handsome as he appeared at the altar, joining his bride there, with Rudie Champny at his elbow. A snobbish-minded lady who was present remarked afterward that for a wedding composed almost entirely of shoddy millionaires it had struck her as amazingly smart. This lady forgot that nearly all prosperous people nowadays dress alike, and that until our aristocrats have found some means of making nature supply them with specializing casts of countenance, such as the invariably patrician eyebrow or the inflexibly select nose, it cannot be said what unholy resemblances may occur.

As the organ burst forth into the wedding-march, and Hilda slipped her kid-sheathed arm within the arm of him who was now her husband, her resolute and determined soul was thrilled by a proud gladness. She knew that every eye was on her robe and her gems, and that these became her as its wings become a bird.

Just behind her was her father, and a little behind him walked Aaron Drummond, with furrowed face, frosted hair and an almost senile stoop of the shoulders. A brief period of time had indeed aged him notably. The general belief had been that his wife's fearfully sudden death had caused this change, though it was never thought that he had greatly cared for her, by those who knew him outside of his cold, shrewd political life. Just as the bridal party were passing the threshold of the church into the little vestibule beyond it, Jacob Stoutenburgh quietly dropped his wife's arm and paused, looking behind him with an air of polite unconcern. At the same moment he drew an envelope from an inner pocket, letting the hand which retained it carelessly droop. Aaron Drummond had slipped to his side in another minute.

"Oh, by the way," said Stoutenburgh, with a splendid bit of assumed carelessness, "here's something I wish you'd glance at. It may interest you."

He handed Drummond the envelope which contained his own two letters, written long ago to Farrish. The alderman had turned white, but his hand was very steady as he took the little proffered square of paper, and his voice was also a model of composure as he at once replied :

" Thank you. I'll look it over while I'm driven up to the reception."

The whole quick give-and-take of the affair had been completely commonplace, and yet it had meant for one of the men concerned in it an unspeakable. relief, a tremendous exultation.

'At last !' thought Aaron Drummond. He had escaped from a grip of iron, but it had laid its lasting mark upon him. There were those who said that half his old nerve and cunning had left him, and that if some day he were the victim of sudden collapse it would surprise none who had of late watched his altered and wandering ways.

Meanwhile Hilda and Casper had gone out across the canopied and carpeted pavement, to enter their carriage. A little crowd pressed eagerly on either side of them, as it always does when a bride leaves the church. The carriage door had been opened. Casper gave his hand to his bride, and she would have disappeared from sight in another second.

But just then a figure darted in under the awning, and with swift, wild hand seized the veil of the bride.

It was Cora.

She had torn the veil quite clear from Hilda's face before Casper could catch her wrist and push it backward. He had not recognized her till then, and then their eyes met. His grasp relaxed as if a sword had cut his wrist in twain. He stared at her face, so horribly changed and yet so incontestably her own. He grew livid, and tried to speak, but his lips only worked like those of a man smitten by sudden dumbness.

Cora clenched the hand that he had released, and raised it above her head. There is no need to write down the tempest of invective that pealed from her lips. Hilda, before it was ended, gathered up her torn veil, and flung herself into the open carriage, horrified, shuddering.

Something desperate and sublime in Cora's demeanor—

something truth-fraught and terrible in her pell-mell words—made every onlooker stand silent and even awe-stricken as they watched and heard her.

"Liar and scamp!" she at length shouted, and flung with a mad force one hand against Casper's lips. The blood gushed from the blow, staining his white-satin necktie, and, as she saw this, Cora gave a laugh than rang for days afterward in the ears of its auditors.

That laugh somehow broke the spell. A policeman seized her by either shoulder and whirled her away from the man she had just assaulted. She did not make the least resistance as another policeman soon joined his mate, and the two bore her off between them.

"I s'pose you'll take me to the station-house," she presently said.

"Yes," growled one of the men, "where such drunken drabs as you deserve to go."

"I'm not drunk," she answered. "I've been drinkin', or I couldn't have done what I did. I made up my mind I'd do it and I took some liquor to give me nerve; but I ain't drunk . . . Well, there's no use grippin' me as you're both doin'. I'll go with you wherever you take me. I don't care."

After a little while they loosened their clutches on her arms. They had begun to see that she had told them the truth. Her pace was firm enough. She did not walk like a drunken woman.

"Is the station-house far from here?" she soon asked.

"Oh, not so very; we'll get ye there quick enough," sneered one of the men with a gruff laugh.

"Nobody's made any charge against me," she said. "Nobody will. You can, if you want—both of you. You can say this, though: that I was a good and pure girl till the man I struck—the man whose bride's veil I tore—betrayed me and deserted me."

A silence ensued. Whether the men looked at one another or no Cora could not see and did not care to find out. She walked with her head bent. The men's hands clasped her arms very lightly ; they had slackened their steps.

"Is there a crowd followin'?" she asked, a little later. "There most always is. I s'pose there must be now, after what happened."

One of the hands fell from her arm. The other fell also, as if obeying its hint. She stood alone, quite still, not turning round, while sounds reached her that told of a throng being roughly dispersed. The policemen both cried out oaths and threats, while a clatter as of scampering feet mixed with their voices. But she did not care to see what was passing. She did not care whether she went to prison or no. An utter apathy of indifference had come upon her. She felt very old and tired. 'Some women would have killed him,' she thought. 'Thank God I didn't want to. I only tried to shame him before *her*. There's no more revenge left in me. If I had my way I'd die and quit it all. I'm dead sick of it. I don't blame anybody now. I've had my fling ; it wasn't much, but it gave me a kind of satisfaction. It let him know I was alive and the poor, mean thing he's made me.'

Almost without realizing what she said she had presently spoken these very words aloud to the men, as they resumed their walk at either side of her.

They began to question her after that, and she answered them with a cold, careless directness, telling her own name, the name of Casper, the name of the woman he had just married, the circumstances which had led to her misfortune, and the earlier efforts that she had made to live an untainted life.

"What a long walk you're takin' me," she at length said, lifting her eyes for the first time since her arrest and glancing about her. "Is it ever goin' to end? I'd like to have it over and see what'll happen. I wish," she added, in sullen undertone, "that it was the pound and I was a dog you were draggin' there to be drownded."

"Oh, you wish that, do ye?" said one of the men; and his voice had such a new soft ring that she veered round and fixed her eyes on his face. It made her start; it was so like Casper's. He had the same jovial, hardy, manful look, and he was watching her with an expression full of the kindliest pity.

"Look here," he said, as they all three paused again; "I guess we won't run you in. You go. I don't say I believe ye, but it looks as if you'd had just the devilish treatment from that chap you tell us you've had."

"Hold up," struck in the other policeman, who was an older man, grizzled and rather grim of aspect. "They see what she done there at the church-door, Bill, an' if we don't run her in they might make it hard for us. Now, if we do our duty, we'll—"

"Damn our duty!" muttered Bill. "I'll bear the brunt of it, John, if there's any row raised."

The speaker, handsome and virile as any soldier, in his bright-buttoned uniform, leaned down and took Cora's hand in his own, pressing it for a moment, while his blue eyes gleamed to her, humid from a compassion that honored and ennobled him.

His next words were too low for his mate to hear, but Cora heard them very plainly. "I wish I'd known you, my girl, before you went wrong like this. There's something about ye that makes me think . . But oh, well, never mind! Anyhow, I ain't goin' to take you in. There, now, get along, and remember this: the world ain't so awful hard and wicked as you think it. There's a chance for you yet if you'll only brace up and try to help yourself. Others 'll help ye if you'll just show some nerve and grit. There, now; take my advice. You've had hard knocks; you've been drove to the wall; you was never crooked till you was forced to be. But there *is* a chance for you yet. Don't forget that. Now . . . so . . . good-bye, my girl, and God bless you!"

Soon afterward Cora stood alone. The policemen had

left her.   She   was   in   one   of   the   western   avenues,
and the limpid winter sky, mild almost as that of a May
afternoon,   arched   over   a   thoroughfare   familiar   to   her
through many a walk with Casper.

"A chance for me yet!"

She repeated the words aloud.   They teemed with a
frightful irony.   The pressure of that big, strong hand was
still on her own.   How like Casper he had looked!   Perhaps if she had met him in earlier days she might have
loved him and married him and borne him children, and
passed with him a happy, honorable life.   He was
in the same sphere as that to which she had once belonged.   He had almost realized how he might have
cared for her.   It had flashed through him there as he
held her hand and looked into her face.   And she had
felt it, too.   She could have loved him if only she had
never seen Casper.   It would all have been so right and
orderly and just!.   Oh, what was the reason of the curse
laid on so many harmless human souls?   What had they
done to deserve their misery?   How could the churches
go on pointing their spires to a so-named merciful heaven
when there was so little mercy ever shown by it?

"A chance for me yet!"

She repeated the words again and again as she moved
onward, and the oftener they left her lips the more bitter
seemed their burden of mockery.

XXX.

"No, I'll give ye no more drink. Get along, now. Ye've had all ye need."

A barkeeper in one of the liquor-saloons not far from the lower portion of the Bowery spoke these words to Cora several hours afterward. They roused her like a sting dealt the flesh, and made her remember where she was and what had brought her into a neighborhood un-visited for months. Lydia had wanted to see her in a certain down-town restaurant ; it had been arranged be-tween them that she should hold a meeting there with the instigator of her recent reckless act at the church-door, provided she should get off unarrested. Lydia held some position in the restaurant named, or so she had asserted ; it was an all-night place, she had declared, and her hours of attendance were from two in the afternoon until nearly midnight. Cora had intended going straight to the address given, but on her way the shattered state of her nerves had led her into frenzies of drink which now be-clouded mind and memory. She could not, for her life, recollect in what street Lydia was to be found, though an unforgotten number still tantalized her drugged brain.

She had never before been so stupefied at such an hour. It meant the beginning of worse things with her no doubt. The thirst for liquor was growing, and soon it would land her among the tramps and trulls over at Blackwell's Island. Why not into the grave before that? If it were possible to buy a little morphine of some apothecary down here, and take it up home with her to her room !

She was in one of the side-streets leading from the Bowery. It seemed to her that for the last ten minutes or so her gait had been quite even. Here she was right, for the slurring words of the barkeeper had produced this effect. But possibly, she reflected, her face was flushed into a scarlet witness of her real state. Not far away she saw the red and yellow lights of a chemist's shop ; they danced a kind of multicolored saraband together while she watched them. Was it of any use to go there and ask for the morphine ? Would not the request be met with scorn, and perhaps with anger as well ?

And yet there was such dead weight of weariness in the thought of waking, faint from excesses of the past night, to the odium and tedium of another morrow ! Dusk had already thickened so densely that the stars had flocked forth into the mild, cloudless heaven above the house-tops. As Cora stood still, unconscious that the light of a near street-lamp was being flung directly across her brow and temples, the faces of all passers had become quite obscure to her. And so, when a man halted at a few yards from where she was stationed, she had no idea that he had even specially heeded her until he drew closer and thus brought some of the lamplight upon his own features.

They were bloated as if by drink. His hair hung matted between his blood-shot eyes and ragged hat-brim, and a stubbly black beard covered his long, heavy jaws and sharp chin.

"My God ! Oweny !" said Cora ; and she drew backward.

He followed her. He had been half-drunk, but the sight of her had sobered him. Still, he did not yet believe in the reality of what he gazed on. He had had two fierce fits of delirium-tremens during the past year or so, and it was easy to rank this aspect which Cora now presented as one among the many repulsive phantasms which had before witched his brain. It must of course *be* Cora ; but in a few seconds her face would look like its old pure, sweet self and lose that horrible blotchy pinkness, that puffed, vicious distortion.

He reached out his hand, thinking she would recede from him. Everybody did, nowadays. He had become the merest drunken castaway, sleeping in cellars and halls of tenement-houses, begging coins in the streets to buy liquor with, and sometimes meeting an associate as low as himself who would help him to a few gratuitous glassfuls of the liquid poison he so loved.

But to his surprise Cora gave him her hand. She laughed while she did so, as if their meeting were a kind of ghastly joke.

"Hello, Oweny, old boy," she said; "we haven't seen one another since that night at the ball; have we? It seems a good while ago, don't it? I guess we've both been havin' some pretty bad kicks since then; ain't that so?" And she swung his hand to and fro while she grasped it—she, this horrible satire on the Cora he had once worshipped.

He worshipped her even yet. Her gross degeneracy awed and sickened him for a brief while; then, having realized that it was no myth of his own drunken madness, the frightful debasement that he beheld in her woke a strange, baleful impulse of congeniality.

"Yes," he said, brokenly and with wide-eyed consternation; "times *has* changed for both of us. An' you—*you!* Good God, Cora! what's made you like this?"

The words ended in a falsetto wail. He lifted her hand to his lips and held it there while she stood and smiled at him. Her smile was like a hideous jeer cast at her former self.

She dropped his hand and stared up at him brazenly. "I got so," she retorted. "Never mind *how*, but I got so. Ain't you satisfied to see me again, Oweny? You used to care for me in the old days."

Horror swept over his wrecked face. "I—I used to love you then—yes—yes!" he muttered. "I love you still. I'd love you, Cora, if you was in the depths o' hell, all on fire, an' it would be the death o' me to take you into

my arms ! That's God's truth ! You might a been my wife
—my decent wife—an' now I look on ye sunk like this !"
He said some other words to her in a tumultuous way—
words that need not be written, but that teemed with
piercing interrogation.

"Yes," she said, in answer. "I've gone right down—
I'm as bad as the worst, now, Oweny."

He gave a harsh, hard cry, such as a brute might give
when a knife strikes it. "I went searchin' after ye for
months, Cora ! I wanted ye so ! I waited so to see ye
once agin ! And to see ye as ye are ! Well, I'm no better
myself. We're a fine pair ; we suit one another this night,
if ever two did on earth. At last we do !—at last ! But
you'd never give a cent for me when you was the sweet
bit of a girl I tried to marry ! An' if we'd married it might
'a been the savin' of us both. I'd 'a kep' straight if I'd had
ye—I'd 'a been your true husband instead of the blackguard ye see me now."

Here was the naked and shameless fact. Cora seemed
to recognize it as she slowly nodded. Then a sudden
question shot from her lips :

"You went like this because of me, Oweny ?"

"So help me God, Cora, I did !"

She clenched her lips and glared for a moment at the
sidewalk.

"Where's your mother ?" she sharply queried, lifting
her glance.

"I dunno. She left me three months ago. She stuck
to me in my drunks for a good while, but one day I got
wild, an'. . . well, they say I was goin' to brain her with
a hatchet. But I didn't."

Cora's next words came cold, slow, defiant. "You used
to get drunk those other times."

"Yes—but I kep' sober for six months on your account.
An' I could a gone on if you'd married me. I could !"

"So you don't ever see your mother any more ?"

"No."

" And you don't work any more, now ? "

" Oh, I guess it's five months an' more since I had anything like a steady job."

Cora nodded again.   " Drinkin' all the time, eh ? "

" Yes," he acquiesced ; " drinkin' all the time." A new
access of amazement seemed abruptly to seize him.   " But
you, *you*, Cora ! you're full o' liquor—you, that never
would touch a drop ! An' it ain't only been to-night. You
must a had lots before ; you're all queered from what ye
was." He put his hand on her shoulder and as it rested
there a great tremor swept through his frame.   " Oh,
Cora, what devil sent ye down to this ? "

She laughed.   It was a sound that some poet in striving
to paint infernal scenes by shrill and bitter tricks of
language might have delighted to imitate.

" Devil, Oweny ? You mean, what man, I s'pose ? Well,
never mind.   All men are devils, I guess.   You look like
one."   And she laughed again.

" I never was one to *you*, Cora ! But it's you I can thank
for bein' what ye see me now ! "

" There's a lie," she cried ; and still again she laughed.

" It's true ! " he protested.   " When I'd made sure I'd
lost ye I didn't care to live decent no more ! I just let
myself go ; I throwed up the sponge.   Where was the
use o' mindin' what become o' me when the gal that I'd a
given my right hand to get was dead to me as if I'd seen
her corpse in its coffin? For I used to believe I'd never
set eyes on ye again."   He looked like some demon
spawned by the vice and crime of the vast city, now, as
he glared at her with quivering nostrils and snapping
jaws.   "Ugh ! if I knew the chap that brought ye down
like this !   Will ye tell me who he is an' where I can lay
hold of him ? "

" No," said Cora.

She began to move along, and Owen walked at her side.
Seeing them, you might have said they typified in their
companionship the worst depravity of the gutters and

alleys, for the very marks of thrift in Cora's dress were more suggestive then if she had been clad with rags.

"You won't tell me, eh? Was it that chap that took ye from me at the ball? Was it, now."

"Never mind if it was or wasn't," she retorted, turning on him with hostile face.

They went onward for some little time in silence. They had reached purlieus of squalor, by this, and Owen at last said, persuasively, even imploringly :

" Look here; couldn't we go into some saloon, somewhere, an' sit down, the two of us, Cora ? I ain't got any money—not a single cent ; but—"

"Here's some money," said Cora ; and she drew forth a few loose coins from her pocket.

His grimy fingers clutched the pieces. "Thank ye!" he gasped. "Come, now.. let's have a talk an' a glass together somewheres.. why not in here?" and he made a motion toward a saloon that had its two cobwebby windows filled with bottles and demijohns, and that was led to from the sidewalk by three or four descendant steps.

Cora shook her head. " I don't want any more drink," she said. "I guess I've had enough. I'd better be gettin' home."

"Cora !"

He caught her dress; there was a look of wild pleading in his brutish eyes.

"Well?" she replied, with sullenness.

"You'll come, won't ye? I—I never thought I'd see ye again, an' now that I have, it sets all the blood leapin' through my veins. Yes, it does, even though you're so mighty different."

She watched him for a moment with merciless irony. "Do you think you'd like to marry me, just as I stand?" she asked sneeringly.

He drooped his eyes. " Marriage ain't for the likes of us," he grumbled.

" I should say not !"

"But I care for ye!" he pursued. "It ain't the same old feelin', but it's love still!"

"Love!" she echoed, in scoff.

"Yes—love! If you was ten times worse than I see ye now—if you was all red with the blood o' somebody you'd killed—if the very face o' ye was battered an' jammed into a jelly an' the sound o' your voice was the only way I had o' tellin' ye for Cora's own self, I—well, by the soul o' me, I'd love ye still! Yes, I'd love ye for old time's sake if nothin' else. An' it's for old time's sake I ask ye to step down here now and take one small drink. Don't refuse me! Don't!"

She made a sign of consent, and he seized her hand, leading her down into the tavern. It was a low-ceiled place, with some soiled and sticky tables here and there, and a lop-sided bar behind which stood a man with the face of a pirate. He was extremely pale, had little tufts of black whisker just below each temple, a white-lipped, cruel mouth, and small gold ear-rings. Two men were playing cards off in the shadow, and from one corner came the snore of a drunken workman, who was clad in blue overalls and whose tin dinner-pail gleamed at his feet. On the table before him stood two empty glasses, and flung beside them was a newspaper bundle from which had escaped, in pathetic sarcasm, a tiny child's shoe, with its little unsoiled sole turned sideways, telling that it was a recent purchase. This saloon, quiet enough at the present hour, had a loathsome repute. So many murders and fights had occurred there during the past few years that it was derisively called "The Pool o' Blood" by both its patrons and foes. But it had contrived to make itself a political necessity for men whom its very existence should have branded with dishonor; and so it impudently throve in the very teeth of reform.

Owen and Cora seated themselves at one of the tables. Drink was served them, and they talked together as they had never done before. Owen, like many another confirmed

sot, gained in poise and balance as he quaffed the deadly
stuff that had sunk him to his ignoble level. By degrees
he grew more like the man he had once been and less
like the skulking loafer of an hour ago. There had been
no hyperbole in his late professions. A hideous romanti-
cism, a ragamuffin gallantry breathed from his demeanor.
As the liquor fed his wasted forces he became like a
blurred photographic travesty of his former self. His
protestations, mixed with blasphemy, had in them the
undercurrent of a barbaric despair. His humor, reckless
and acrid, was but the threadbare cloak of an ink-black
sadness. All had been lost with him, and he knew it. A
little strength remained, but health had been fatally shattered, and to attempt any ordered routine of work would
have proved almost as idle as to retain it. A semblance
of his old fierceness broke through his manner as he drank
amply of the fiery fluid that Cora merely sipped. She
already felt her brain reeling again, and to lose consciousness in quarters like these would have been a deed of
insane rashness. But she became aware that responsibil-
ity was drifting from her, and that to reach her up-town
lodgings would require all the self-control she could
muster. Not that she cared much what became of her.
But to sink senseless here might only mean the sort of
disaster from which death would bring no rescue and for
which a pitiless continuance of living must proffer the
harshest sequence of pain.

There was something measurelessly pitiable in the
meeting of these two destitute and accursed human souls.
Each had made its own earthly hell, and amid the horrors
of such a doom they sat and gazed at one another. Not
far from them the immense hopeful push of human life
was progressing. The innocence of childhood, boyhood,
girlhood, kept its purity unsullied. Ambition, thrift, the
delight in life, blossomed like hardy flowerage on sturdy
stalks. Household peace and ease, domestic love and
joy, honor of self, parental tenderness, confidence in the

future, wisdom of temperance, hatred of soiling habitude, calmness of virtuous old age, wifely and husbandly devotion, filial fondness and obedience—all, in short, that sums up what we name the nobility and worthiness of society flourished but a few streets away from these two outcasts, and yet all was so abysmally distant! For them destiny pointed to one sure path. They could blame its misusage and cry out against its hardships as bitterly as they chose. It had left them nothing more dignified to do than to pass from a world which neither needed them nor could console them. It had left them nothing better to do than to die!

"I—I must go, now," at length said Cora. She rose, a little staggeringly, from the table, but soon gained fair steadiness of step as she moved toward the door.

"Don't go so soon," said Owen, following her. "Set down again an' have just one more."

"No," she persisted. "It's gettin' late. I must go."

She opened the door and passed out. Once in the air she reeled somewhat. Owen put his arm into hers, and they walked on for some time in silence.

"I'm . . I'm so tired," she said, presently. Her tones were sleepy and thick. "Are we goin' right?"

"Oh, yes."

"I mean, is this the way to the Sixth Avenue Elevated? I want to take it and get home . . ."

"Well, we'll be there soon."

"Are you sure."

"Yes—sure?"

She was leaning heavily on him. A stupor had come over her, and she was making efforts to shake it off. Suddenly she burst into a bleak, hysteric laugh.

"Oh, I wish I was dead!" she cried.

"So do I," said Owen, "now that I've seen you."

"Seen me! I was a fine sight to see!"

"*I* thought you was."

"Such as you found me!"

"Yes—such as I found ye. Better that than not findin' ye at all!"

They chanced, just then, to be passing a structure that was in course of demolition and that loomed ruinous from the verge of the sidewalk, with gutted walls and masses of tumbled bricks and timber. Owen saw a certain passage-way that seemed to lead within the dismantled pile, gleaming vaguely off the lamplit street.

Cora did not see the glitter that had crept into his eyes. "Come in here for a minute," he said, "an' let's look what they've been doin' with our old house."

"Our old house?" she murmured. "Why, this—this ain't Prince Street, is it?"

"Yes." He drew her with him into the narrow, ragged passage-way as he spoke. "Here's the old tenement-house where you an' mother an' me used to live together. They're pullin' it down. In a day or so there won't be nothin' more left of it."

She looked up through a great chasm made by the walls of the houses on either side, and saw the stars, remote, scintillant, mystical. She looked about her and saw great heaps of rubbish that the darkness and her own cloudy brain changed into fantastic, repellent shapes, as though they were goblin gods of the huge sinful city that surrounded them.

The stars were better to look at. She lifted up her eyes again, to watch their stately silver calm. Not that they had any friendliness; but they were so pure that they fascinated her and made her think alike of the peace and the chastity that she had forever lost.

"I'm very tired," she faltered, after a few moments. "I must get home soon or I shall drop down somewhere. Come." She turned gropingly toward Owen. "Which is the way out of this place?"

He did not answer, at first. Instead of speaking, he laid a hand on each of her shoulders and forced her, hot rudely but quite gently, to seat herself on a heap of loose matter that was close to where they had paused.

"Rest for a minute or so," he said.

And then she felt one of his arms tighten about her neck, and in the darkness perceived that his lips were seeking her own.

"No, no," she said.

But he pressed upon her lips, the next instant, a kiss that shot horror through all her frame. She was too weak to struggle with him, and if she had striven to cry out the strangling kiss would not have let her. It was the first of that sort he had ever given her—he who had loved those lips of hers when they were stainless as an opening rose ! Here fittingly, in the darkness and engirt by ruin, he, with his darkened soul and ruined life, gave proof to her of that strange and stubborn love which no profligacy had stifled.

The caress revolted, sickened her. When it was over she gasped like one just saved from choking.

"My neck !" she cried, in a voice of pain. "You've hurt it so with your hand pressin' into it so hard."

"Forgive me, Cora," he said, and sank down beside her. Then he searched in the gloom for her hands and found them both, and as he kissed them and sighed over them she was conscious that his tears were falling on them, heavy and hot.

"Oh," he sobbed, "if ye'd only make believe ye cared for me, just once—just once ! If ye'd only put both arms about me an' say two or three kind little words, whether ye meant 'em or not !"

As he held her hands and wept over them a sudden compassion stirred her. She rose from the rough seat on which he had placed her and drew her hands quickly m his clasp. Then she stooped and threw both arms ınd his neck.

For Owen the darkness became luminous. And as though spirit had won the power to leap aloof from flesh

22

and quite transcend it, all his foulness of the few past months fell away from him like a noisome garment. He felt crowned with hope and vigor ; he was a man again, and more than this, an impetuous, passionate lover. The woman whose arms clasped him was the unstained Cora of old ; not a trace of sin had ever touched her ; she was and had always been as a vestal that guarded the white flame of honor. Suddenly it seemed that her face, just as he had last seen it here where their former home lay crumbled about them, bloomed for him from the darkness in perfect similitude of what it once had been. The gold-brown eyes—the auburn hair, mutinous and fluctuant about her delicate head—the little mobile mouth, and, dearest of all, that pink of the eglantine on her milky cheek—these lived again with delicious restoration ! The Cora that the gloom had hid from him was no more. This lovely ghost had come to take her place ! . . .

Presently through his delirious imaginings a subtle voice seemed to whisper : ' Your joy must soon die. You know what devils will get you when it does. Cut yourself loose from the old cursed moorins' with that knife you've got now next your heart. The blade of it will point ye just the way ye want to go. It'll be into darker darkness than this, but you're sick o' the light, an' so is she. *Take her along with ye.* She said she wanted to go. Two's company, even in hell—if there is one ?' . . .

It was some little time after this that Cora said moaningly : "Come, now, Owen, let us get away from here."

And Owen replied, in a hushed, uncertain voice : "Yes—we'll both get away soon, very soon."

The next instant she felt something cold against her throat. Perhaps no pain followed, for as she sank to earth, half supported by him who had given her the quietus that she craved, not a single shudder shook her frame . . .

Next morning, in the chill of the winter dawn, two workmen found them lying side by side. Owen's face was buried from sight. One of his arms had fallen across Cora's throat, so concealing her wound, and by some accident there was no bloody disfigurement of her features, which looked almost as placid as though she slept, and to which death had given back much of her native beauty in tender resuscitation.

END.

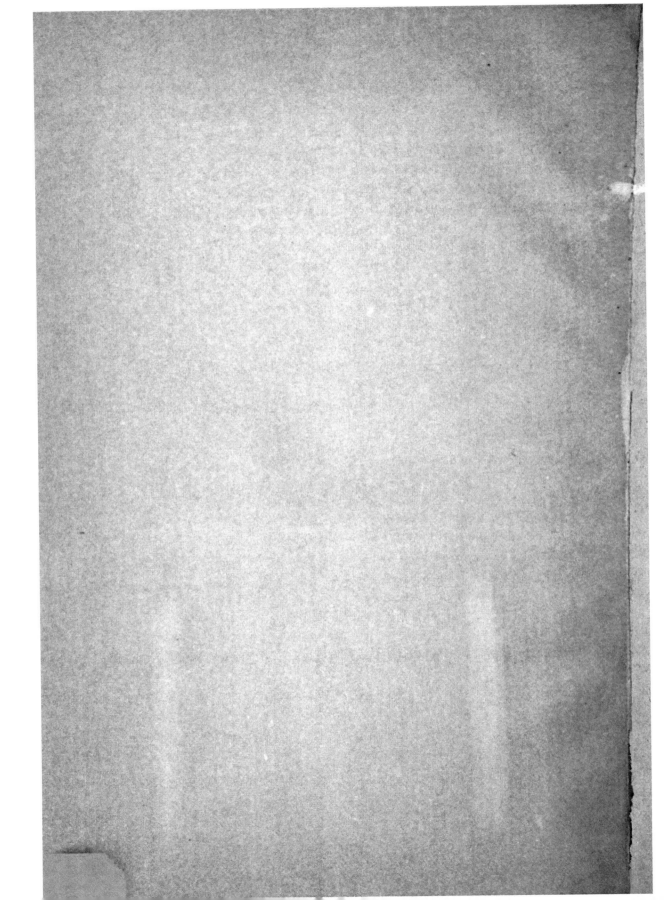

PT1
654

CPSIA information can be obtained at www.ICGtesting.com
Printed in the USA
LVOW132200091211

258742LV00003B/58/P

9 781173 771256